The Inside...

Getting Started
in Christian Music

Reed Arvin
General Editor

A CCM Book

HARVEST HOUSE PUBLISHERS
Eugene, Oregon 97402

Cover design by Left Coast Design, Portland, Oregon

The acronym "CCM" is used throughout this book in reference to the music genre popularly known as "contemporary Christian music." CCM ® is a registered trademark of CCM Communications, home to *CCM* magazine, *CCM Update,* and other Christian music publications.

GETTING STARTED IN CHRISTIAN MUSIC
Copyright © 2000 by Gospel Music Association
Published by Harvest House Publishers
Eugene, Oregon 97402

Library of Congress Cataloging-in-Publication Data
Getting started in Christian music / Reed Arvin, general editor.
       p.   cm.—(A CCM book)
       Originally published: The AGMA music curriculum. Nashville, Tenn.
 : Academy of Gospel Music Arts, 1999.
    ISBN 0-7369-0267-8
      1. Contemporary Christian music—Writing and publishing.
2. Church music—Instruction and study. 3. Contemporary Christian
musicians—Conduct of life. I. Arvin, Reed. II. Academy of Gospel Music Arts. III. Series.
MT67.G37 2000
782.2'2'023—dc21
                                            99-43231
                                          CIP

Printed in the United States of America.

00 01 02 03 04 05 06 07 08 09 / BP / 10 9 8 7 6 5 4 3 2 1

Contents

From the President

In the early 1990s a vision emerged about how the members of the Christian music industry could more effectively give back some of what they have learned to emerging songwriters and artists. After years of planning and study, the Gospel Music Association launched the Academy of Gospel Music Arts (AGMA) as the official educational and talent competition effort of the Christian music industry for unsigned talent.

It was never our intention to only help people in search of recording and song publishing contracts. Even though this has happened many times over, other successes have also occurred. At every turn, we have urged our students to be faithful to whatever platform God puts before them. Some are called to write or sing for millions and to deal with immense wealth and fame. Others are given local and regional platforms of influence while they maintain their "day job." Most importantly, all are called to create excellently for an audience of One.

Our educational vision included the eventual publishing of a curriculum that would include written and recorded media which would archive and reinforce what was being taught in live AGMA settings. As in the classroom, we wanted to adhere to high academic standards that include qualified presenters, effective communication and accurate material. We also wanted to address and reinforce the very important spiritual dimension that covers all creative and business endeavors by Christians.

The vision and generosity of the Sparrow Foundation has made this project possible. Founded in 1976 by Billy Ray Hearn, Sparrow Records has consistently modeled what it means to be Christian and creative. The Sparrow Foundation was created to assist God's people for years to come in imaging His creativeness. We are deeply grateful to Billy Ray Hearn, Bill Hearn, Holly Whaley, and the Sparrow

Foundation Board and Grant Committee for their unwavering support of, and guidance in, this project.

A massive project like this is just not possible without a capable editor to manage the entire effort. Reed Arvin possesses expertise in several disciplines. He is a very gifted musician, producer, composer, author, educator, and editor who has capably led the team contributing to this curriculum. As Academic Dean of the Academy, Reed's mission, which he has faithfully executed, has been to ensure that learning takes place. GMA owes Reed Arvin its deepest gratitude, along with all the contributors he has recruited, whose talent and commitment have made this important project possible.

Frank Breeden
President
Gospel Music Association

Welcome

Since I am coming to that holy room,
Where, with thy choir of saints for evermore,
I shall be made thy music; as I come
I tune the instrument here at the door,
And what I must do then, think here before.
John Donne (1572-1631)

Welcome to the Academy of Gospel Music Arts Curriculum. This project is the effort of many talented and dedicated people. Their gifting is in the area of music and in the management of musical talent. Their dedication is in communicating this expertise to people who are committed to learning.

The quote that begins this book is there for a reason. John Donne, a seventeenth-century pastor whose theological work still inspires, was also a romantic who wrote some of the most beautiful and passionate love poems of his day. His was a totally integrated faith, in which his beliefs and his art mingled with inspiration and highly individual expression. But he was not just a brilliant savant—he was a tireless worker whose sheer output in words rivaled that of Bach in music. He didn't merely create haphazardly; he took time to "tune the instrument here at the door."

It is the hope of the GMA that Donne could be an inspiration to you as he has been to many of us. Live your life in such a way that God is continually glorified. Create at all times, and not just with your eyes toward heaven, but sometimes to reflect others upwards by what you observe and create in the world around you. Sing a new song—to God, and also to each other. And like Donne, "think here before." Spend time developing your craft and your art in a lifetime pursuit of excellence. God will be glorified, and the people of Earth will be delighted.

Reed Arvin
General Editor

ARTISTS AND SONGWRITERS

Music, Ministry, and Fame
By Reed Arvin

Is it possible to succeed in a selling profession and also be content with the rear table? Only if you are willing to pay a price to live as Christ lived.

I am a professional Christian. I am writing on a computer paid for by Christians who bought records that I produced or a book that I wrote. I wear clothes and live in a house bought in the same way. Every dollar that I make comes from the church. Jesus is my living.

I have found this life to be very difficult to live with integrity. There have been times that I thought I understood it quite clearly. There have been times I was convinced it was impossible. Mostly I live in the in-between.

This chapter is about trying to live this very improbable, very strange life. My words are by no means definitive. In your journey you will hopefully seek the counsel of many, sifting through ideas until you prayerfully make your own decisions. Listen to everyone with experience. There is only one type of person to mistrust: Turn away from those who will not or cannot see a conflict. To live this life well requires a willingness to confront conflicts honestly. Pretending they don't exist is not a step toward that goal. Living as a professional Christian requires that you suture together two often-unwilling partners: the gospel of Jesus Christ and your personal financial ambition. To do this at all is difficult. To do it glibly is certainly a mistake.

If, as many of you do, you dream of creating and being paid for art that comes from a faith perspective, there are certain principles that have helped me greatly in the search for living this dream with integrity. I do not present them as unalterable truth. They have helped me, but they have not solved my dilemmas, thus proving their insufficiency. Or perhaps it is my unwillingness to live by these principles that is at fault. But even living by them, I still find myself sometimes facing difficult decisions.

> Although life has great clarity when we are determined to be completely honest, life as a professional Christian is full of subtle distinctions that make black-and-white definitions difficult.

Much of this chapter will read like a cautionary tale. It may be tempting, halfway through, to decide that to pursue this life is simply not worth the risk. That would be a rational thought. But there is a powerful reason to attempt it. It is my hope that when you encounter this reason at the conclusion of the chapter, some of you will find it compelling enough that you will decide to attempt this dangerous path.

Principles for Living as a Professional Christian

The first principle that any search for truth must embrace is that God does not lie. And conversely, we know that the devil is the deceiver. This may seem self-evident, but living according to this simple principle can be remarkably difficult.

Although life has great clarity when we are determined to be completely honest, life as a professional Christian is full of subtle distinctions that make black-and-white definitions difficult. There are many reasons for this, but most of them stem in some way from the dynamics of selling.

Selling, almost without exception, involves hyperbole, or lies. There is subtle or grand exaggeration in nearly all advertising, and we've come to accept this through the sheer repetition of marketing in our lives. A recent ad for the new cola product Pepsi One says, "There's something missing in your life. This is it. This is all you'll ever need." We understand that this is a lie, because we are accustomed to and accepting of the dynamics of selling. No one sells floor wax with the ad line, "Buy this floor wax—it's pretty good." Floor wax, like other mundane products such as cola, is presented as revolutionary, ground-breaking, and even life-changing. The husband enters the home, sees the sparkling floor, sweeps the wife into his arms, and we are free to infer that, "If you buy this floor wax, it will actually change your life." Pick a product; the principle remains the same. Every month or so a new movie is released as "the motion picture event of a lifetime." There is no embarrassment when another film is similarly described, even when released by the same studio. How can this be? It's made possible by the tacit acknowledgement of the sleight of hand endemic to selling. Some naive people believe that because they recognize that the ads lie, they are unaffected by them. But of course the people who make them understand that this realization does not diminish their effectiveness. All that is required is sufficient repetition so that a positive feeling is associated with a high degree of brand recognition. It's in no way necessary for the target to literally believe the claims. Everyone knows that household products perform with remarkably little differences. But standing in the grocery store before a row of identically-performing floor waxes, the vague happiness of the ad flickers in our minds. It's not important if we believe that our lives will be changed by floor wax. What matters is that we reach out and select the correct product.

Into this swirl of exaggeration Christian music pushes, vying for attention in the thronging, clanging noise of a selling culture. It was inevitable that out of a sense of survival, and also from both conscious and unconscious imitation, there would be a substantial glossing of the image of Christian artists, as artists are the selling vehicle of almost all recorded music.

Like the floor wax example, you will never see an ad for a Christian artist that says, "Buy this record. It's pretty good. It's recorded by a person who has a fairly conflicted relationship with God. Most of the time she's convinced that Jesus is divine. There are times she wonders. She prays irregularly and has some bad habits, including often not being entirely honest with herself."

This would be a pretty fair description of most Christians, including most Christian artists. It's lousy advertising, however, and so you won't see it. Don't blame record companies; it's not their business to promote themselves with lousy advertising. It's their business to use highly effective advertising, which by its nature has an implicitly disingenuous message: "This artist walks closely with God, and by buying this record, you will have a transcendent experience."

The difficulty, of course, is that we expect a higher calling in regards to matters of faith. Although not everyone has the language to express this sense of incoherence, the great majority are able to feel it. "They're selling Christian music like floor wax," we feel intuitively. This leaves many with an uncomfortable taste. Inevitably, our cynicism grows and we begin looking for someone to blame.

You may be surprised and encouraged to discover that many people in Christian music are aware of this awkwardness. No one, however, has been fully able to solve it. Selling will always be selling. As a Christian artist, you must make your own decision about whether or not you can allow yourself to be packaged like floor wax.

But I will give you this warning: If you align yourself with a record label, some degree of packaging will certainly happen to you. This is because the packaging of artists is essential to selling them.

You may make peace with this reality. I hope some of you can, for the reason stated at the end of the chapter. But I hope that you can't do it easily or without inner conflict, because that would indicate a need to think more deeply about what it means to become a commodity. It's not my place or anyone else's place to tell you what to do. But it's essential that you are aware of this process and can respond in a mature, thoughtful way to its pressures.

The Unspoken Deal

If the salient feature of floor wax is its ability to clean and polish, the equivalent quality in a Christian artist is not, interestingly, musical talent. Talent is an important, but not determinant, side quality. The center of the selling bull's-eye of all artist-oriented Christian music is the personality behind it. Essential to this personality is a public perception of a deep, expressive faith in Jesus. Before the music finds its place in the Christian marketplace, there must be an understanding reached with the buying public: "This artist is a strong Christian who talks to God every day. He reads his Bible. He goes to church. His Christian experience is relatively uncluttered with darkness or sin. He hears from God in ways you probably don't. You may think of him as a spiritual role model." This understanding is reached in both subtle and not-so-subtle ways, depending on the artist and his intended target audience. The careful use of Christian symbols in advertising, cover art, and the tone and wording of press releases all contribute to this understanding. The artist will also normally be personally introduced to radio programmers and retail distributors in a group context, and on promotional tours in order to cement this understanding.

> In order to maintain this essential fiction, a "poster image" of the Christian artist must be created, usually with the implicit cooperation of the artist.

My experience in Christian music does not support this implicit contract between buyer and seller. I find that Christian artists are neither more nor less spiritual than the average believer. They are, instead, generally more intelligent, more ambitious, and very much more creative than average. They possess an ability to communicate and rephrase truth in new and compelling ways. These are positive qualities and they empower Christian artists to survive in a highly competitive environment. But these qualities are not, strictly speaking, a part of the implied contract with the buying public. The contract implies a spiritual depth and experience far above the norm.

In order to maintain this essential fiction, a "poster image" of the Christian artist must be created, usually with the implicit cooperation of the artist. If you have a small career, this image may be fairly manageable. If you become highly successful, however, you will discover that this "poster image" has more effect on people than your actual personality will, simply because it reaches many more people more often than you can possibly do in real life. In the same way that actors are appalled to discover that people talk to them as if they were the characters they play on television, you will find people speaking to you as though you and God were inseparable, intimate lovers that speak of things mere mortals cannot comprehend. You will discover friends you never knew you had. If you become a star, it will become routine for you to meet someone at the conclusion of a concert who trembles wordlessly before you, tears welling in their eyes. The occasional marriage proposal will end up in your record company's mailbox, even if you are already married. These are real examples that would be familiar to any highly successful Christian artist. But even though a relatively few of your fans will be so over-whelmingly moved, almost everyone who meets you will be subtly impacted by your poster image.

Even people you knew before you became famous will be impacted, and some may grow resentful. You may grow comfortable with this image, and try to maintain it. You may grow cynical about it and even come to despise the people who believe in it. There are a small number of artists in Christian music who have succumbed to this cynicism. But what is most likely—and I say this after many years of observing Christian music from very close range—is that you will develop a powerful love-hate relationship with your image. You will love it, because it supports your career, your lifestyle, and your ego. It also protects you from having to be yourself, and although almost every person has some kind of public mask, very few have a professional marketing team employed to maintain it. This is a seductive luxury that only a very determined person can resist indulging. But you will also hate your poster image, because it makes real relationships much more difficult, and because you know it has the power to bring out the worst in you. Fame, you will dis-cover, is generally not ennobling.

Who Can We Blame?

To whom shall we ascribe responsibility for this cynical, selling approach and the damage it inflicts on buyer and seller? It may be tempting to blame record companies—after all, they reap the greatest financial rewards for a successful record. But ultimately this isn't a very interesting or productive exercise, because it starts from the assumption that companies of any kind can and should truly reflect the nature of Christ. Any reasonable examination of the life of Christ and the structure of how business operates will expose this as mostly untenable. I know there are a lot of books out to contradict this, books which describe Jesus as the ultimate CEO. But Jesus was not a CEO,

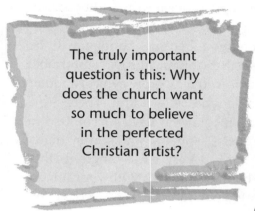

The truly important question is this: Why does the church want so much to believe in the perfected Christian artist?

He was a Savior, and that is a powerful distinction. The best such books can do is to describe the personal qualities of Christ and encourage us to go and do likewise in the business environment. This is invariably good spiritual advice, but not invariably good business advice. Jesus routinely took actions that were completely out of character for a CEO and would not be tolerated in any normal corporate environment. Corporations generally will not and cannot reflect Christ, simply because Jesus wasn't in the selling business. Jesus was completely and utterly in the "giving away" business. Businesses will never be and can never be in the "giving away" business. Business is not sin. But business is also not a reflection of Jesus, because Jesus had almost nothing to do with it. He had very little to say about it, and what He did say was mostly by way of warning.

The next logical place to turn is to blame self-serving Christian artists. After all, they benefit as surely as the record company. But for different reasons, this is also not a terribly interesting proposition. In the end, there are only a very small number of professional Christian artists, and who can know what is in their hearts? This is an individual question, settled one person at a time. Although the motivations of corporations may be generally assumed, no one is in a position to judge the motives or calling of another individual. But there is an important—even essential—question that remains. This issue affects millions, not hundreds. The truly important question is this: Why does the church want so much to believe in the perfected Christian artist? Why, in other words, do so many look up to the poster image? This question is ultimately the only one that matters. As long as human nature persists, people on stage will always be affected by their fame, and record companies, like all companies, will always seek profit. But the church has a higher calling. It is intended to be, in every sense of the word, nonprofit.

The Christian Currency of Acceptance

For many years I have taught Sunday school to college students at a Baptist church. Every semester I ask the new group of students a simple but telling question: "Where are you most real?" I want them to imagine the place of their greatest comfort, the place where they are most likely to reveal their innermost secrets. Over the years, hundreds of students have answered this question for me. Their answers are remarkably consistent. The vast majority—at least 80 percent— say that they are most real, "with their friends at school." They describe a dorm room with a small cadre of friends, secure in their peer group. A small minority find this freedom at home, with family. None—not a single student—has ever answered "church." Think of it: Of the hundreds of students asked, not a single person felt most safe to be himself in the house of God. I believe that the reason why this is so universal an experience is a key to why the image of the perfected Christian artist is so powerful in our lives.

Every culture has what might be termed a currency of acceptance. In basketball, it's the ability to play that sport at a very high level. If the skills are high enough, almost everything else is tolerated. Recently an NBA star attacked his coach, physically striking him, leaving the arena, and returning to attack him a second time. In spite of this assault, he was allowed to continue playing for another team after a relatively short suspension. He possessed the currency of acceptance—the ability to help his team win. In business, it may be the ability to close a sale. We all know people who rise through a corporate hierarchy in spite of a less-than-winning personality. They do so because they excel in the currency of acceptance of that subculture—the ability to make money.

Christianity is no different. The currency of acceptance in the church is as clearly and narrowly defined as in any other segment of society. This currency could succinctly be described as "a close walk with God." Everyone thoroughly churched knows what this phrase implies: a daily quiet time, a vivid prayer life, no hidden sin, and a substantial biblical knowledge. And above all, it implies a peace that comes not from above but from never having to wonder about the basic precepts of the faith. Doubt and questioning is not a part of the currency of acceptance in the Christian subculture. The higher up in the subculture, the fewer questions are tolerated. New believers can ask basic questions for a short period of time. Conversely, the pastor, residing at the pinnacle of the subculture, must never ask. He must always have answers. You will see this reality played out next Sunday in your church, if you're observant. The odds are overwhelming that your pastor will not ask a question for which he does not already claim to know the answer. If you're impatient for this demonstration, you may turn on a television to Christian programming. Televangelists are, as a class, the most evidently confident people on earth. Theirs is an image of truly impervious security in every tenet of faith, and indeed of life.

Contrast this attitude with Nicodemus, who did the unthinkable. When Jesus told him that he must be born again, Nicodemus gave a thoroughly logical and almost required response. He simply asked, "How can that be?" By asking this question, Nicodemus became a serious student of truth. "How can that be? Should I go back into my mother's womb?" Jesus gave him his answer, and having encountered the real Nicodemus rather than a poster-Nicodemus who never wondered, the seeker was changed. Now think: When was the last time at your church someone raised his hand and asked, "How can that be?" Imagine some mysterious precept being taught, a precept that frankly, few, if any, of us understand. Take the divinity of Christ, for example: Imagine the pastor telling us that Jesus was all man and all God. Now imagine someone in your church asking, "How can that be?"

We understand intuitively that in most churches such a question would be cultural suicide. This is because of the currency of acceptance. We do not celebrate those with questions, we celebrate those with answers. For this reason the words, "I really don't know," are generally not a part of the public pastoral vocabulary. It may well be that some pastors long to speak this honest, imminently sensible statement, but they understand the currency of acceptance in their subculture too well to hazard it. If any among us raises questions or, much worse, admits to doubts, the church turns to settle and silence the questioner as quickly as possible. Real, extended discussion is very rarely tolerated. Understand that no one will say out loud that this type of questioning is not tolerated. It will merely be understood and scrupulously obeyed.

In our deep selves, however, we understand that we are at times conflicted in our faith. We do wake up some mornings and wonder if Jesus was divine. We do wonder if he rose from the dead. Our faith lists to the side, and we hold it in, understanding that admitting our doubts to the whole group or even to a small gathering of friends is perilous.

Into this picture floats the image of the perfected Christian artist. We see him stride confidently onto the stage, deeply talented, deeply spiritual, touched by the hand of God. Surely, we unconsciously think, Steve Green prays every day in the secure knowledge that God hears him. Surely Margaret Becker doesn't wonder like we do. Surely Michael W. Smith doesn't think impure thoughts. And so we raise a hero, a place to hide our own conflicted lives. We raise many icons into this vacuum—pastors, church leaders, famous evangelists, Christian authors. They are the chosen ones who walk so intimately with God that they no longer have doubts or questions.

Some Christian artists are able to maintain the fiction of spiritual perfection over the course of a career. But what happens when the hero falls? Then the misplaced dependence on a surrogate for our faith becomes the root of bitterness. We feel cheated, as though the artist had personally lied to us. But think about the nature of the transaction; we don't actually know the artist at all. Nothing has transpired between us but smoke and mirrors, and we have been willing participants in a charade.

There are two culpable parties in this hoodwinking. On the one hand, Christian artists are only too willing to allow a picture to be painted of them that they know in their hearts isn't accurate. The pressure to capitalize on the public's need for a hero is palpable. But the audience, also, is responsible. We have to release these artists from our expectations and allow them to be real people. This must start in every individual church. It will not start until individuals find the courage to raise their hand in Sunday school and say those powerful, liberating words: "How can that be?" Because our churches are not a safe place to ask this soul-revealing question, we are trapped between expectation and reality, longing for a place to be ourselves but understanding perfectly the currency of acceptance in our subculture. This tension is unhealthy and is one reason why so very many among us who are sick stay unwell. It's simply not prudent to bring out into the light our aberrations and have them handled. Better to suffer silently and maintain connection with the group.

If we face honestly what these universal Christian experiences mean in the context of professional Christianity, we now find our answer to the question, "Who is to blame for the image of the perfected

Christian?" The true answer is that we are all to blame. And I will, in fairness, personalize and say that I am to blame. I am to blame because I don't raise my hand and ask, "How can that be?" when I am sincerely confused, thereby making it easier for the next person to do so. I am to blame because I have been unwilling to do my part to overthrow a currency of acceptance that is based on performance and not on love.

> What an extraordinary release it would be to know, walking on stage, that people were fully and honestly prepared to accept you for who you are.

Imagine for a moment a church that people described as the place they found it easiest to be real. Imagine a church in which people brought their frailty and sin, confessed to one another, found healing and ministering. And now imagine what it would be like to bring your art there as a Christian musician. What an extraordinary release it would be to know, walking on stage, that people were fully and honestly prepared to accept you for who you are.

The Ananias and Sapphira Percent of Hype

Ultimately, concerns about blame must become productive and turn toward taking responsibility. Responsibility tends to be individual, not corporate. Whether or not the church has fostered an environment receptive and needful of the poster-Christian, the artist must carry responsibility for his or her personal decisions to exploit this receptiveness. The Bible makes this clear in the story I believe is most relevant to Christian artists, that of Ananias and Sapphira.

To have been a part of the young church during the time of Acts must have been absolutely thrilling. Convinced that Jesus was going to return imminently (say, next Thursday), believers pooled their resources for the survival of the group. Belongings were sold, and in some cases people had enough faith to sell everything, bringing the proceeds as an offering. I have no doubt that there was a great celebration attached to those offerings. Watching them from a distance were a husband and wife named Ananias and Sapphira. They were extraordinarily generous; they were willing to sell a field and give most of the proceeds as an offering. Think of it as a mega-tithe; keep a little, give a lot. By my way of thinking, that's above-and-beyond giving and worthy of praise. But Ananias and Sapphira noticed that those who gave everything seemed to receive a greater measure of affirmation, and they were desperate for that extra percent of adulation. It's important to note that they didn't represent themselves as completely different people than they were. They did, in fact, make a terrific sacrifice in giving most of the money and keeping only a small amount. But by pretending to be only slightly more than they were, God's wrath was invoked.

Peter's response to them was to the point: *Wasn't the field yours to do with as you wished?* By this Peter was forcing them to take accountability for their actions. This unhealthy need to be more than you really are in public is your issue, he was saying. Yes, the congregation may have been giving too much credit to men and not enough to God. But we must walk our own path and be responsible for our actions. Peter repeated himself, just to be clear: *Even after you sold it, wasn't the money yours to do with as you pleased?* In other words: You walked in the door with this need to be celebrated. You should have at least given us the chance to accept you for who you were.

And so it is in Christian music. When given the opportunity to speak to aspiring Christian artists, I never tell them that I'm afraid that they will be completely different on stage than they are in real life. In my experience, this is almost never the case. The real danger is that they will get on stage and be subtly different. They will, in effect, take the "Ananias and Sapphira percent of hype" on stage with them. Maybe it's only 10 percent. Maybe you'll adopt a tone of voice that makes you seem more spiritual than you really are. Maybe you'll state categorically things which you only hope to be true. Maybe you'll praise Him more exuberantly than you have ever done on your

> The first step in living this life with integrity is one of the most difficult; you must become intimately involved with what is said about you on your behalf.

own. Perhaps you will learn how to push the levers in the audience for an exuberant response, using the name of Jesus like a cheerleader. But whatever it is, the pressure to be a little bit more than you are will be enormous, and no one will have to explain it to you. If you've grown up in church, this pressure will be as natural to you as breathing. The message of this pressure is clear: Never doubt. Never wonder. Above all, never ask, "How can this be?"

Think for a moment about being on stage. Think about being interviewed by a Christian publication. How will you walk through this dangerous minefield? How can you make a clear path through pressures that have controlled the public image even of strong personalities?

Take Responsibility for the Way You Are Marketed

The first step in living this life with integrity is one of the most difficult; you must become intimately involved with what is said about you on your behalf. However, to do this successfully in a relationship with a record company will take sensitivity. Running a record company is publicly glamorous but actually quite a difficult proposition. Record companies understandably and rightly place a premium on artists who have a cooperative attitude and don't create problems. This is because these companies have a great many artists to promote, and if there is a perception that the artist is resisting the efforts of the marketing department, the whole enterprise can become a frustrating, uphill battle. There are far too many skirmishes to fight on the outside to have them internally between label and artist. Therefore, it is very much in your interest to cooperate with the record company wherever and whenever possible. However, there is an important distinction for you as the artist to remember: When the ad copy is written and the promotional materials are sent out, the marketing department does not have to walk out on stage and be the person that they have described. Only you have to do that. Only you must carry the weight of that image with you into every conversation of your life, including those you have with God. While you are struggling to be yourself in what you will find to be a highly artificial environment, the people who created your image will be drinking coffee and working on the next project. So because you are being described, you must ultimately be responsible for how you are presented.

In order to reach this consensus with a record company, the ability to listen will be a strong and necessary asset. It is probably a fact that the people working with you have knowledge of the market that you lack and experience in successful promotion from which your career would benefit. So it's essential that you demonstrate respect for this expertise and the interest shown in your project. To lose the enthusiasm of your record company over mundane issues would be a terrific mistake for any artist, so you must make sure that there is something important at stake before you determine to raise your hand. But it is also important to remember the first principle: All truth is God's truth, and all lies are the devil's lies.

It is not only signed artists who face these issues. Even regional and local artists create promotional materials. How will you live in this crucible? What will you do when you see pictures and read copy about yourself that describe the best fifteen minutes of your life, rather than the way you really live? And more importantly, what will you do when you hear yourself giving an interview or talking from stage as though you were more spiritually mature and settled than you really are? The difficulties are complex; even the image of humility can be a badge for the proud, and you will sometimes see this quality intentionally displayed for its effect.

> Through simple repetition, the word "gospel" has little meaning to many people who work in Christian music, and much less to the people outside it.

Remember Always the Actual Life of Jesus

Although you may be working in the field of "gospel" music, you will quickly learn that this word has become mostly amorphous and meaningless. As the cultural memory of the actual good news of Christ fades, a once-powerful word has become little more than the description of a musical style. We associate it most facilely with a black gospel choir, resplendent in velvet robes. But when such a choir appears in a Madonna video singing background while the artist has simulated sex with a Peter icon on an altar, we may be assured that the actual meaning of the word has been thoroughly drained. It is sometimes abbreviated as an acronym; the GMA, or Gospel Music Association is an example. Such a name is devoid of spiritual meaning; it describes a musical style and possibly, a vague collection of cultural affinities. Through simple repetition, the word "gospel" has little meaning to many people who work in Christian music and much less to the people outside it.

The actual life of Christ, however, is something different. Unlike the acculturation of words, His life doesn't change. The things Christ did and said are locked in history, although our interpretation of them can certainly shift. But the fact will always remain that Jesus did not pursue wealth or comfort. He owned only what He wore; He did not pursue the adulation of men; He lived well and for His reward got murdered. Most disturbingly, this killing was conducted with the approval and logistical support of the church itself.

While alive, Christ made some powerful statements, including one deeply troubling to all professional Christians, whether in music or otherwise: *Do not*, Jesus said, *seek to sit at the head table and be asked to move back. Sit at the back, and be asked to move forward.* But think: If you are a professional Christian, you will certainly employ the use of a publicist at some point. The sole purpose of a publicist can be described in a simple, crystalline sentence: Get your client to the head table.

That's it. There's no other reason for the existence of a publicist. Locate the head table, and make sure your client sits at it. It's fascinating, when rare television appearances become available for Christian artists, to see publicists doing exactly what Christ warned against—fighting for appearances and on-air minutes for their artists, and doing it vigorously, often with a distinctly competitive flavor.

Is it possible to succeed in a selling profession and also be content with the rear table? Only if you are willing to pay a price to live as Christ lived. It's not that the believer should "trust God" to always bring us to the head table because we demonstrated our humility by not seeking it on our own. On the contrary, it's fair to assume that there will be many times that having humbly not promoted ourselves, no one, including God, will take up the slack. It's not a life that tricks God into being our divine publicist. It's a life lived not in the pursuit of the adulation of men, and therefore, many times lived without it.

The More Famous You Become,
the Less Freedom You Will Have

Surprised? Most people assume it will work the other way. "Surely," one may imagine, "when I have power I will use it for good."

A great many classic works of literature have taught generations the world over that this is almost never true. Frodo, in *The Lord of the Rings*, toys with this lie, but soon sees the danger of it. He cannot possess the ring and stay himself. If he takes this power, he will resist for a time, but in the end, he will be changed by it. He must choose. Fame is like the one ring of Tolkein's tale; we assume that we will be benevolent dictators, our favor landing lightly on small and large alike. But this is very rarely the case.

There is another more practical reason why success and freedom work against each other. When a career gains momentum, other people align themselves to it so that any decision the artist makes affects many others.

No one's career illustrates this as effectively as that of country superstar Garth Brooks. Some time ago Garth and his wife were blessed with a new baby, and Garth held a press conference announcing that he was retiring from touring for some time in order to be with his growing family. I remember turning to my wife when I heard this and saying, "People all over town just got their plans changed." And it was true. Band members were out of a job; his publicists could only say, "Garth's at home with the kids again today" so often; the sound and light companies lost a hundred and fifty shows in a year; concert promoters lost a sure money-maker. The list goes on and on.

Literally hundreds of lives were affected by Garth Brooks' decision. Now, I don't know Garth Brooks. I've never met him, and I've never seen him. But I do know that it wasn't very long before Garth was back out on the road again. And it's easy to imagine conversations that might have been held to convince him to do it.

"Garth," the record company people may have said, "the music business is a timing business. You're the first country artist in history to be No. 1 on the pop charts. You're white hot, and even though you're huge, times like this don't necessarily come back around. And you want to take some time off *now*?"

Maybe Garth's a nice guy; I have no idea. Like all famous people, you can hear anything you like about him depending on whom you ask, so all rumors are therefore meaningless. But if he is a nice guy, maybe he just looked at his wife one day and said, "You know what? We're deciding for a hundred and fifty other people what their year is going to be like. I don't want to do that."

If God calls you to play the guitar for the next six months in a prison chapel, chances are you can do it, at least part time. But for an artist with a band on salary and a host of other people depending on him, that choice would be very difficult. Or even if you work alone but have allowed your lifestyle to float upwards based on your new income, such a choice would be extremely difficult. The more successful and famous you become, the more difficult your choices can get. Managers don't get paid when their artists don't work, and it's not rocket science to understand that they tend to lean in that direction. You have freedom now. Revel in it. Use it. If your dreams come true, it's possible you may lose it.

If You Are Completely Palatable to People, You're Not Accurately Reflecting the Gospel

Jesus wasn't really that popular of a guy. He had His moments, like His triumphant entrance into Jerusalem. But not too much later a lot of those people were calling for His head. In my book, that means they weren't really His friends in the first place. Any friend of mine that later wants to kill me is pretty easy to leave off my Christmas card list. But there is a reason those people turned on Him: He wouldn't keep quiet and leave His popularity well enough alone. He did bring comfort (the part of the gospel that televangelists and "seeker-oriented" churches emphasize), and if He had left it at that He would have been, as Leonardo DiCaprio so famously said in the film, *Titanic*, "the King of the world." But He didn't leave it at that. He went on to say a great many things that ticked people off in a big way (the parts of the gospel that televangelists and "seeker-oriented" churches mostly leave out). He had the temerity to bring up the cost of the cross and mention a white-washed tomb or two. People, the record supports, did not like that.

It is a great misconception that the power of the gospel is mostly in its message of comfort. This is an idea sometimes held by people who spend too much time only with other Christians. If you spend a lot of time with non-Christians, you will find that the average person in today's society is much more self-satisfied than he is desperate for answers. We find ourselves living in the most affluent nation in the most affluent time in the history of the world. In a time like that, people are not mostly craving comfort. Even in the time of Jesus a great deal of what He preached was intended to disturb the self-satisfied, the self-made man.

And today it is even more important that we do not deprive the message of Christ of its greatest power, the power to disturb. Selling records and getting concert bookings doesn't leave much room for that kind of holy risk-taking. It requires, almost by definition, that you be liked, liked very much, and liked all the time. You must be admired. You must be desirable as a friend, as a spiritual fantasy, and even, if we're honest, in many cases as a sexual fantasy. Maintaining those fictions is pretty hard work, I think you'll find. And it's hard to fit the

> Jesus probably could not win a Dove award. He would certainly have ticked off the establishment too thoroughly for that kind of unfettered affirmation.

occasional "you brooding pit of vipers" comment into that image.

Jesus probably could not win a Dove award. He would certainly have alienated the establishment too thoroughly for that kind of unfettered affirmation. But He never displeased people casually or for effect. He was committed to truth, and by not catering to the expectations of men, He bought His freedom to always be truthful. That freedom was bought at a terrific price.

So what to do? How can we be honest when necessary and still be a professional Christian dependent on the good graces of the church? Steve Green has dealt with this issue in an innovative, gentlemanly fashion. Steve explains that his office never calls churches or promoters to try to book dates. Even if he is performing on Friday in, say, Kansas City and again on Sunday in Minneapolis, he won't try to book a Detroit date on the open Saturday. In a lot of ways, booking such a date makes a great deal of sense. Why sit in a hotel room when you could be out performing? But Steve has instructed his office to wait for people to call him with their invitations for him to sing and speak.

Naturally, I was curious why. Steve explained that he feels very uncomfortable delivering any hard words to a congregation if he has invited himself to be with them. It boils down to good manners.

If I invite myself to your house and then try to give you advice on how to raise your children, you might conclude I wasn't much of a dinner guest. If, on the other hand, you invite me to be with you knowing that I'm something of a straight-shooter, you get what you paid for and no hard feelings. Not that Steve usually goes into a church with a hard message; it's very seldom that this issue comes up. But when it does, it seems essential that the invitation be extended in one direction so that he can be free to speak without reservation.

When Steve explained this to me, I asked an obvious question: "Sure, Mr. Promise Keepers phone-rings-off-the-wall-booked-into-next-year-recording-artist, it's easy for you to sit around and wait for people to call you." But Steve replied that this was a commitment he made early in his career, determined to live with the consequences.

It doesn't follow that because Steve was faithful in that way that God just filled up his calendar. No doubt there are many days that he doesn't work that he could if he simply pursued it. He's free, but he paid the price to have that freedom. That may not be the way you decide to pursue things. There is, in fact, a great deal of helpful advice in this very book about how to book yourself in churches. But Steve's system of dealing with this issue is a kind of gold standard for how an artist can maintain the freedom to portray the words of Jesus distinctly apart from the selling atmosphere.

Maintain Accountability to a Group of People

The word "group" here is used intentionally. There are far too many unbalanced people in the church for it to be safe to be accountable to one person, especially if you are in a position of visibility. I once met a girl at an airport who was disaffected with the church; when I asked her why, she explained that as a teenager her pastor had told her to flush her contacts down the toilet. He had done this because he felt that to possess them limited God's power to heal her eyesight.

> There are far too many unbalanced people in the church for it to be safe to be accountable to one person, especially if you are in a position of visibility.

Needless to say, being accountable to him would have been a mistake. But to be accountable to a group of people can be an important backstop in your journey. The group needs to be level-headed and spiritually mature, and not necessarily interested in or knowledgeable about music. They just have to be interested in and knowledgeable about God and about you. And hopefully, they will be people who occasionally ask, "How can that be?"

The gold standard for accountability was set, in my mind, by the late Christian artist Rich Mullins. As his producer for eight records, we naturally talked about every subject under the sun. During one album, I asked Rich what his income from publishing was like during a typical quarter. Tacky, I admit, but you'll just have to accept that at 2 A.M. on the thirtieth day of recording, you're pretty much past the formalities.

But Rich's reply aroused my curiosity. "I don't know," he said simply.

At first I interpreted this to be the result of indifferent business acumen, of which Rich was legendary. But I was to learn that the actual reason he didn't know how much money he made was far more compelling. I pressed him: "Don't the checks come to your house? Think back. What's typical?"

He shook his head. "The checks don't come to me," he said.

"A business manager?"

"Nope. To my church. Well, a board of elders at my church."

"How come?"

"Because I don't feel like what I do is any more important than what anybody else does. So I tell them to pay me the average salary of an American worker."

"I still don't understand why you don't know how much there is."

Rich answered without the slightest hesitation. It was obvious he had given this subject a great deal of thought. He said, "Because if I knew, it would be so much harder to give away."

That is a gold standard of accountability. It was very expensive, but remarkably, towards the end of his life Rich decided he needed even more freedom. He took a vow of poverty, determined to live on $1,000 a month. In so doing he moved toward the way Christ lived.

I do not have the faith to follow his example. Or perhaps it's not a lack of faith; perhaps it's much simpler and more venal, nothing more glamorous than an unholy attachment to things. But Rich wanted freedom more than he wanted money or what it could buy.

Consider the freedom that Rich's sacrifice purchased. Imagine yourself in an A&R meeting with him trying to get him to move in a particular direction in order to sell more records. I suspect he would look at you and say, "I think I'm going to make my thousand bucks a month either way." So he was poor and he was free. If you have a lifestyle to support, meetings with A&R departments could be much different. You pay your money and you take your choice. But freedom costs.

Have an Artistic Center

At first this may seem tangential to living a life of integrity as a professional Christian. But you'll find that having a true artistic center liberates you from many business pressures. If you know who you are, others won't be able to remake you in the image they prefer. If you don't, the pressure of fads in the marketplace will lure you into one image after another.

A friend of mine in A&R tells a story about meeting an eager young singer looking for a record deal. "What kind of music do you do?" my friend asked. "Whatever you're looking for!" the singer exclaimed. Not exactly the answer of a true artist. And that kind of pliability doesn't bode well when push comes to shove. Needless to say, my friend passed on the singer.

Christians should intuitively seek the arts as a way to express their faith, and do so with personal integrity. Where the marketplace has not overwhelmed the arts, this is actually happening. My brother-in-law is a southern Baptist missionary in Nepal. Nepal is an extremely poor country with very few Christians. The idea of an Nepali Christian market is absurd. But there is already a Nepal Christian Arts Society. I love that—it's exactly as it should be. And people who pursue a true artistic soul are not just better artists—they're on much safer ground when it comes to compromise on other issues.

What Do We Need Artists For, Anyway?

I warned at the beginning of this chapter that one might conclude that the life of the professional Christian is too risky to attempt. But I also promised a motivation that some may find compelling enough to do so. I believe for a few it is a risk worth taking, for one powerful reason.

The writer Madeline L'Engle defined art in the following way: "Art," she said, "is the thing that makes truth new all over again." I love this definition, because it tells us why we need Christian artists: We need them to make the truth new all over again. The risk of living as a Christian artist is too great if we take it only for fame and fortune. Jesus asked, "What good will it be for a man if he gains the whole world, yet forfeits his soul?" But to make the truth new again for ourselves and for the world is a beautiful way to live, a high and spiritual calling.

> If art makes truth new all over again, every person who calls themselves a Christian artist must therefore be able to succinctly answer the following question: "What truth are you making new?"

If art makes truth new all over again, every person who calls himself or herself a Christian artist must therefore be able to succinctly answer the following question: "What truth are you making new?" If you have an answer, you may consider yourself an artist, although you have yet to know if you are truly talented. But no matter how talented you are, if you cannot answer this question, you are probably just a singer or a performer. There is nothing wrong with those professions, but they are little different from banking or manufacturing. To be an artist—to live the creative life—asks more and gives more.

Tonight all over America, people will get off work, sit in comfortable chairs, and pick up the remote control of a television. Many of them will seek nothing more than entertainment. But a surprising number of them will, mostly unconsciously, be longing for something more significant. They will, in fact, be longing to have the truth made new for them. When they watch a film or a television program they will watch with open eyes, looking for connections to their own lives. They will watch what happens to the characters in these fictions, drawing conclusions about their own circumstances. And if the people of Christ can through the media make the greatest truth ever known new to them, then the great commission can be powerfully fulfilled. It is essential that Christians take up this cause.

Because of the pervasive influence of television in our society, a new and startling phenomenon occurs many thousands of times every day in our world. While switching between, say, HBO and Fox, many millions of viewers each day pause momentarily on Christian television programming, or what is sometimes referred to as inspirational programming. Because the cultural memory of what Christ actually did and said is largely lost to our society, a shocking percentage of the people who briefly watch this programming will have a thought that no one who grew up in a church would dream of having: "Oh," they will say, "it's Christianity. I've heard a lot about it. I wonder what it's like?" And for the four or five minutes that they stay on the channel, what they see will quite literally be the only answer to that question they ever get. They have never been to real church, except for a funeral, or, with increasingly less frequency, a wedding. So there is no basis for comparison between what they see and what a real church is like, between the outlandish, seductive claims often spouted on Christian television and what the Bible really says. Jesus did not call us to be always happy, to never suffer, and most certainly to be rich.

Even the least-observant unbeliever can see that this is not how Christians actually live, and the sense of our hypocrisy that forms in them is inevitable. And so, predictably, great damage is done to the cause of Christ, and derision for our faith is given unlimited fodder.

But what if a generation of Christian artists were to arise that were dedicated utterly to making the real truth of Christ new? What if, in full knowledge of their peril, they humbly became not stars but foot-soldiers, wielding the weapons of their gifts, their discipline, and God's inspiration? What if, when these foot-soldiers were given the opportunity to impact the media, they eschewed this contemptibly ersatz God, this Santa Claus, this heavenly honey-bear, and pointed people to the actual living Christ?

That is why I beg you to consider your life carefully, humbly, and in all wisdom. I beg you because you may have a calling that will lead you to a life of adventure, suffering, joy, risk, and glory. And I beg you because, if you become nothing but spiritual floor wax, you will achieve none of these goals.

One day, while preparing a Sunday school lesson, a famous passage of Scripture hit me very hard. Like most of you, I had read it many times. It begins in 2 Corinthians 5:19. "...And he has committed to us the message of reconciliation. We are therefore Christ's ambassadors, as though God were making his appeal through us."

I realized that I had been missing the essential message of this passage. Like most, I had focused on the responsibilities of being an ambassador for Christ. But what I had missed was whose appeal I was making. Most Christian artists think when they prepare a concert that they are preparing their own appeal on God's behalf. They put their evening together, crafting moments, working out details. But that is not our calling. We are actually making His appeal. We don't own it, and if we mess with it and sweeten it and compromise it or, most fatally, use it on our own behalf, we are literally coming between God and His people.

The life of an artist of faith is a beautiful life. To live it with integrity and dignity will sometimes require going against the grain of the expectations of others. But in so doing you may be able to make the truth new for the world. I encourage you to be brave and committed, to live your life with the dignity appropriate to the One whom you serve.

Reed Arvin is the managing editor of the AGMA curriculum. He has produced recordings by Rich Mullins, Amy Grant, 4HIM, Michael W. Smith, and many others, which have garnered 24 top five and 11 No. 1 songs. He is the author of *The Wind in the Wheat* (Thomas Nelson) and *The Will* (Scribner/ Pocket Books).

The Role of Music in Worship
By Harold Best

CHAPTER 2

To think of church time as worship time
without connecting it to the seven-day-a-week
liturgy of being living sacrifices is to miss the
entire biblical point of worship.

THE NATURE OF WORSHIP

Nobody Doesn't Worship

There are innumerable definitions of worship, in just as many books, that emphasize such things as love, mystery, adoration, praise, devotion, awe, grandeur, and glory, especially as these are informed by the character, nature, and expectations of God. Other definitions, while not overlooking these, focus more on the centrality of Christ through whom all worship is mediated and by whose Spirit it is directed and empowered. Interestingly enough, there are no real compact textbooklike definitions of worship anywhere in the Bible. To be sure, there are abundant references to worship and varied examples of what happens in worship, from the Old Testament models to the description of the gatherings of the early church. But if we are to find out what the Bible says worship truly is, we have to look beyond definitions and activities, and inquire into deeper principles.

As rich and useful as the textbook definitions are, virtually all of them miss a fundamental point, namely this: Worship is fundamental

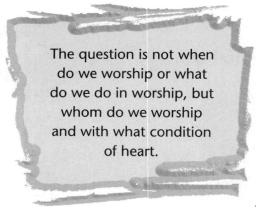

The question is not when do we worship or what do we do in worship, but whom do we worship and with what condition of heart.

to life itself, so much so that we can safely assume that it goes on all the time, all around us, inside of us, and, in a paradoxical way, in spite of us. So before we talk about Christian worship, we must first of all understand that there is no one in this world who is not, at this moment, at worship in one way or another; consciously or unconsciously, formally or informally, passively or passionately. For worship does not just apply to specific religious activities and to the deeply religious people who have strong feelings about a nameable god (Christian or otherwise), and how that god is to be pleased, placated, served, and worshiped. That is but one part of a larger picture. The question is not when do we worship or what do we do in worship, but whom do we worship and with what condition of heart. The answer to these questions literally constitutes the difference between heaven and hell, for the worship of every human being will be consummated in one of these two places.

So let's try a very broad definition, something that goes beyond specific events and religious practices and takes in the most fundamental issues about who we are and how we live. Worship constitutes a comprehensive choice that we make about who or what masters us and how we give ourselves over to that choice through devotion and service. As Jesus said, no one can serve both God and mammon, but it is inevitable that each of us will serve one or the other, to one extent or another. This is a fact and there is no escape from it.

This fundamental law of worship cannot be fully understood without taking two realities into account. The first is that God originally created us to worship Him continuously. The second is about how the darkness of the fall cut into the splendor of this original truth. We were created to live worshipfully—not just worshiping at certain times, but continually—to be in adoring submission, serving the One whom we cannot help but adore and being adored by the One to whom we cannot help but submit. The depth and extent of this relationship is based on the uniqueness of God creating us in His image and in the indescribable intimacy made possible by this. God intended that this relationship be a continuous exchange of gifts in that both He and the worshiper are givers. Worship was thus to be a marriage of a double willingness: the willingness of God's all-sufficiency bonded to the willingness of our dependence; the willingness of His sovereignty bonded to that of our submission; eternal and unconditional love bonded to our responding love; infinite and transcendent worth bonded to our finite and created worth.

I wish there were a word that would at once include both living and worshiping in an indivisible union, because that's what God originally intended, and this was certainly how Jesus lived—33 years a living sacrifice—no moment spent not worshiping. It is His life that shows us in absolute clarity what the law, the poets, and the prophets were trying to say to us, namely that we were created continuously to adore and to serve. We were created as naturally to honor, to adore, to fellowship with, to depend on, to submit to our Maker as we were to breathe in and out. It is in this fullness of life that God intended worship to be simple, normal, and ongoing.

Worship and Sin

Just as the original creation was all about ceaseless worship, so is the fall and our fallenness. Somehow, in the mystery and chaos of the fall, Adam and Eve turned from the complete truth to the complete lie even though the desire to worship was kept alive and active. While dead to God but being kept alive as worshipers, Adam and Eve simply exchanged gods. With the only true God removed from the picture, they had no choice but to fall under the spell and dominion of creatures and powers around them. Consequently, falling under the dominion of the very things over which they were initially given dominion spells the difference between false worship and true worship. There is only one word for false worship, in its numberless guises: idolatry. This is the remarkably blended act of choosing, even shaping, a god, only to be shaped by the very god that we have chosen or shaped. There is, in fact, a double blindness in all of this. On the one hand, by making a choice as to who or what "god" is, we assume a kind of lordship; we are deluded into thinking that we are in charge when actually we are enslaved. But because we have chosen to fall down before things that we have shaped or chosen, we are enslaved by them as well. Our self-enslavement, as well as that imposed on us by what we have chosen and shaped, combine in a hellish and chaotic death dance. We end up neither servants nor masters, but confused and blinded slave-gods. This is the ultimate schizophrenia of fallen worship. With the true God absent, but with worship continuing, countless self-made religions, manufactured righteousness, and self-justification have rushed into the vacuum. And it is God alone who can take this chaotic, upside-down-and-backwards mess, this maze of contradictions, lies, and confusion, sort it out, and, through the blood of Christ, turn us back again towards the true worship of the one true God.

> We cannot forget that we are still fallen, that we sin, and contrive innumerably subtle ways to re-create our idols.

But the problem is not just with fallen worship, but with fallenness in our Christian worship. By this I do not mean that, for instance, we worship Jesus alongside of a clay goddess or, having sung a song to Jesus, we turn around and perform a blood-letting sacrifice to an ancient spirit. It's far more subtle than that. If idolatry is the act of shaping something and then allowing it to shape us, then we must look around to discover the ways we still depend on things, or acts, or buildings, or people, or music, or art, or any other thing to cause or even facilitate a state of worship, determine the worth of our worship, or

> We were created as naturally to honor, to adore, to submit to, to depend on, to fellowship with our Maker as we were to breathe in and out.

define the extent of God's presence with us. And how often have we heard worship leaders talk about the power of music, or music as a tool, or creating a sequence of songs that "lead up" to worship, to empower worship or bring it to a conclusion. We will be dealing in more detail with this problem later, but for now, I want you to see that being a Christian and being at worship is not an automatic release from false worship and idolatry. We cannot forget that we are still fallen, that we sin, and contrive innumerable subtle ways to re-create our idols. This is why the Scriptures spend so much time on idolatry, on the danger of our returning to former ways, creating new gospels, and worked-up worship.

Here's what we have said so far: All of life for all of humankind comprises some kind of worship; therefore worship is always worship, it's only the gods that change. All liturgy is liturgy, whether Christian or pagan, only the content and intent change. All actions are acts of worship, whether we are under the spell and dominion of Wall Street, the arts, a snake in the Eastern highlands of Papua New Guinea, an evil spirit in the tenements of Hong Kong, a rock pile in Zimbabwe, a frog in the rain forests of South America, a guru in Waco, Texas, or a misguided worship leader in a local church gathering.

Worship and Our Redemption

Now we come to the nub of the matter. If the urge to worship is created in each of us and if all of us are somehow at worship all the time, how do we talk about true worship? When is worship really and truly worship? The answer lies only in Christ, in whom, by whom, and for whom worship becomes Christian worship. In order to offset the darkness and inversion of fallen worship, and to ensure that our Christian worship stays clean and unadulterated, we have to go to the very root of the gospel, for the root of the gospel is the root of true worship. We have to return to the tried and true concepts that supercede worship styles, worship times, worship music, and liturgies. We cannot assume that if we think good thoughts about God, repeat a call to worship, turn on the organ, strap on a guitar, fire up a synthesizer, or hire the best worship team, true worship will take place.

Here's the first tried and true concept, so familiar that we can lose sight of its profound significance: The just shall live by faith. Let's put this another way: Faith is the only thing the just shall live by. Whatever we do, it is all by faith, or better yet, faith as a stepping stone into yet more faith, not faith into something else. Consequently, it is in the midst of completely and continuously living by faith that true worship takes place. It is living by faith that allows us to discern between the mere activities of Christian worship and the faithful (that is, faith-full) condition that makes them into a pleasant aroma. All worship is by faith and unto more faith. Living by faith means worshiping by faith, and worshiping by faith encompasses the whole of living by faith. There is simply no other option or condition for the professing Christian. But we must go further. If, among faith, hope, and love, love is considered the greatest of the three (1 Corinthians 13:13), then love raises the whole of faithful living and continuing worship into a gracious, celebrative, unfussed, uncontrived, unmanipulated offering to the Lord. In Galatians 5:6 Paul puts it this way: "The only thing that counts is faith expressing itself through love." This is the way of Jesus, whose way is the way of continued worship, and this is certainly what Paul must have meant when he said that we are living epistles (2 Corinthians 3:2-3 NKJV). And it is only this kind of living that allows us to say that the best witness is overheard worship. This concept is powerfully explicated in 1 Corinthians 14:23-25 where Paul speaks of unbelievers entering a gathering of believers, hearing prophecies (that is, the speaking forth of truth) and being led to bow down, to worship, and to declare that God is truly among those who worship this way.

We can now turn to some of the passages in Scripture that will directly confirm and integrate these thoughts. Meanwhile we must bear in mind that the Scriptures include or allude to every approach to worship there is: organized, spontaneous, public, private, simple, complex, loud, quiet, silent, brief, or extended. It is sheer presumption for us to think that, under the guise of being "contemporary" or creative, we can come up with new ways to worship. There simply are none. The Holy Spirit saw to that millennia ago.

Of the many passages that lie at the heart of all Christian worship, three in particular stand out. The first is Romans 12:1. Here we have a clear, compact, and all-encompassing statement. The message is unequivocal: Whatever we do as Christians we do as living sacrifices. Because of the once-for-all sacrifice of Christ, it is no longer necessary for us to keep placing creatures and goods on the altar as symbols of our need for right standing. From now on, to use an oft-quoted phrase from one of Eric Routley's hymns, it is both "our duty and our delight" to become and remain once-for-all living sacrifices as a response to Christ's once-for-all sacrifice for us.

This stunning pronouncement means nothing other than a return to the kind of continued worship that God originally intended for us before it was turned upside down and backwards by the fall. For the Christian, this can only mean that there is now but one call to worship.

It comes when we are born again, when in sincere repentance we admit to having worshiped falsely, trapped by the lie and enslaved to false gods, before whom, all along, we have offered ourselves as dying sacrifices. Since the call back to true worship comes but once (not every Sunday, as mistaken as this concept is), we are free to understand that the carpenter, the surgeon, the garbage collector, the engineer, the artist, and the public servant are to continue their worship of God within the constructs and sequences of their daily work.

It is more than coincidental that the word liturgy was originally a secular term signifying an agreement to perform and complete some kind of ordinary service: tile setting, carpentry, and the like. Thus, being a sacrifice for as long as we are alive constitutes our agreement to be at work worshiping as the people of God, in all circumstances and places. Consequently, a liturgy is nothing other than the ongoing work of those who, as living sacrifices, are authorized to call all of their work worship. In all walks of life, therefore, our daily work, undertaken by faith, motivated by a desire to excel, and given over to loving God and serving humankind, can be likened to the perfume that Mary poured over Jesus' feet. We must remember that it is the supreme worth of Jesus that should motivate us to make every living act, whatever its name or condition, into the rich perfume of faith-driven love, adoration, and worship. This is the moment-by-moment stuff of Romans 12:1. This is where the joy is. This is where the celebration is.

Now what about corporate worship? Corporate worship is the special and occasional liturgy within the grand liturgy of the moment-by-moment Christian walk. Put as simply as possible, we do not go to church to worship. We go to church to worship corporately (that is, in common—in communion with each other) only to continue what we should have been doing all week long: praying, singing, listening, offering, speaking, being silent, confessing, growing, and being broken. To think of church time as worship time without connecting it to the seven-day-a-week liturgy of being living sacrifices is to miss the entire biblical point of worship. Yes, there are "special" times of worship, for which we plan and to which we congregate, but they are meaningless unless they are a seamless part of the life of continuous worship to which Romans 12:1 calls us.

The second scripture is taken from Jesus' conversation with the Samaritan woman: "Yet a time is coming and has now come when the true worshipers will worship the father in spirit and truth, for they are the kind of worshipers that the father seeks. God is a spirit, and his worshipers must worship in spirit and truth"(John 4:23-24). During the course of the conversation the woman attempted to change the direction that Jesus was taking and tried instead to talk about worship. And why not? Given what we have already said about the all-pervasive nature of worship, the confusion of worship with religiosity, and the way we tend to think that worshiping is a form of self-justification, her tactic makes a certain sense. Furthermore, she reduced the issue of worship to one of location, time, and tradition, which is what a great deal of today's "worship talk" is about.

However, Jesus would have none of this. In His profound wisdom, He decided to respond to her query, but in a way that at once kept Him on the subject of her need for salvation and on a rad-ical re-definition of her mistaken concept of worship. In a brief but powerful statement, Jesus subsumed the entire worship history of time, place, tradition, and protocol under a new law: that of worship in spirit and in truth. Jesus looked far ahead into Romans 12:1 and reiterated the grand principle that goes clear back to the creation of Adam and Eve: True worship is continual while location and circum-stance are incidental. In effect, Christ was saying that spirit and truth are to be made manifest as much in the workplace as in the grand sanctuary, for being in the spirit, worshiping in spirit, and living according to the truth are the Christian's only option and continual obligation. Being this way, in that sense that Jesus described it, is being at worship. He was talking about a worship that precedes, embraces, subordinates, and above all, validates liturgies, systems, planning committees, techniques, music, art, architecture, teamwork, preludes, postludes, and interludes. He was implying that reducing worship to such things, or depending on them, violates the principle of spirit and truth, because spirit and truth constitute a continual domain while the rest constitute a procedural and transient domain as evidences and not causes.

The third scripture is Psalm 29:2. This psalm begins with a commandment to ascribe glory to the Lord, immediately followed by a parallel commandment to worship God in the beauty of holiness. Once again we are brought face to face with the reality of worship as an ongoing state, simply because holiness itself is a continuous state to which all Christians are called. Holiness is a beauty seen fully in Christ Himself, who has promised personally to dwell in the living sacrifices who continue their worship daily by working out their salvation (Philippians 2:12) and by pursuing holiness, without which no one can see the Lord (Hebrews 12:14). This is the worshipful holiness of the twenty-four hour day, the state of being saved, of continuing as a living sacrifice, of being led by the spirit to live completely in the truth.

We can now summarize these three passages with another one from the Old Testament: Deuteronomy 10:12-15, 20-21. Verses 12-15 state in detail what Paul in Romans 12:1 says in principle. Then verses 20-21 add even further force and specificity: "Fear the Lord your God and serve him. Hold fast to him and take your oaths in his name. He is your praise; he is your God, who performed for you those great and awesome wonders you saw with your own eyes." In other words, God is truly worshiped (verse 20) only to the extent that the kind of life described in verses 12-15 and 20-21 is lived.

Let's put all the preceding thoughts together: Christian worship is to be undertaken as an act of love, driven by faith, architectured by hope, and saturated with truth, whatever the content, context, time, place, style, or circumstance. Our corporate worship is acceptable and effective only to the extent that we are moment-by-moment living sacrifices, doing everything in the spirit and according to truth, seeking out the beauty of holiness as our only path and our only walk, holding fast to God, who alone is our praise and our worship. If these conditions and actions mark our entire way of living, then they will mark the entirety of our corporate worship. There is simply no exception to this principle. It is simple, uncluttered, and within reach of every believing Christian.

Once we get the faith-love-worship issue straightened out, once we submit to the scriptural principles stated above, once we truly understand that Christian worship can only lead to more and more of itself, then we will make a startling discovery. Church going, as it is typically perceived and practiced, will most likely turn out to be artificial because of the ways we have separated it from the biblical concept of worship unto continuing worship. We will also come to realize that what we do in church says less about who our God is and how faithfully we serve Him (or them), than what we do the rest of the week. But if we understand worship as a seamless garment comprising all of faithful living, made startlingly new by the blood of the Lamb and brought to full strength by the Holy Spirit, then Sunday morning will be something splendid and different, and our worship planning may well have to undergo deep revision.

As has already been implied, Christian worshipers should be continuing on Sunday what they should have been doing all week long. A worship service has but one uniqueness, namely that it is corporate, for it is only through this kind of worship that the entire resource of a local congregation, its ministers and its many actions can be gathered, centered, and directed toward its Lord, its spiritual well being, its nurture, and its outreach. To borrow on a musical concept, Christians worshiping corporately are to do everything together, both "in unison"—spiritual unison—as well as in "parts"—spiritual parts. That is, the spiritual unison grows out of what the Apostles' Creed calls the communion of the saints:

We are one in Christ. We are all saved in exactly the same way: by the blood of Christ; we are mastered by the same Word of God; we have a single life's goal, to glorify God and to enjoy Him forever, and we are all, without exception, to grow up into the stature and fullness of Christ Himself. We are, in Paul's words, members of the household of God, built upon the foundation of the apostles and prophets, with Christ Jesus as the cornerstone. In Him the whole structure is joined together and grows into a holy temple in the Lord; in whom you (we) also are built together into a dwelling place for God (Ephesians 2:19-22).

In the next chapter of the same epistle, Paul literally begs the Ephesians to "bear with one another in love, making every effort to maintain the unity of the Spirit in the bond of peace because there is one body and one Spirit, just as you were called to the one hope of your calling" (Ephesians 4:3-4). Spiritual unison is every Christian's responsibility and no amount of liturgical and creative variety can ever displace this concept.

The concept of spiritual parts, on the other hand, means that even as we are one in Christ and one in each other, we are variously gifted, variously mature, variously repentant, and variously at work, both in spiritual and vocational ways. We are different to and for each other, even as we are one in each other. It is in this sense of being different even as we are one that prompts Paul to use the analogy of the human body with each of its members in profound need of all others. In corporate worship, all of this oneness and variety come together as in a cohesion of which God alone—not a worship style—is the coordinator. After all, it was He who decided in the first place against any two things—creatures, or people—being alike. Only a sovereign, all-powerful and all-knowing God could pull this off and still require unity while providing the means for achieving it.

Therefore, while everyone in worship is doing the same things together at the same time, they are doing the same things differently. So we must remember that the styles we choose should in no way account or substitute for the magnificent unity-within-variety that is represented in the single act of Christians coming together in the same place and submitting themselves and their worship to the same Holy Spirit who made sense out of the "chaos" and clamor of Pentecost. In fact, if we depend too much on the unifying properties of musical style, we may forget or even undo the deeper principle of union in Christ which is far and away more crucial than anything else we can think of or do.

WORSHIP AND MUSIC-MAKING

Some Simple Instructions from Scripture

We can now deal directly with music in worship. At their best, worship, worship styles, and music are a seamless garment. However, it is still necessary to briefly discuss music-making as a separate subject, as simply as possible, in order both to validate what has been said so far and to prepare the way for a discussion of other issues.

Let's repeat this principle once more: We do not gather together to worship but to continue our worship in union with Christ and in communion with each other. This truth radically repositions music-making, especially for those who hold that music is the door to worship or the facilitator of worship, or even the sum and substance of worship itself. If we are already at worship before we gather together, music-making cannot possibly be considered an aid to worship or a tool for worship or a means to worship. This would put music-making outside of worship and place the Holy Spirit at the mercy of musical action. Neither is music an end in itself because that would reduce worship to a doormat for music and would further imply that music is for music's sake. Music is, purely and simply, an act of worship or idolatry. It is God alone who is both means and end, Alpha and Omega. And since Christ Himself is both the Author and Finisher of our faith and sincere worship is of no effect outside of the exercise of faith, it has to follow that music-making is always subordinate: a wonderful servant, but an evil master. It is in this sense that the joy of the Lord, the joy of His continuing presence, the joy of the knowledge of salvation, the joy of making offering to Him, bring a joy to music-making that it does not possess by itself.

We do not, therefore, make music in order to worship, to create a "mood" of worship (it is near blasphemy to think of worship as a mood), nor should we depend on it to take us to the spiritually higher state that some Christians even liken to entering the Holy of Holies. Instead, we make music because we are at worship, because we adore Christ so much that we cannot help but make music, because we have a high priest who Himself entered the Holy of Holies once for all, not time after time (Hebrews 8:12). By trusting Christ we are permanently in Christ; Christ has once for all entered into the holy place, having done away with the entire sacrificial system and having sworn us to continuous worship, irrespective of time or place, so we are drawn back to the sweeping truth that He is our worship. Therefore, we do not have to "arrive" at worship or approach a condition of worship that is not already a continuation of the worship to which we are permanently called.

All of this brings a new luster, a new freedom, and a new responsibility to music-making. No longer is the burden on music, the music-makers, and the so-called worship leaders, teams, and bands. The burden is where it is supposed to be, squarely on the shoulders of the Holy Spirit, squarely in the hands of the Savior Himself, and borne up by God who is at once Creator and Sustainer of all things. No longer need we fret over whether or not the music is doing the right job. No longer need we fear those who claim they could not worship because of the music. No longer should we feel especially at ease or proud when others say God seemed so much nearer because of the music.

Why? Because the true worshipers are offering music instead of depending on it, even when it is not "their" music; even if they may not completely understand or appreciate it. Biblical worship places the emphasis where it should be: on the giver and not on the gifts. Thus, we are free to worship in spite of the music but never because of it. Furthermore, we must rid ourselves of the idea that worship is limited to the making music parts of worship, or that music and worship are one and the same. Whenever you hear someone say something like this: "We'll worship" (meaning we'll sing/play) and then we'll (whatever follows next in the service)" reject it out of hand. It is wrong. Quietly but firmly correct the one or ones who have been taught this in error and truncated worship this way. The music is just one of countless acts of continuing worship.

> There is no circumstance in life for which music-making is inappropriate.

In the many references to music-making throughout the Bible, this one principle emerges: There is no circumstance in life for which music-making is inappropriate. From weddings to wars and from temple to synagogue to the early church, the Scriptures cite music-making. In fact, God directly commands us to make music. There is no option. "Sing (play) to the Lord a new song" does not beat around the bush. In its directness and simplicity this single utterance contains three interrelated commands.

1. "Sing" (and/or play): As already stated, no one is excused, even those who might not want to sing or might not like the song being sung at the time. Worship, in the time/place/circumstance

sense, is not mentioned in this commandment. Rather, the commandment to sing assumes the ongoing as the commandment to worship.
Therefore, singing and worship go hand in hand, day in and day out.

2. "To the Lord": The preposition "to" is the key word. If we are to
be continually at worship and if we worship the Lord without need of
any intermediary except Christ, then music, faithfully made, can go
only in one direction. It is meant to go directly to the Lord. Only then
can we allow it to serve our co-worshipers. This principle is so
important that it goes beyond church music and applies to every
Christian who makes any kind of music in any place. The story of
Mary pouring expensive perfume over Jesus' feet (John 12:1-8) is the
perfect metaphor for our music-making. It is but one of countless fra-
grant offerings that we as living sacrifices lavish on Jesus' feet. We
must not make the mistake of offering music to people or programs or
markets or results. Doing any of these reduces the Lord to an
observer or a bystander and raises up new idols in His place. When
we sing to one another (Ephesians 5:19-20 and Colossians 3:16), we
must understand that we do this only in light of singing first of all to
the Lord. In fact, Paul says specifically that our melodies should be
made in our hearts to the Lord. Therefore, singing to each other in the
biblical sense is not an independent act, but a contingent one. We sing
to each other and we instruct each other only because we have first
directed our songs to the Lord.

3. "A new song": Here we have two commandments wrapped up
in one. Those who are created in the image of God are given the
capacity to dwell in newness because that is what God does and that
is what He expects of us. Of course, our kind of newness, even the
best of it, is not quite God's kind because He creates whatever He
wants out of nothing (no-thing). We cannot create out of nothing; we
need raw materials, advice, example, surrounding context, and time.
We create out of something into something else. Thus, a music maker

makes a song out of the musical examples and contexts around him or her. If there is any newness, it lies in the creative difference, the originality, and in some cases, the cutting-edge qualities that the truly imaginative musicians possess. If they are truly creative, they will then create such newness that they will be imitated by others. And so the chain of human creativity goes on from leader to follower and from generation to generation.

> The trouble with many Christian musicians is that they begin and continue by imitating. Therefore, they have nothing new worth imitating.

The trouble with many Christian musicians is that they begin and continue by imitating. Therefore, they have nothing new worth imitating. But imitation continues nonetheless and we end up imitating imitations. This may be the most serious problem with present-day Christian music, whether traditional "contemporary" or Christian contemporary. We have learned to cover this up by calling it ministry, seeking comfort from those who say that they have been ministered to when they have merely been made to feel good. With few exceptions, things are bound to continue this way as long as cutting-edge creativity, whatever the style or type, is kept out of the religious mainstream by those who strategize along lines of customer satisfaction and choose shallow emotional substitutes and spiritual quick-fixes over deep-down mystery. "God gave me this song" is a dangerous way to describe God's generosity when these supposedly divinely given songs are so un-new, so ordinary, and so lifeless. We need to be careful with our words about God, just as much as we need to be careful about God's words to us.

Nevertheless, the commandment to make new songs continues to stand lonely, but real, awaiting something truly new, something that would shake us to our boots—that is, if we have the faith and courage to celebrate the God of newness—even if we literally have to cling to each other for support.

We can also turn the adjective new into the adverb newly. We can then say, "Sing to the Lord a song newly." A song newly sung can be a new song becoming old, as with the so-called praise/worship songs, or an old song that has lived through the ages and deserves to continue to live. In both cases, newness comes about only by the exercise of a lively faith. Every time we repeat a song, we must make it new again, otherwise we will be guilty of what the Scriptures call vain repetition. It is entirely possible to take the Lord's name in vain while we are gathered in the sanctuary singing, praying, or preaching if we do not literally and intentionally mean what we say and sing as if it was for the very first time.

Repetition is necessary. We repeat things that are truthful simply because truth must be repeated over and over. We say (and sing) the Lord's Prayer. We sing the Doxology. We sing "There is a Redeemer." Faith alone can make these new. In this sense we can say of our music and lyric: "Old things (that is, their chronological oldness) have passed away and all things (whatever their age) have become new." Put into context of the Genesis creation story, we should live, day unto day, as if it were always in the first day when everything was new: brilliantly, disturbingly, diversely new. If church music followed this example, all of it—new, old, simple, complex, long, short, familiar, and strange—would be in a far more splendid condition.

What can we learn from Jericho? The story of the defeat of Jericho by Joshua and his people (Joshua 6:2-20) cannot be fully understood without reference to the music that was made as the people marched around the city. The story is so familiar that it does not need to be repeated here, except to say that the making of music was among the things God told Joshua and his people to do, and the walls did not fall down until the trumpets were blown.

There are at least two ways to interpret the musical part of this story. One interpretation is biblical, and the other is not, yet each is commonly lived out in present-day Christian circles. The unbiblical interpretation goes this way: People blew their trumpets and brought the walls down. Simple, isn't it? It was the music that did it, that brought the culmination about. And this is what many of us say about music in worship: It is capable of bringing great things about. It is capable of bringing people into a state of worship; it somehow brings God nearer and brings results.

The biblical interpretation goes this way: As people blew their trumpets in obedience to God, He knocked the walls down. When we view music-making this way, we understand it is God alone who does the work that He wants done as we make our music, not because we make our music. Our task and privilege is to follow His commands and to bring our work and music to Him first. Then He can do whatever He pleases and we can take no credit for what He has done. If He works mightily when music is made, let us be sure that we do not credit the music and then build on that presupposition, for if we do, we are bound to expect music to repeat the glory when it is God's business alone to repeat the glory, music or no music. If you are truly honest with yourself, you will have to admit to those times when you or other worship leaders have strained and strained to repeat the glory, to maintain the "high" through some pretty superficial devices. Avoid this.

It is crucial for church musicians and worship leaders to understand the profound difference between these two interpretations, for either one can become the foundation upon which music ministries are built. One is equivalent to building on sand and the other upon rock, and it does not take a genius to figure out which one honors God. Yet, as each of us knows in times of deep heart-searching, it is quite tempting to depend upon the music instead of the God of the music. Be careful.

Music in Contemporary Culture

Like it or not, we cannot forget that cultural conditions impinge heavily on contemporary church music practices. What the church and its leaders choose to do with these conditions is another matter, but they must be recognized in any case.

The first condition is fairly obvious. There is more music in more styles made by more people from all walks of life, available in more ways to more people, than at any time in history. There is no way for anyone except the most gifted cultural critics to account for this explosion. Even the experts who dig intelligently into as much music as possible cannot do more than scratch the surface. In the midst of this explosion, we are all making choices. Some have chosen to eliminate all but two or three styles and others whose tastes and discernment range over dozens and dozens of styles: jazz, classical, rock, folk, ethnic, gospel, and so on. This latter group, unfortunately, is in the minority throughout secular culture, but even more so among church and Christian contemporary musicians.

Second, there is not only more music than ever before, but more music is being made in more places and contexts than ever before. Music is virtually omnipresent. There is no escape from it. It is an integral part of a massive sight and sound environment. It is in this sense that music has become, for lack of a better term, insignificant significance. Culture is glutted with music, not so much because there are so many great artists around, but because we have to find ways to keep filling the huge maw of musical consumption.

While it is historically true that a lot of music has been made while something else is going on (music as background), there has probably never been a time in history where so much of it is made among so many other competing contexts. Today, it takes an enormous amount of effort for the average person Christian or non-Christian, in or out of the church, to face the music for what it is in and of itself. Most of us simply hear music; a smaller number take time to listen to it, and fewer ever truly encounter it, deeply engage with it, with any degree of intellectually and emotionally informed involvement.

Third, this glut of music-making is embedded in a culture that pays less attention to the importance and precision of words and their connection to truth-telling. Carefully chosen speech, meaningful speech, is becoming more and more the exception, even among those for whom it should be a regular habit: teachers, preachers, public servants, and media leaders. The advertising industry, which is essentially professionalized exaggeration, has robbed us of the ability to discuss issues precisely, subtlety, and dispassionately. All products, from pizzas to sexual experiences to skyscrapers to music ministries are "unique," "awesome," "mind-boggling," "incredible." Standing ovations, formerly reserved for isolated instances of extraordinary worth, are now accorded nearly every performer at the end of carefully manipulated, climax-producing events. In describing nearly everything with superlatives, we are left with the irony of everything being on equal footing. This in turn renders us incapable of making truly qualitative judgments based on fairness, reason, and above all, truthfulness.

> Carefully chosen speech, meaningful speech, is becoming more and more the exception, even among those for whom it should be a regular habit.

Fourth, even though our language has been devalued and our verbal communication blurred, we still need to communicate and connect with each other in some manner. Consequently, we have become drawn together more by the nonverbal, the gestural, and the "spiritual." We use music to create and identify, to connect up with each other, perhaps as in no other time in civilizational history. On the surface, this appears to be somewhat harmless, because who does not love music and who, in one way or another, is not deeply moved by it and bonded to each other in its making?

But the whole combination is dangerous. While music, even in its glut and insignificant significance, can powerfully affect emotions and bind people together in almost a tribal way, it has absolutely no capability to express moral qualities or propositional truth. It is morally neutral; it is completely "dumb" as to any ability to state anything outside of itself. As with no other art form, music depends on association—repetition in the same environment—to gather to itself any semblance of "moral" or "truth" meaning. But when the music does come to the forefront, when it is the primary bonder, as it presently appears to be, it becomes, as George Steiner has said, the new literacy, its own kind of truth. Everything is wrapped up in music: how it is done; how it affects people; how it may be used to accomplish a variety of tasks; and how it appears to be responsible for the way people behave.

> Music is now irreversibly linked to something inherently foreign to it, namely consumerism and money.

In short, music has grown larger than itself (another way of describing an idol). It has more and more become the culture-shaper. It persuades, it binds, it identifies, it manipulates. We have become addicted to it for all that it does for and to us. Furthermore, music is now irreversibly linked to something inherently foreign to it, namely consumerism and money. It is an industry among interconnected industries masquerading nonetheless as an art form or a ministry. It no longer stands on its own as something to be carefully and temperately used, intellectually encountered and wisely distributed. It now dominates where, biblically speaking, it was only intended to be offered up and to serve. It now manipulates where it was only meant to express, and it must be produced in greater quantities, not so much to satisfy a deep love, but to ameliorate a gargantuan habit.

Now, let's take all of this to church and to current trends in church music and ask some questions. Why is music itself more and more dominant? Why does so much hinge on music? Why is music so heavily depended on to produce worship? Why are music and worship virtually equated with one another? ("We'll worship for awhile and then we'll be led in prayer and then we'll hear from God's Word.") Why are lyrics so shallow, so thin, so repetitive and theologically imprecise? Why do we hear theologically shallow church leaders say that if we want to grow a church, we'll have to change worship styles? Why do people say that while they can worship with one kind of music, they cannot worship without it or with another kind? And why is preaching less powerful, theologically accurate, and verbally precise, and why does music seems to take its place as the worship *glue?*

How much singing and playing is a religious form of addiction? Why does it take a leader or a team to get worship started and to keep it going? Why has a significant part of so-called praise and worship turned into something similar to a mantra, with its lack of variety, and its seeming dependence on repetition and formula? Have we bought too much into the norms of culture and failed to see that church music can be something radically different without having to become an unintelligible or intellectually arrogant substitute for the best a culture can come up with? These several questions have been asked in order to prompt you to examine your methods and to question the methodologies that you have adopted or you may have been erroneously taught. Watch out for the pithy sayings, the formulas, anything that places the relevance of music over the power of biblical thought. Watch out for musical practices that move people into thinking God is moving them. Watch out for those times when you literally feel you have people in the palm of your hand and you know exactly what musical move to take and make them feel God's presence. And then you make that move, knowing full well you are leading them into error. Wake up to the idolatry in this. Get broken, plead for humility. Plead for the actual disappearance of music from your life and the life of your congregation until you and they have so come to depend on God that true worship in the most powerful sense of His presence are realities in themselves without one note of music.

Then let the music come. Let it come in its rightful newness because God is there, not the reverse. Get out of the way. Set your heart and mind against the next cliché, the next move, the next contrived climax and still another repetition of the music that has worked so well for so long—why change it? If you are called to be a leader, then be one, even if it means that there is less music but more significance, less repetition and more freshness, less of self and more of God; even if it means that you must confront the senior pastor who may be senior in all respects save artistic integrity, biblical thought, and good theology.

Musical Diversity and Musical Quality

Even though we discussed the danger of too much music, we need to distinguish between glut and variety. Even though we may cut back on the amount of music that fills our lives, we still need many kinds of music. There are only two ways to treat musical diversity honestly. The first is to say that diversity, in each of its countless parts, exists, but there is no need to bring it together in one place. Just let one sector of diversity remain true to itself, making whatever type of music it prefers and changing or adding to it when it internally feels appropriate to do so. Classicists can be classicists, country west-erners can be country westerners, praise and worship people, praise and worship people, rappers rappers, jazzers jazzers, and so on. In church, traditional worship can be traditional, praise and worship can be praise and worship, and contemporary can be contemporary. This approach is very tidy but not very exciting. It will work as long as repetitive practitioners do not turn separation into prejudice or develop a kind of inbred snobbery and staleness that comes from keeping a practice to itself.

The second approach is far more desirable and equally complex. A world of music literally means a world full of diverse musics that exist in their own right. Furthermore, a world of imaginative musi-cians means that diversity won't stay put. It is continually on the move and continually changing. Stylistic and practitional boundaries blur and merge, only to separate again. In a word, truly creative people are truly eclectic. They will want to keep experimenting, adding, shifting, paraphrasing, and fusing. In the spirit of the great Wesleyan hymn, a thousand tongues will never be enough.

Where does church music come into this glorious whirl? We must admit that most of our solutions are quite superficial partly because, as we have already said, the truly creative are not particularly wel-come in Christian music and church music; partly because church music does not have to be particularly diverse to be healthy; but mostly because the typical Christian concept of artistic creativity falls short of a biblical theology of the same. We have our reasons: our fear of losing people; our propensity to choose the familiar over the strange; our tendency to depend more on emotional response than faithful encounter; a failure on the part of traditionalists to under-stand how creative a tradition can be and a parallel failure on the part of contemporists to understand how quickly the new becomes old. Consequently we keep getting caught up in second-rate solutions.

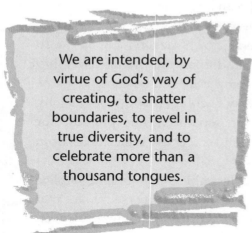

We are intended, by virtue of God's way of creating, to shatter boundaries, to revel in true diversity, and to celebrate more than a thousand tongues.

Either we blend what little variety we possess or we separate it into 8 A.M. and 11 A.M. worship clubs.

Likewise, the blended is often nothing more than stylistic tokenism: adding X to compensate for Y so that Z will contain enough to please everybody some of the time. Meanwhile the contemporary, as stated elsewhere, can easily denigrate into a narrow, increasingly repetitious body of songs interspersed with talking/praying about coming into the presence of God and helped by look-and-act-alike worship teams. ("Blended" is a terrible term even though it enjoys widespread use. It implies mixing everything up into a generic whole in which all the individual flavors are lost—a kind of musical health food drink. Is there a better word? I do not know; maybe diversified—or eclectic—is better, although each comes with its own baggage. Just be sure you do not get sucked under by labels, especially as they are tossed around at conferences and how-to-do-it sessions. People who have the floor love labels!)

So why have church music at all, if things need so much fixing? The answer is simple: to sing to the Lord new songs; to sing old songs newly; to teach and admonish one another in the ways of holy newness; to change things in Jesus' name while striving to become better today than we were yesterday; and to understand that a biblical theology of faith, creativity, and worship summons the Body of Christ to be ready for anything and to celebrate this readiness.

Human beings are created creators. We are intended, by virtue of God's way of creating, to shatter boundaries, to revel in true diversity, and to celebrate more than a thousand tongues. Why? Because that is

how God is and that is how God acts. His creation—His handiwork—
is infinitely varied and wildly imaginative. Our handiwork should be
too, and what better place is there to celebrate the redeemed wildness
of our creative imaginations than in corporate worship? Were we to
do this in Jesus' name, were we to depend solely on His power to empower what we can only offer to Him, were we to be cleansed of the
idea that it is music doing the work, maybe the world would be
turned upside down. Not because of our wildly redeemed creativity,
but because we fearlessly worship the One who has commissioned us
to be wildly creative and to speak in His name as if He were making
His appeal directly through us (2 Corinthians 5:20).

Now this wildness does not
mean creative idiocy and artistic
intemperance—musical binges
for the sake of binging and
artistic license for the sake of art
alone. Rather, it means creative
authenticity and corporate integrity. This further means that
diversity is a deliberate and inventive way of thinking and
acting, based on local conscience
and local resources. The reason
why so much church music sounds
so inauthentic, so "ordered out,"

> The reason why so much church music sounds so inauthentic, so "ordered out," is because individual churches seem afraid to be themselves and so prone toward imitating success.

is because individual churches seem afraid to be themselves and so
prone toward imitating success. They seem reluctant to ask, "Who
are we in this place in Christ, and how can we fulfill the glory of
Christ in us and in this place without having to act like the church
down the street, or adopt the programs of the big-budget mega
churches or feel inferior or ineffective because we are small and
poor?"

Diversity does not mean a headlong rush into every idiom and style available. No one can do this and no one should attempt it. But it does mean that experiment, change, variety, and even dislodgment are to be sought in preference to stay-the-same practices, whether traditional, contemporary, or blended. In a time when it is obvious that churches are trying to outgrow and outdo each other, where growth-by-envy might be more real than apparent, it is vitally important for each local church to spend time, thought, and prayer as to what it can authentically be and do in its local setting, with its limited resources and with God-given desire to be exactly what He wants it to be. It is only in this sense that church musicians and worship leaders must pray for the gifts of theological insight, prophetic wisdom, and unrelenting excellence, but in relation to this one inevitable question from God: Given the command to grow up into the stature and fullness of Jesus Christ, what is your next move forward? How much like Abraham are you willing to be? Then, if you are a traditionalist, you will discover that there is far more diversity in tradition than most people allow. If you prefer contemporary styles, do not limit yourself to the way most churches define contemporary. If you prefer something blended, make sure the blend is not tokenism, bringing the usual tradition and the usual contemporary into some kind of nervous accommodation. Make sure that it is a truly honest search into the best of as many styles as you and your creative brothers and sisters can creatively handle.

I remain personally convinced that we should not limit ourselves and our worship to one style, or divide an otherwise unified congregation into "traditional" and "contemporary" encampments. When we do this, we deny the capability that people have for being stretched, even though they do not recognize this capability or want to admit it. A congregation, truly enlivened by faith and willing to go deep and wide for Christ, should be as stylistically diverse as is possible. Then within the theological mandates for newness and familiarity, it should seek out that which, for it and its resources, is appropriate.

We must remember that we who call ourselves Christians—we who are truly living by faith—are, of all people on earth, the most capable of facing, handling, and celebrating variety, newness, change, and mystery. After all, we are saved by the creating and sustaining Savior and we claim to worship the most diverse Creator imaginable. There really is no option. Our worship should strive with all its might to burst into a veritable Pentecost of styles—again, a thousand tongues will never be enough—simply because we, as redeemed images of God, created to celebrate the infinite wonders of an unlimited Creator, fall short of the glory of God when we break worship down to a few paltry alternatives. For sure, people are going to say that this "didn't meet my need" or "I can't worship unless they do my music." But this is where the gospel stands tall and reminds them that to think this way is to depend on things rather than God. And, as we have said already, depending on handiwork instead of God is nothing short of idolatry.

Before we fall into the usual trap of "picking the right worship style" we need to remember the deep-down theological mandates that make faith, not style, the arbiter. Worship leaders have a serious responsibility in this respect. The worship style of a given congregation will only be as imaginative and creative as its gifts are developed. It is therefore of utmost importance that worship leaders themselves be people of immense theological and creative width, as well as people with exceptional stylistic expertise, not just technical licks, not just a passing acquaintance with so-called alternatives. After all, it is the Lord Himself who is being worshiped, not just in a functional sense, but worshiped for all that He is and all that He can be, despite our tendencies to worship safely and predictably. And since it is our task to be ambassadors of Christ, we have to keep coming back to this thought: The best and most complete witness is the overheard witness of continuing worship.

Above all, be sure of this: Whatever music styles you decide on, they should be far less important than the biblical principles that have led to their choice. In all of this, your congregation must be carefully taught, first, to understand that the music they hear and do is far less important than the Christ to whom it is offered, second, to understand that all the music in the world is but a lisp when compared to the splendor of the Godhead, third, to understand that being limited to just one musical style is like limiting our appreciation of God's creation just to liking pine trees, fourth, to understand that even if it were possible to bring the heavens down with the greatest music ever conceived, Jesus will always be more splendid, and fifth, to believe that no music ever written will ever be able to express what a simple, childlike, hungry, faith-driven and spirit-filled heart can, in complete silence, experience.

Then let the music come! Let a thousand tongues break out! Let our songs be ready for Him instead of getting Him ready for our songs.

Worship, Music, Feelings, and Emotions

Present-day culture is dominated by emotional experiences and, as a result, many music-worship experiences are emotionally driven. There is no way that we can rid ourselves of feelings. Were we able to do this, we would cease to be in the image of God, for as we well know, God is not a nonperson. He is not depersonalized, detached, or disinterested. He loves, He hates, He grieves, He rejoices, He laughs, and He weeps. We do these very same things because He does these things, despite the fact that we cloud and distort them with sin. We do not emote because we are sinners any more than God emotes because He is holy. Rather, we do and God does because we are persons, wondrously related and, because of Christ's wonderful work, we are deeply in love.

It stands to reason, therefore, that whatever we do as human beings we will do with feeling. A good carpenter will rejoice over a finely-crafted joint; a good surgeon laments over the discovery of cancer in a patient, even though he will experience happiness over being able to remove the cancer, and he will feel satisfaction over a suture that is closed with skill and precision. Life cannot be lived without deep feeling. The knowledge that all of life can be lived out as a continuous act of worship is one of the most heart-warming, joy-giving emotions that we can have. Likewise, knowing that we are riddled with sin—not just now and then, but always—fills us with ongoing grief of such depth that only the ongoing joy of repentance and forgiveness can offset it. Corporate worship is not only under-girded by these emotional constants, but filled with the occasional and variegated feelings brought about by the particular acts we undertake. A moment of confession highlights the ongoing sadness we have over our sin, just as the promise of forgiveness highlights the ongoing joy we have because of Jesus.

And within all of this we make music, and without a doubt music-making is a deeply emotional experience. However, the expressive power of music and art, as well as any sequence of litur-gical events, should never be mistaken for the presence of God or the increase of faith. When it is, we have just made a sacrament out of musical action and emotional response. How many times have we heard someone say how much nearer God seems if the music is just right, or how many times are we as musicians tempted to bring Jesus just a little closer by choosing just the right tune, chording, or color?

To the person living by faith, God does not appear in incremental doses that are related to our feelings, doings, and music-making. Before all of the Sundays of history ever got under way, before anyone decided anything about contemporary or tradition or blended or anything else, before we got ourselves so fussed up about the power of music, we must remember this stunning fact—God is always here. God is always here before, during, and after all the doing is done. God is now here, from everlasting to everlasting. God is now here, and when we try to get Him to be more here, to dress up His presence with music, artistic action, device, and tool, we are going to grieve the Holy Spirit. As Brother Lawrence so simply said: "He is within you; seek Him not elsewhere."

> Worship is forthright, ongoing stuff, isometric stuff—striving, wrestling, hungering, thirsting, honest-to-goodness and down-to-earth stuff.

Going to church or attending a worship service is not how-will-my-felt-needs-be-met time, nor is it what-kind-of-experience-will-I-have time. Worship is not what, at any perceptual or aesthetic level, just might happen to feel good; nor is it my job as a worship leader to even hint at the idea that music-making, feeling good, and the presence of God are one ball of wax. Worship is forthright, ongoing stuff, isometric stuff—striving, wrestling, hungering, thirsting, honest-to-goodness and down-to-earth stuff. It is not titillation. It is not show-off. It is not superficially emotive, sacramentally orgasmic stuff. Sunday worship is simply and powerfully the corporate synergy of all its moment-by-moment parts.

Now if the music deeply moves and pleases me, that is quite all right. This simply means that I add my feelings to my offering to the Lord instead of depending on them to make Him seem closer. I make a faith-driven offering of my music and my feelings. If I am not moved or pleased, that is all right, too. I am still obligated to make a faith-driven offering and to celebrate the One the worship of whom is infinitely beyond my feelings and understanding. In all cases it is faith unto faith and love unto love, not faith or love conditioned by my response to music, art, preaching, or environment. To the truly faithful, it is the giver and not the gift that has pre-eminence.

WORSHIP LEADERS, TEAMS, TECHNIQUES: SOME CONCLUDING SUGGESTIONS

It does not take a rocket scientist to figure out that worship can take place without a paid or even volunteer worship leader. Many churches continue to worship in significant ways without a named worship leader. Other churches seemingly cannot wait to redescribe and reposition themselves by creating a position of worship leader or minister of worship and creating worship teams to assist them in what they describe as worship. Here are some general suggestions, based on principles already outlined, that must be considered without fail and in any situation.

The term "worship leader" is in itself a questionable term, if worship leadership is limited to responsibility for planning a sequence of activities that include virtually everything but the sermon. Biblically speaking, a worship leader should be someone who sees to the spiritual growth and well-being of the congregation in terms of the biblical concept of worship as a way of life. In other words, worship leaders should include the senior pastor and the entire pastoral team, irrespective of their titles and job descriptions. But since worship leaders are hired and described with a more limited construct in mind, and since it seems nearly impossible—outside of a deep and penetrating theological reformation—to turn this limited and erroneous concept around, it would do ministers of worship well to understand that they labor under a weighty biblical concept. Thus, without usurping authority that their particular form of church governance might disallow, they can still understand that, in the biblical sense, they are charged with something far more comprehensive than planning and doing worship times.

Related to the above, the term "worship team" is even more flawed, given biblical concepts of worship. While this term is likely to be around for some time to come—at least until the next wave of labels and descriptives strike church leadership—it would be well to understand that the real worship team is the congregation and those who are up on the platform, behind mics, slide charts, and synthesizers are, at best, coordinators and caregivers. Thus, for them to overwhelm, stand out, or give any appearance that they are to be followed or highlighted—as to sound level, gestures, movements, dress, and the like—is to denigrate the congregation and its role as a gathering of priests unto the Lord. Each member of the Body of Christ, it must be remembered, has direct access to God through Christ—with no need whatsoever of the loud, swaggering, and acoustically superior trappings that many worship teams have. Do everything in your power to guard against the assumption these are indispensable. Leading worship is not the same as giving a concert or mixing concertlike activities with congregational song. Remember that the heart of church music is the song of the congregation, not the specialized work of the teams and leaders. Given the performer-spectator atmosphere in American culture, it becomes all too easy to perpetuate this in a worship setting. Do not forget that many Christians are literally unable to separate worship from entertainment and they expect you to entertain. Do not buy this. Examine yourself, and in a spirit of brokenness and openness, visit church after church and observe the extent to which a performance atmosphere infects what should be a congregation-centered approach to God. Where you see humility and brokenness instead of strutting, loudness, and hype, give thanks and go back to your workplace and do likewise.

> Each member of the Body of Christ, it must be remembered, has direct access to God through Christ.

None of this is meant to imply that we should not have Christian concerts. On the contrary, we need them—but not mixed in with corporate worship. Once we understand the nature and place of music in corporate worship and once we understand that the congregation is the chief body of music-makers, we will do less leading and concertizing. But when it becomes appropriate to present full-fledged concerts, the roles are changed. The congregation becomes a true audience and the musicians can truly become performers. And in both situations, corporate worship and concertizing, the music first of all goes to the Lord and only then to and among the worship-hearers.

A worship leader is, above all else, a teacher. The teaching is above all else verbal, conceptual, and biblical. It must be these even before it is musical, for a theology of music should always derive out of a theology of worship, and a theology of worship should be nothing less than a theology of daily life. Putting technological concepts and ideas before musical ones means that the worship leader-as-teacher should be known for the ability to guide a congregation about more than how to make it through the next hour or so of activity. Worshipers must understand that what they are about to undertake is not the be-all-end-all. It is not "brought on" by the team and the music—as exciting and enticing, as "spiritual" and God-reminding as it can be—because it is not spiritual power; it is not "God with us." Instead, because God is already with us, because Jesus is the same yesterday, today, and forever, because He does not change personalities or have more personal clout just because He is found in a church building—because of these things and more, worshipers must be taught that everything they do is because God has done it first, and corporate worship is a witness to this and worshipers give testimony to this. The only other alternative is for worship time to be constructed as a time of gradual buildup, so that worship will somehow be achieved and God will somehow eventually manifest Himself. Guard passionately against the temptation to say that by worshiping, or beginning worship, we are entering into God's presence or that God's presence is something to be invoked, as if He were merely one of those who came in the front door and was handed an order of worship so that He could see exactly when it was His time for His Presence to be felt. Guard against calls that imply a chronological beginning to worship. Rather employ calls to corporate worship, or be sure that any opening remarks, printed or improvised, are statements of worship, not start-ups for worship.

In everything you do, strive for excellence and do not hide mediocrity behind the idea that the only thing God wants is purity of heart and right motives. Of course He does, but once we biblically examine what it means to be pure of heart and possessed of correct motivation, we discover that these are more than disembodied qualities. Purity of heart means pursuing a more excellent way, and pursuing a more excellent way means that all of life, from hammering nails to performing open heart surgery to making music is an engagement in pursuit of excellence. Seeking the highest quality should not be thought of as elitist, but as normal. Pursuing excellence, for the Christian, is the norm, not the exception.

So, what is excellence? A good and entirely biblical question. The secular answer goes something like this: "Excellence is winning. Excellence is doing something perfectly. Excellence is doing something better than somebody else does it." Stated directly or in any number of cultural, personal, and emotional disguises, it is these kinds of answers that make neurotics out of some people, push others to intolerable limits and, ironically, keep everybody from doing even as well as they were created to, whatever their level of capability.

There is, however, a completely biblical approach that applies just as much to an individual as it does for a local congregation. It is healthy, it is for real, it is achievable, it requires discipline and hard work, and it is based on God's direct and intelligent act in creating each one of us as unique individuals—no two of whom are of equal talent and capability.

Here it is: Excellence is the process of my (or a congregation) becoming better than I (or it) was yesterday. The pursuit of excellence is not just for a select few, the virtuosi, for the beautiful people, for the culturally advanced, for those with biological, musical, or socio-economic head starts. It is for everybody. We are unequally gifted—no two people are alike—hence no two people can equally achieve. But one thing is true of all of us: We must strive to become better than we once were or we shrivel up into less than we once were. There is no neutral condition.

Furthermore, becoming better than we once were means that excellence is not perfection. Perfect, perfection, perfectionism are demon words. They are neurosis-provoking words. They constrict, they maim, they inhibit—even kill—true excelling. Ironically, none of us knows what perfection is because literally nobody exudes it, even those who seem light years ahead of us, even for a micro-instant. They, too, are still striving for something yet beyond them, or they, too, atrophy. Yet we talk of perfection as if it should just be around the corner; we pursue it, this haunting ghost of a thing, this abuser of the creative spirit. And when we think we've found it, we are recounting mostly the measurable stuff: no wrong notes, good tuning, the correct note values, and an occasionally well-turned phrase. And we know way down inside this was really not perfection but at best only a fleeting hint of something better, or at worst, a transient and superficial correctness. But the rest—the stuff of which real and lasting art is made—is the domain, not of the perfect, but the immeasurable, the profound, the variable, and the ongoing.

When seen in this light, excellence is a process, a way of living. Like faith and worship, it is a continuum. Just as faith is unto even more faith and worship unto continued worship, excellence is unto continued excelling. Becoming better than I was yesterday is to be seen in such biblical conditions as striving, hungering, thirsting, wrestling, growing up into, seeking, confessing, repenting, pressing on, getting up after falling down, and not looking back. While we are instructed to look to each other for example, we are not instructed to become the same as someone we admire, or seek to become better than they are, or gloat because it turns out to be true we are actually better.

When we translate this concept into worship leading and music-making, we can understand how important it is to avoid the kinds of perfectionism that haunts so many artists, and on the other, the kind of slop and spiritualized carelessness that marks so much of church music. How can anyone press on if they are already perfect and how can anyone continue to be sloppy when they are commanded to press on? Paul puts it all together when he talks about pressing on toward a goal, yet understanding that he has not yet arrived (and on this earth, never will).

> Excusing artistic mediocrity and slop for spiritualized reasons is the antithesis of excelling.

While striving for excellence does not mean becoming the same or better than someone, it certainly means we cannot overlook the examples that the best of those around us have set. Music-making is a severe and demanding discipline. Church music has suffered time and time again for several reasons. First, less-than-gifted musicians have assumed that being less than gifted can be compensated for by God's power, without any personal effort to enter the disciplines of improvement. Second, gifted musicians have come to assume that "it's just church music" or "it's only prayer meeting" or "we have to give people what they want and giving them what they want is not that big a deal." Third, truly gifted musicians who think biblically and are artistically disciplined are forced out of the church because the first two kinds of musicians have won the day and most congregations and pastors do not know the difference or simply do not care. Excusing artistic mediocrity and slop for spiritualized reasons is the antithesis of excelling.

> While striving for excellence does not mean becoming the same or better than someone, it certainly means we cannot overlook the examples that the best of those around us have set.

At the same time, we must remember that many churches cannot afford any professional help and must rely on some pretty sad examples of music-making. The biblical concept of excellence applies just as well here, as long as becoming better than I was yesterday drives the untrained and untalented in the same way that it drives the gifted and true professional.

Examine yourself constantly under the guidance of Scripture and within the protection of Jesus' blood. Are you self-satisfied and artistically dead in the water, even though you have come a long way? Are you satisfied that you have got it all together? Are you under pressure (from a senior pastor or congregation) to stay as you are because things are working so well, or to change for less than biblical reasons? Do you feel you are in great shape because there is no church in town whose music can quite compare with yours? Do you shun the very best examples of music-making and disciplined advice from the truly artistic because you do not want to appear unspiritual?

Do not easily assume that these questions are for somebody else. If you are a typical sinner, or if you are anything like the typical Christian (and 99.9 percent of us are both), then look closely and be ready to be broken. Once you are, you will be on the road to the kind of excelling that Scripture demands, your congregations will be taken all that much further, and you might even come under heavy criticism for being what a true church musician biblically is: a true prophet, unafraid to take yourself and your people to depths for the sake of Christ.

Harold M. Best served for 27 years as dean of the Wheaton College Conservatory of Music and has written widely on issues of arts education. He served as president of the National Association of Schools of Music. His book, *Music Through the Eyes of Faith,* was published in 1993.

CHAPTER 3

The Creative Christian Life, Part 1
By Charlie Peacock

Focus on Christ is essential to the Christian life, for it is Christ that makes us Christians. In Christ Jesus, God is making all things new. Our praise for such a glorious reality should never stop. Even so, before God began making all things new, God made all things. This is where the story begins.

All Christians are people of the story. No healthy professing Christian is exempt from this designation. As keepers of the kingdom story, we ought to be the greatest and most prolific of all storytellers. Guarding and communicating the true story is a part of our stewardship work. It is our privilege and responsibility to care for the creation and the story of its grand beginning. In like manner, we tell the truth about both our glorious beginning and our present sinful condition, and we communicate the answer to the question of who will save us from ourselves—namely Jesus. To the degree that we fail to tell this true story in the most comprehensive fashion, we fail to do the privileged work of redeemed humanity. To communicate anything less than the full true story of creation, sin, redemption, the kingdom at hand, and the kingdom coming is to tell something other than the story. Though the story we tell should be informed by the whole counsel of God, this doesn't mean that every song we sing must tell the whole story. On the contrary, both our songs and our individual lives build upon one another to complete the story God is telling in history.

Acknowledging that we are people of the story is the starting place for awakening the Christian music community to its lofty creative potential as God's image-bearers, and most importantly, for steering all of us—artists, industry, and audience—toward a grace-dominated life of living for God everywhere and in everything.

> Only by knowing God's story can we ever hope to interpret our own.

Though our individual stories are important and should be told, they do not, on their own, make sense of life. Only God's story adequately makes sense of our own. For this reason, people of the story start by acknowledging that the Word of God is the story we must first know and understand. Only by knowing God's story can we ever hope to interpret our own.

The Facts of God

The spiritual health and scriptural knowledge of everyone involved with Christian music (artist, industry, and audience) has a direct effect on its ability to maintain an environment where faithfulness to a comprehensive kingdom perspective and mission is understood and encouraged. It is for this reason that addressing the audience is just as important as addressing the artists or the industry. The artist, the industry, and the audience are mutually dependent and mutually responsible. Love for God requires that we know the facts of God. Knowing the facts of God equips us and inspires us to serve and love one another.

According to G. Earnest Wright, "The realism of the Bible consists in its close attention to the facts of history.... These are the facts of God." [1]

For Alister McGrath, "The biblical witness, itself narrative in form, illumines our self-understanding and enables us to make sense of the story of our life." [2]

For David Wells, God's narrative makes sense of our own story because God's true story reveals objective truth. "The importance of the story form in the Bible...lies in the fact that as a narrative of God's acts in the external world, it has yielded truth that is as objective as the events to which it is wedded." [3]

If truth is the light which illumines our own understanding, then getting at the truth ultimately requires getting at God's Word—the means by which God clearly communicates with His children. And while I believe that the Scriptures are nothing less than God's Word to Israel and the church, we must not forget that the Scriptures themselves reveal Jesus, a living being and not a proposition, as the ultimate embodiment of the Word (John 2:11; 20:30).

The Good Story of God Acting in History

God's Word isn't merely a series of doctrinal statements gathered together in what we know as the Bible. It's also the story of God's dealings with humankind. The doctrines are woven into the story. We need to understand both the importance of what constitutes belief and the truth that God acts in history. If we celebrate the doctrine and dismiss the narrative (the story), we risk living a truncated version of the Christian life—one void of sufficient truth. Knowledge about God does not equal knowledge of God. Knowledge of God comes only by walking with Him, or in the biblical case of Jacob, wrestling with Him. On the other hand, if we are faithful to celebrate the narrative but dismiss the doctrine, again we risk living a life less than God would desire. Knowledge about God comes only by knowing the Scripture. Doctrine is meant to interpret our experience and to test it.

The good story of God's actions in history is something all Christians need to know and be able to communicate in a compelling and accurate way. In its simplest sense, it's a script that even Steven Spielberg would envy. Consider the opening scene: The Creator of all things seen and unseen creates man and woman in His image and places them on Earth, a small planet revolving around a star called the sun located within the Milky Way galaxy. These two fleshly image-bearers mirror God in imagination, creativity, and holiness. In this way, unlike any other created thing, they are like God. Considering everything that God has created, men and women are greatly privileged. They are unique and set apart from all of creation. They are made for fellowship with God and there is no impurity in them. They are of two sexes, male and female—a perfect match intellectually, emotionally, and sexually. Both the man and the woman receive God's blessed commission to govern the earth as co-rulers.

This is certainly an extraordinary beginning, isn't it? Unfortunately, we seldom communicate the story of our beginning with the same delight and fervor with which we communicate the story of our redemption. Still, it does make sense for Christians to focus on redemption and on God as the Redeemer. After all, redemption is something we have experienced and are experiencing daily in the Christian life.

Focus on Christ is essential to the Christian life, for it is Christ that makes us Christians. In Christ Jesus, God is making all things new. Our praise for such a glorious reality should never stop. Even so, before God began making all things new, God made all things. This is where the story begins.

God Is Creator

"In the beginning God created the heavens and the earth" (Genesis 1:1).

Through this scripture we encounter the Creator, the maker of all things. He is the origin of everything that has been made. He is the Author, the Inventor, the Artist. Max Lucado describes the Creator as a "tireless dreamer and designer."[4] This is an apt description, for God cannot tire of Himself. In the Creator dwells the fullness of imaginative creativity and He delights in using it. He absolutely loves being who He is—the Creator. Like God, we too should love being who we are and find great pleasure in using our intelligence to think, speak, and act in imaginative, creative ways.

We Are Men and Women Created in the Image of God

"Then God said, 'Let Us make man in Our image, according to Our likeness; let them have dominion over the fish of the sea, over the birds of the air, and over the cattle, over all the earth and over every creeping thing that creeps on the earth.' So God created man in His own image; in the image of God He created him; male and female He created them" (Genesis 1:26-27 NKJV).

While the world increasingly teaches and lives out its belief in the insignificance of the human, Christians teach that men and women are the most significant of all God's creation, since the privilege of being an image-bearer of God is given to them alone. The image of God in humankind is extrinsic in that it has been imparted to us and imprinted on our being by the Creator. For this reason alone it should be esteemed.

> What then is the very first thing we can know and understand about ourselves? An image-bearer is to be creative, as God is creative.

This good gift and privilege has come from God and is a reflection of Him, and as such ought to be treated like the priceless gift and privilege it is. As I've pointed out, the very first thing we can know about God in Scripture (Genesis 1:1) is that He is Creator. The first thing we find out about ourselves is that we are made in His image (Genesis 1:26). What then is the very first thing we can know and understand about ourselves? An image-bearer is to be creative, as God is creative.

Created to Be Creative

Creativity is at the heart of our reflection of God's image. "In creating man God completes his activity and in obedience to God man continues God's creativity."[5] As image-bearers we are to mirror God's creativity. We are in truth created to be creators. We are to use our intelligence to think, to speak, and to act imaginatively and creatively.

> We are image-bearers, yet utterly dependent on the One whose image we bear, for in God we move and live and have our being.

We are made, in a very real sense, to partner with God in continuing the process of creating the world and all that is in it. Our work is to flesh out the incredible creative potential of what God has created. God is the origin of everything, the true throne of originality belongs to Him alone.

Only God can create out of nothing because in Him is the very power of being, what theologians call aseity or self-existence. When we make something new, something never seen before in history, we create out of what God has called into being. We are image-bearers, yet utterly dependent on the One whose image we bear, for in God we move and live and have our being.

God Is Holy

When the Scriptures speak of God's holiness, more often than not they speak to everything about God—His transcendence, His moral perfection, which sets Him apart from all else. He is "majestic in holiness" (Exodus 15:11). God's holiness permeates all His attributes. In all ways God can be nothing short of holy. Holiness speaks to God's completeness and His perfection. He loves completely and perfectly. His justice is perfect and complete, whether it be His wrath against sin, or His justification of sinners by grace through faith in Christ. There is no darkness in God, only purity and light.

Created to Be Holy

Because of God's holiness, the image of God in humankind involves a moral dimension as well as a creative dimension. We are like God in that we are moral beings, and as such are created to be holy. We possess reason and will and the ability to make choices and to follow through on those choices. We are to choose well and, by so doing, mirror God's holiness.

Our choices are to be fueled by holy love, holy justice, and holy mercy, just as are God's. We are to be holy as God is holy. Holiness is integral to the Christian life. The very idea of human integrity is founded in holiness. The special dignity of being human, according to J.I. Packer, is that, "As humans, we may reflect and reproduce at our own creaturely level the holy ways of God, and thus act as his direct representatives on earth. This is what humans are made to do, and in one sense we are human only to the extent that we are doing it." [6]

Humanness Made Complete

Our humanness is made complete by living as God made us to live—as holy caretakers, imagining and creating to the benefit of everyone and everything under our care. Our creativity should be a testimony of faith expressing itself through love—an outward sign of the inward reality that our imaginations have been captured by the holy, creative mind of God.

Ephesians, chapters 4 and 5, teaches us to be imitators of God, children of light, men and women captured by the gospel. We are to be made new in the attitude of our minds, putting on the new self, "created to be like God in true righteousness and holiness" (Ephesians 4:24). Our ways of thinking and doing are to reflect our maker. We are to be set apart from the world's ways of thinking and doing, ways which are contrary to God (2 Corinthians 6:17).

God has clearly shown us what is good and what is required of us. We are to act justly, to love mercy, and to walk humbly with Him. This is the high and holy calling of the image-bearer. It is the calling which the artists, industry, and audience of Christian music must take very seriously.

Abraham Heschel writes: "We become what we think of ourselves,"[7] and "What determines one's being is the image one adopts."[8]

In order for those of us involved in the artistry and industry of Christian music to think rightly about ourselves, we must of necessity have the story straight. We must first know and understand that we have been born with the image of God, and now through our adoption as children of God, the sin-tarnished image is being made new in the likeness of Christ.

This being so, we are to mirror God in holiness and creativity. This is the straight story. This is the starting place. Only by owning God's story will we live out the good story which He has graciously equipped us to tell, that God has equipped us to mirror Him is the absolute truth.

Even so, at times it can be difficult to believe and act on. When it is, we must remember God's truth-telling nature.

God's Truth-Telling Nature

If you come to this book with a greater understanding of the holiness of God than the simple overview I've included in this chapter, then give thanks and be grateful. If God's holiness is not a topic you've studied a great deal, then let me point you to the connection between God's holiness and His truth-telling nature. Without this connection it will be nearly impossible to receive the full benefit of what this chapter strives to offer. The whole idea that Christians are people of the story, and that we are to be imaginative, creative, and holy, rests on the foundation that God is who He says He is, that He has spoken, and that what He has said is true and worthy of human trust. I believe this, but it's you the reader, who must come to this conviction. The Scripture makes plain that because God is holy, He can be believed and trusted. Consider these texts:

In the book of Leviticus (22:32) the Lord tells Moses, "I must be acknowledged as holy...." The psalmist listens and obeys with this hymn: "Exalt the Lord our God and worship at his holy mountain, for the Lord our God is holy" (Psalm 99:9). The writer of Proverbs reminds us that "Every word of God is flawless..." (Proverbs 30:5). And in Revelation 21:5 John records these words: "He who was seated on the throne said, 'I am making everything new!' Then he said, 'Write this down, for these words are trustworthy and true.' " Trustworthy and true indeed.

A high belief in the trustworthiness of God is the fountain from which all God's faithless and fearful children must eventually come to drink. The men and women of Christian music are no exception.

The Beginnings of Imagination

Imagine with me if you will: It is the 1960s, sometime between JFK's assassination and the arrival of the hippies to San Francisco's Haight-Ashbury district. I'm just a child, one child among several seated in a classroom. There are four neat rows of desks with six desks to a row.

Each desk, constructed of wood and steel, has a hole at the top for an inkwell. Since the universal conversion from ink to No. 2 pencils, the only activity the inkwell enjoys is the rush of gravity as a crumpled piece of paper, or a wad of Bazooka, drops from the hand of a student into the cavity of the desk. What pleasure.

I'm lucky. I have my pleasures, too. My desk is number four in the row next to the windows that look out onto Plumas Street, the main street of Yuba City—my hometown. From my coveted position

I have a reasonably unobstructed view of the front door of the corner store where I will most certainly purchase cinnamon toothpicks when the last bell rings and I am set free.

Still I have my wistful days, when the autumn breeze dances through the open windows with such enticement and abandon that I cannot resist climbing aboard for a ride. Straddling the wind, I hold on for life and carefully navigate the slender gap between the open window and its sill. Wide open space. I rocket into the sky, then fall and dart like the swallow. High above the street, I conclude there are more rich people in my little town than I had thought—so many swimming pools.

When I tire of flight I'm back in my seat, busy, shrinking. I make myself small enough to walk along the top of my teacher's desk. I climb onto the open pages of her grade book and look for my name. I don't find it; I hear it.

"Chuck, turn around in your seat and face the blackboard."

And with those words I'm brought back to size. I've been caught imagining. Again.

Have you ever been caught imagining?

Imagination and Creativity

Imagination is the power at work in us which allows us to make images within the mind, to see or hear something before it actually exists.

> The breadth, height, and depth of the imagination is never known in full by any one man or woman.

When you think of the imagination, think of it as making images or sounds which start in the mind and remain in the mind. To imagine is to dive deep into an ocean of possibilities. What can the imagination see with eyes closed?

What can it construct without moving a finger? What can it taste though the tongue is locked up tight? What can it hear? Innumerable things, infinite images, choices, and sounds, far more than we can describe or name.

In truth, what the mind can imagine is so great that you or I could never think of, or catalog it all, in a lifetime. The breadth, height, and depth of the imagination is never known in full by any one man or woman. It's too vast, and truthfully, too good to be known by us in such a way. The fullness of imagination is God's and God's alone. Nevertheless, each of us has an important role to play in contributing to the collective imagination of our time. Every contribution is significant to history. There are no insignificant roles.

Now it's time to link the imagination with creativity. While these two words are certainly connected, they should not be thought of as synonymous. Imagination acts as the soil out of which creativity grows. It is not creativity itself. Creativity is fruit born of seeds planted in the soil of the imagination. For example, with regard to music, if the role of the imagination is to germinate melody, then the role of creativity is to nurture and draw forth melody from the soil of the imagination (the mind) into the light of everyday life (fingers on a keyboard). The imagination is responsible for musical dreams, while creativity is responsible for making musical dreams come to pass. One thinks, the other acts. The imagination asks "What if?" Creativity answers with, "Here it is." Yet, sometimes creativity does not answer, and what's been imagined is never actually created. You can imagine without creativity, but you cannot have creativity without the imagination.

It's important to remember that imagination is not neutral. The presence of sin ensures that the imagination of men and women will be sinful as well as good. For example, the good imagination helped Handel create "The Messiah," but the imagination also helped King David see in his mind's eye what it would mean to possess the beautiful nakedness of Bathsheba. While Handel's imagination created beauty, joy, and worship, in King David's case the imagination was the soil in which sin took root, and David's sin led to pain and death. Such is the power of the imagination.

Naming the Animals
By Billy Crockett

> *"I have a name for my pain. It's Batman!"*
> —The Riddler

I love it most when someone responds to a song of mine by saying something like, "That's what I am feeling. I just didn't know how to say it."

Life often seems a litany of the obvious, the routine, the getting by. We live on automatic pilot. But the mystery that makes for meaning is mostly not obvious nor automatic. It is hiding under the words of a conversation, or beyond the facts of the police report, or in the dark corners of our hearts too scary or embarrassing to look.

In the middle of the business as usual God speaks, "I am making all things new." Where do we suppose that is happening? Could it possibly be in the terms of our own lives? So we listen to life...breathe... notice...feel... and try to name it. We can't allow what we'd rather see or what we think we should be feeling to obscure the essential true thing. What fear exactly? What lump in the throat? What gasp? What welcoming warmth? What revulsion? What hope exactly? How does it feel? How can you tell? Where are you now? What might this mean?

This is the common ground of artists and people of faith. Naming the animals. We are Jacob wrestling with an unknown stranger, pinning it down until it gives its name. Such tenacity. It is not enough to struggle and survive—he must know what it means. And the reward for Jacob and for us is that we get named in return. With every act of naming we are closer to knowing... and being known.

And that's the good stuff.

Billy Crockett is a recording artist and songwriter living in Dallas, Texas. He is founder and president of Walking Angel Records.

The Good Imagination

For now, though, let's consider the good imagination. Immeasurable acts of creativity are born out of the simplest of imaginings. For centuries children had imagined the ability to fly like a bird or to shrink themselves so small as to travel in places where the human body could not go. Today in our time, we do fly—in rockets, jets, and gliders—and through laproscopic surgery shrink small enough to travel inside the human body. How did this come to be? Someone went beyond imagining to the tangible reality of these extraordinary inventions. What they imagined, they created. And what once did not exist, now exists.

> In order for the people of Christian music to become known as the people of the good story, we must of necessity understand who we are and what we are specifically to be about.

This is the way God has worked through fallible humans all throughout history. He can be trusted to work in this way. God's trustworthiness should give the artists, industry, and audience of Christian music ample reason for hope. It seems entirely possible that with our image-bearing abilities, specifically holiness, imagination, and creativity, we might imagine holy solutions to the problems we've created. With God's help, these good imaginings might serve to create new and faithful chapters in the story of music and the children of God. The work we do matters to God.

He wants us to tell good stories through our lives and the work we do. It doesn't matter whether our work is songwriting or retailing, God wants us to live good lives that contribute to the grand story He is telling in history. In order for the people of Christian music to become known as the people of the good story, we must of necessity understand who we are and what we are specifically to be about. Who we are is God's people. What we are to be about is God's people, in God's place, under God's rule. Specifically that means everyone, everywhere, and in everything living out good stories entirely for Him.

Tell Stories That Reflect the One in Whom You Claim to Believe

In summation, your labor and your play within the Christian life is about telling a good story with your life that reflects the One in whom you claim to believe. But don't automatically think that your labor and your play must somehow become more religious—that they must testify in some direct scriptural way. You needn't put a Jesus sticker on your boat in order to justify boating. Every moment is a testimony to God's grace. It's your story of His grace. And your story is eternally important because it contributes its chapter to the grand story of God and His creation, a creation in which each of us plays a God-assigned role. It should be our goal as storytellers to tell good stories, to as the Bible says, "Live such good lives among the pagans that, though they accuse you of doing wrong, they may see your good deeds and glorify God on the day he visits us" (1 Peter 2:12).

Christians Belong to God, Not the World

Telling a good story, whether it be within an individual life or a community of believers such as Christian music, requires that we remain focused on known aspects of the story which has already been told. For example, a believer belongs to God and to God's purposes in the world. We are called by Him, to Him, and for Him. We've all heard that we are to be in the world not of it, but many of the world's ideas and systems are eager to trip us up in this regard.

One striking reason for the lack of demonstrative evidence of Christians living out their calling to be holy, imaginative, and creative people is that we are often consumers before we are holy image-bearers. This should not be. Consumerism is the enemy of the spiritual life. By living out the destiny of the consumer rather than the destiny of the image-bearer, we consume and accumulate to create a lifestyle rather than living imaginatively in order to create a life honoring to God. Whereas a lifestyle is constructed of the energy of man, which is easily exhausted, life is what God is helping you take hold of right now in the kingdom at hand as you move ever closer to eternal life with Him in the kingdom coming. By pursuing life instead of a lifestyle, you become liberated to live creatively as both a part of and a re-teller of His story.

It's a Huge Story, a Kingdom Story

It is my belief that the Christian music community must come to understand that the significance and ultimately the quality of the work we do and the lives we live will be determined by our understanding of the story in which we are taking part. It is a huge story—a kingdom story. It is not a small story about the American church. Neither is it a small story about the importance of contemporary Christian music. The story that is given to us to live out is the only good and true story worth living.

Again, the story worth living is to be God's man or woman in God's place under God's rule. It is to live for God everywhere and in everything. There are no small roles in this huge story. The question is: Will we—the artists, the industry, and the audience of Christian music enter into it with faith and imagination—and with reverence and awe for the extraordinary story it is?

Ten years ago my friend Margaret Becker sang these simple but essential words: "I commit."

Will you?

Charlie Peacock is an award-winning recording artist, producer, songwriter, and teacher whose songs have been recorded by Amy Grant, dcTalk, and Russ Taff. In addition to his own recordings, he has produced records by Avalon, Out of the Grey, Margaret Becker, and Sarah Masen.

Text adapted from Charlie Peacock's book, *At the Crossroads: An Insider's Look at the Past, Present and Future of Contemporary Christian Music* (Broadman & Holman, 1999).

1. Quoted in: David Wells, *No Place for Truth* (Grand Rapids: Eerdmans, 1993), p. 258.

2. Alister McGrath, *A Passion for Truth* (Downers Grove: InterVarsity), p. 108.

3. David Wells, *No Place for Truth* (Grand Rapids: Eerdmans, 1993), p. 259.

4. Max Lucado, An excerpt from *In the Eye of the Storm,* quoted in *The Inspirational Study Bible,* New Century Version, Max Lucado, General Editor (Dallas: Word Publishing, 1995), p. 4.

5. George Carey, *I Believe in Man* (Grand Rapids: Eerdmans, 1977), p. 32.

6. J. I. Packer, *Concise Theology* (Wheaton: Tyndale House, 1993), p. 71.

7. Quoted in: Douglas John Hall, *Imaging God* (Grand Rapids: Eerdmans, 1986), p. 1.

8. Ibid.

9. Eugene Peterson, *The Message* (Colorado Springs: NavPress, 1993), p. 453.

The Creative Christian Life, Part 2
By Reed Arvin

There is a reason why we tend to repeat our mistakes over and over again and so seldom live up to the potential of our blank pages.

The Blank Page

An interesting exercise begins with holding up and examining a completely blank piece of notebook paper. I have always liked the clever ways of describing this object: a cloud on a china plate, a lamb dancing the tango with a snowman, a polar bear stacking cubes of sugar. But of course these are all simply games with words. The page is actually blank.

As you look at your blank page, consider that this is exactly what Beethoven's "Fifth" looked like before the first note was written; it is just what *Finnegan's Wake* was like before the first word; it is precisely as the Mona Lisa appeared before the first brush-stroke. It's empty. For the right person, the blank page is the most enticing, hopeful, and tempting thing in the world. It is the beginning of a possible masterpiece.

Few of us achieve the goal of creating something truly masterful. For many people, the blank page can be as intimidating as it is full of possibility. Bach, whose creative output is a musical legend, habitually wrote the letters "J.J." on the top of each blank page of music. The letters stood for, "Jesus help me," and I suppose that if you had to come up with a new cantata every week or so, you would probably begin every day's work with the same prayer. So you shouldn't worry too much at this point if you don't feel like Beethoven when you sit down to write a song. But how you do feel—the emotional relationship you have with the possibilities in your life—is terribly important to your creative output. It will dictate how much you create, how often you try to create, and to some extent, the quality of what you do create. It will certainly control how well you live up to your potential.

Every person has a long relationship with blank pages, beginning with the earliest school years. As summer ends, a ritual is happily indulged by schoolchildren all over the world: They are ushered into department stores and new notebooks are purchased for the coming year. These notebooks—which are nothing but collections of blank pages—are highly symbolic to us. Does it matter if there are still unused pages in our old notebooks? Not at all. We insist on new, clean notebooks. Even old pens are discarded; if we could, we would have new rulers, new lunch boxes, new calculators, new everything. And the reason we want the new blank pages—along with everything else—is because these objects symbolize for us the possibility for change. Even into college this symbolic relationship continues. Clutching our fresh, clean notebooks, we tell ourselves, "This is the semester I'm going to be different. This is the year I'm not going to procrastinate. This time I'm not going to try and be brilliant on caffeine and donuts the night before a paper is due."

Not surprisingly, these resolutions rarely come true. In spite of the optimism of these new beginnings, most of us engage in disappointingly predictable patterns of behavior. By the third week of school our resolve is weakening; by the fifth, we're making old choices; by the eighth, we're firmly entrenched in the original patterns. This is why college admissions counselors weigh high school grades so heavily in the admissions process; through experience, they've learned that no matter how inspiring an essay a student writes, nothing predicts his performance in college as accurately as his high school transcript. We buy new notebooks but keep on doing the same things year after year. In school, this can be a real problem. Creatively, it can be deadly.

There is a reason why we tend to repeat our mistakes over and over again and so seldom live up to the potential of our blank pages. Scientists have proven conclusively that we use relatively little of our brains, and much of what we do not use is the part that is intuitive and creative. So why do we find it so difficult to go to new places? Why do we continue to work at the same level, writing and rewriting the same "song" over and over again? Why do we work in the same patterns, even though we know we aren't living up to even a fraction of our potential?

I believe that although we think the blank pages of our lives are empty, they are in fact absolutely covered with invisible ink. You have to look hard to find them, but all our blank pages have subtle, highly individual messages written upon them. What those messages say can dictate what we do creatively in every area of our lives.

The Four Messages in Invisible Ink

There are at least four messages in invisible ink and, of these, the easiest to find is our self-concept. Self-concept is just another way of saying how we feel and think about ourselves. Psychologists call this a script, or a predetermined idea we carry inside our heads about who we are and how we respond in certain situations. The script is comprehensive and covers most of life. If you'll think about what the word "script" actually means, you'll get an idea of how important a role it plays in our lives. Suppose that you are an actor in a play and the author gives you the words to memorize. In every performance, no matter how often repeated, you will be forced to say the same things. The play will unwind every night, full of apparent tension and possibility. The audience may be on the edge of their seats, wondering which of several possible endings will unfold. But the conclusion will be foregone. Night after night the story will end identically.

In our real lives each of us has a script as well, telling us how things will end. Faced with a thousand exciting possibilities, we tend to make the same choices over and over again, ensuring the same results. We meet a new romantic interest; the plot begins to spin outward with a flush of initial excitement. Briefly, as though in a play, it seems as if anything can happen. But within a few weeks, we hear ourselves repeating the same words from previous relationships, as though reading them from another source. If we were jealous before, we find ourselves dealing with those emotions again. If we were controlling, or lazy, or selfish, or fearful, we tend to repeat the same destructive behaviors. Conversely, the script can be a force for good in us, telling us not to settle for poor behavior in the people around us, moving us toward healthy relationships. The script affects every area of life, but our creative lives are particularly susceptible to its effects.

Leader. Loner. Needy. Giving. Loser. Winner. These are words that form our self-concept and play out in our scripts. For example, you may sit down to write a song. But the invisible ink of your blank page whispers to you, "You're not talented enough to write a great song." Or perhaps, your invisible ink tells you, "Don't worry about finishing this. You always procrastinate anyway." Or perhaps you dream of writing a larger work, like an opera. But your invisible ink whispers, "This task is too large for you. Don't attempt it." Perhaps you are a super-perfectionist; if so, this script may be stopping you from finishing what you start, or cheating you out of the pleasure of creating. There are many scripts, and many messages within them. But what yours says is important.

Particularly devastating in the Christian self-image is the role of habitual sin. This invisible ink may prevent you from writing about your relationship with God, or worse, force you to put on a religious cloak when you create. It may whisper, "You know who you are. You're not worthy to write anything truly worshipful." Or you may hear in a faint whisper, "Put on your Sunday-self when you write. Don't be honest. Present yourself as more spiritual than you really are." The messages of self-image can be very specific. Ideas such as these can literally dictate the songs and performances from a person, holding creativity in chains.

It's important to remember that we don't literally hear these words in our minds. Rather, general impressions and emotions cloud our thinking and keep us from working up to our potential. Fortunately, it's not true that in order to be free creatively we have to entirely remake our scripts. Our scripts are set in adolescence and are extremely difficult to dislodge. To do so is a lifelong ambition. If we are to begin to be free now, we have to learn how to manage our scripts rather than wait for them to dissolve or fully change them. In time, this may happen. But we must not be held captive to them now.

The Super-Creative

Some people with extraordinary talent leave little to show for their abilities. Conversely, other less-talented individuals leave a huge legacy of work. Very rarely, talent and effort converge perfectly, and a lifetime of brilliant art emerges. These highly creative and motivated people work through

> I can remember being told by a brilliant producer that he was convinced that with every record he makes, he will be exposed as having little or no talent.

their destructive inner scripts intuitively. They are constantly reinventing their possibilities, moving in new directions. Most of what they think of attempting they end up doing. It would be a mistake, however, to think that the super-creative and highly productive are simply lucky people with uplifting, healthy, and empowering scripts. On the contrary, some of the most brilliant voices in the world have been the most tortured. They have simply learned to work through their inhibitions and insecurities and become productive in spite of them.

In my career in music, I have been fortunate to observe and work with many fantastically talented and productive people. Although their personalities differ, in two important ways they are a remarkably homogenous group. First, most of them consider themselves lazy but actually work incredibly hard; and second, most of them don't think they are actually very talented, and consider the work of their peers superior to that of their own. Sometimes, this humility is so unexpected that encountering it can almost give one a sense of vertigo. I can remember being told by a brilliant producer that he was convinced that with every record he makes, he will be exposed as having little or no talent. A part of him believes that he has merely fooled everyone so far into thinking he has ability, and that it's only a matter of time before the truth comes out. A wall full of awards and gold records would argue against this idea. But his experience is remarkably consistent in the creative community. Most people in it are secretly terrified that they lack talent. Their success means that you don't have to wait until you can remake yourself to revolutionize your creative life. You can work through your script and begin to change now.

> Change takes work, and one thing we all learned from school is that the notebooks don't end up doing the changing for us. We have to do that within ourselves.

Think about your own life. Are you growing creatively at a rate that satisfies you? Project outward ten years from now. How many songs will you have written? Is your output high enough? If you only wrote four songs last year, will you magically write fifty next year? Or will you repeat your old behaviors? Have you bought a new notebook, thinking that it would change your behavior? Change takes work, and one thing we all learned from school is that the notebooks don't end up doing the changing for us. We have to do that within ourselves.

What Others Think of Us

If we are held in thrall by our self-image, another powerful force that limits us creatively is what other people think of us. The expectations of others can literally change what you feel is possible. For example, if you grew up in a family in which being a musician was not highly regarded, it's likely that your creative output will be negatively affected. Some people believe that a life working as a musician is something a serious person would never do. "Sure," they may say, "play guitar. But make sure you can get a stable job, too." It would take real courage to dedicate a life to musical expression in such an environment.

The expectations of others can also control what you feel is appropriate to write about. For example, in some churches only overtly Christian topics are considered worthwhile. Some themes as well as certain musical styles are considered off-limits. Only the most holy of attitudes can be freely expressed. The creative soul cannot thrive in such circumstances.

The controlling force of the opinions of others is often expressed by fear of rejection. It's possible that you long to perform but are unwilling to endure the possibility of ridicule from your peers. Ours is a blunt, critical age. Having heard your friends tear other performers apart, you may be hesitant to expose your own weaknesses to

> Just because you don't sing like Sting doesn't mean your gift is less important. You must come to terms with the gift you have, accept it, and dedicate your life to growing it to its maximum beauty and expression.

them. For adults this can be particularly difficult. No one knows how many closet singers or actors work in banks or law offices simply because they are unwilling to endure criticism.

One particularly insidious expression of this type of control occurs when an artist is held captive by his heroes. I endured this control myself for several months while traveling on the road with Amy Grant. My time traveling with her was lovely, and for two years of this experience I shared keyboard responsibilities with Michael W. Smith. Michael is a remarkably talented and, incidentally, almost completely uneducated musician. I joined the band just out of graduate school, where I had received a master's degree in piano performance. So I foolishly imagined that I was likely to be a superior musician to Michael, who can barely read music.

Each night in concert there came a time when Amy would talk to the audience, and Michael had a tendency to play piano softly behind her as she did. Each night was different, and each night was worthy of recording. It was remarkable, on the fiftieth or sixtieth evening of those tours, to hear Michael find new and memorable tunes effortlessly from his creative center. It did not, frankly, come from a place of discipline. It was pure gift, and he proved night after night that no amount of effort would ever close the gap between us. It was, although I would never have admitted it, quite intimidating.

I actually stopped writing music for several months during this time, although it was much later when I understood why. Without realizing it, I had found a hero—who might have inspired me—and allowed myself to be held captive by him. I needed to remind myself to love the gift I had, even though it wasn't Michael's. I needed to release myself to be who I was. It took a conscious decision to push through that and begin writing again. It's possible that you have a hero who holds you captive. Just because you don't sing like Sting doesn't mean your gift is less important. You must—*you must*—come to terms with the gift you have, accept it, and dedicate your life to growing it to its maximum beauty and expression.

Who We Think God Is

The third message in invisible ink on our blank pages is who we think God is. For many people, another way of saying this is that the law is on the page. It is initially difficult to see, but once recognized, we begin to understand its enormous effects. We are consumed with the idea of not displeasing God. This is a worthy idea, but what, exactly, displeases Him? Does creative searching and exploration? Many evangelicals unfortunately believe that this is the case. Their creative output is maimed as a result. Clyde Kilby, in the book *The Christian Imagination: Essays on Literature and the Arts*, puts it this way:

> *Evangelical Christians have had one of the purest of motives and one of the worst of outcomes. The motive is never to mislead by the smallest fraction of an iota in the precise nature of salvation, to live it and state it in its utter purity. But the unhappy outcome has too often been to elevate the cliché. The motive is that the gospel shall not be misunderstood, not sullied, not changed in jot or tittle. The outcome has often been merely the reactionary, static and hackneyed....Pastors seem beset with the conviction that statement is the only correct way. I am starkly admonished, for instance, to love, as though I did not know this fully as well as the preacher, as though I had not already beaten myself a thousand times with this cudgel. What is needed instead is the opening of some little door through*

which I can enter, some little path through the tangle of my own
selfishness, some glimpse of a person who practiced love last week.
But what is the use of repeating to me, as though my soul were
blind, what my conscience and the Holy Spirit habitually tell me? [1]

It's easy to recognize the "art" that comes from this philosophy. It is typically judgmental, uncreative, and predictable. A lot of what I call "you songs" fall into this category. They have lines like, *You've been running for so long,* or *You've turned away from God,* or *You need to meet Jesus.* You, you, you. One can almost picture the wagging finger as the song is sung. Robert Sterling, in his chapter on poetic devices, describes these songs as "Sunday school lessons that rhyme."

Kilby's words challenge us to use new pictures to tell what Charlie Peacock and others have called, "the story." As Charlie's chapter points out, we are all telling, in some way, our part of God's story. And the need to "open some little door through which we can enter" is the greatest creative challenge facing the community of faith.

The Last and Most Secret Message

One last thing hides on your page, most inscrutable, most mysterious. It is, ultimately, far more powerful than anything else. Hiding secretly on all your blank pages is the real, living God. Not who we think He is—that's a separate category entirely. Even the most illuminated of us doesn't really understand or know God. Paul admitted that we see through a glass darkly. But the real God is there. Improbably, with great politeness, the real and actual God settles on your pages, above you, behind and before you, beneath you, ready to do what is in His divine nature to do: set people free. This is God's job. It is not God's purpose to enslave. So it is wrong that so much Christian art and life is narrow. It is, in fact, God's passion to set us free. And nowhere is this more necessary than in our creative lives.

How, we are desperate to know, does God do this? How can we be made free to create? More than anything else, we want there to be a simple answer. But Christianity is not a faith for those with a limited imagination. Think, for example, of the way the Old Testament describes the beginning of time. It's so clear, so decisive. "In the beginning God created the heavens and earth." A simple statement, declarative and unambiguous. Now consider the New Testament version of the exact same moment: "In the beginning was the Word. And the Word was with God, and the Word was God." These two descriptions of the same event are very different. With the coming of Jesus, we are forced to deal with metaphor and contradiction. If you must have your world perfectly ordered, Christianity will be a frustrating experience.

Who Is This God on Our Blank Page?

What's the first thing we know about God? As many have pointed out, the first thing we discover about Him is that He is Creator. Before we know Him as Savior or Provider or Redeemer or Father or anything else, we only know Him as Creator. And we learn that we are created in His image. And many Christians have made this connection—that because God is the great Creator, we are to be creative as well. This is essential and inspiring to know, but not in itself truly life-changing. Unless we take the next steps, we're smarter but no wiser. We have to think about how God creates, and we need to take the step of dominion.

When God gave us dominion over the world, what was He doing? It certainly wasn't ownership; the Bible clearly states that, "the earth is the Lord's, and everything in it." So what was it? The word dominion actually means to take what God has made and make more good with it. To make more good is a very open-ended idea. In giving us dominion, God was doing nothing less than giving us both a mandate and a method to create. "Here is the world," He is saying. "Here are the raw materials for your inventiveness. Here is earth and metal and wood and water and light and color. Now make more good with these things, and do it in the ways that I have done."

> In the context of dominion, we see that songs of praise cannot be considered more worthy than love songs or other songs, because this is not the way that God creates.

This idea of dominion definitively answers a lot of plaguing questions that have bothered Christians for some time. For instance, it resolves a long and unprofitable debate over whether worship, or "Christian" music is inherently superior to "secular" music. In the context of dominion we see that songs of praise cannot be considered more worthy than love songs or other songs, because this is not the way that God creates. God is not making and has not made a universe of crosses and religious symbols. Look out your window—do you see in God's creation any religiosity? What is the religious sub-text of a frog? Of the color yellow? Of the planet Neptune? God is not creating a landscape full of Bibles. Neither is He establishing a hierarchy of creativity, where some kinds of invention are superior to others. He simply has created and is creating in orderly freedom. Planets. Textures. Animals. Stars. Plants. Light and darkness. The laws of physics. All created by Him, all worthy of admiration, all perfect in their way.

And so, therefore, should we create. This is the mandate of creation, the continuation of His creation. Like God, we should let our creativity flow outward without reservation. Gardens. Dinners. Houses. Friendships. Clothing. Painting. Photographs. Music. We must never fall into the trap of thinking that creativity is limited to the "spiritual" and still less to the "arts." Creative freedom and energy should animate every aspect of our lives. To creatively live—to remake into newness everything around you—may be the single thing you can do that is most like God.

Think, for example, about the giving of gifts. The greeting card industry makes millions of dollars every year creating innocuous, ready-made gifts for people who are unwilling to bring their own energy and creativity to the task of communicating to another person that they are appreciated.

Once in a great while we meet a person who is living the creative life. Contrast a greeting card with the following truly personal, creative gift: When I moved to Nashville from Miami, I found myself missing the ocean a great deal. The sound and feeling of the ocean gets deep inside you, as anyone who has lived near the water can attest. I was commiserating with the girl I was dating at the time about this longing. One day I returned to my little apartment to discover that she had turned my living room into a beach. She had covered the floor with plastic, brought in three inches of sand, put up cardboard palm trees, had surf sounds on the stereo, put two beach chairs in the sand and, wearing a grass skirt, served me a Piña Colada in a hollowed-out pineapple. She was not locked into a narrow expression of any prefabricated greeting card. She was free to really create. Was I impressed? I married her.

The beach story is a great example of taking what He has made and making more good with it. Take the sand, the cardboard, the pineapple and make a good thing. No area of our lives is exempt from this creative scope. In this context, planting a garden is understood to be as deeply a spiritual act as prayer itself. Or the building of a house—our homes must never be designed as drab, efficient boxes. The Shakers, for example, have for decades made furniture—the quality of which surpasses anything possible by machines—as an act of worship. The individual character and superb quality of each piece is an altogether appropriate demonstration and homage to God's way of creating. Christians, I am convinced, should be the most free creators on the face of the earth.

The One Caveat

If our only conscript is to make more good, we're left with an important question we must face squarely: "What is good?" We can answer this question in two ways, both with scripture. First, Philippians 4:8: "Finally, brothers, whatever is true, whatever is noble, whatever is right, whatever is pure, whatever is lovely, whatever is admirable—if anything is excellent or praiseworthy—think about such things." I love this list—it doesn't say anything about church! I've seen architecture that fits on this list—especially the "true" part. Have you ever seen an expansion bridge and been struck by its "trueness"? And likewise, what is true is also beautiful. Richard Feynman, the remarkable physicist who solved the mystery of the space-shuttle Challenger explosion, once rejected a particular theory to describe nuclear fission as untrue. His colleague asked, "How can you be sure without doing the math?" Feynman smiled and answered, "Because it's not beautiful. The truth couldn't possibly be that ugly." And Feynman was right—the bogus theory was ultimately disproved, and the real answer turned out to be elegant and much simpler. Conversely, all of us have seen shoddy workmanship that violates this scriptural set of qualities. Christians must never do shoddy work, at any time, for any reason. It violates our very purpose. To take what He has made and do poor work with it is not acceptable. We must do good with it, and we must let our standards of what is good be challenged by excellence at every stage.

Second, consider the law of love—to love God with all our hearts, minds, and souls, and to love others as we love ourselves. By this standard, anything that adds value to our concept of human life or of God is good; conversely, anything that diminishes these ideas is not. Living by these standards opens us up to a way of living most people would find very strange, which is probably a good sign. For example, there are some movies that certain prudish people would not approve of that I would say meet this criteria and happily attend. By the same token, a movie like *Terminator II*, while technically superb, in my mind diminishes the value of people through its pornographic, incredibly lifelike violence. Therefore by this standard it is not "good"; it makes human life less valuable in the souls of the audience. Every person must make application of these verses on a personal level, but they are the biblical standard both for what we create and what we consume.

Having met these standards, we should be utterly free to create. Let no one make a corral around your ideas when God has ordained you to be free. And more than ordained—He has demonstrated this freedom in abundance. Create as He creates: in orderly freedom. Take another look outside; let that be your inspiration.

All Things New

One other characteristic distinguishes God's creativity: God has never repeated Himself from the beginning of time. Every person, every tree, every living cell, every inanimate stone, each breath of wind—none is identical. The standard of never repeating is one way in which God shows that His ways are above our ways. We can never hope to accomplish this goal. Imagine composing music for eternity and never repeating a single phrase. Imagine never repeating a lyric line, not a single word. Imagine making everything new every second of every day forever. If you are seeking something about which to give Him praise, a place of genuine wonder, here is something truly awesome. We are in His image, but we are not God. We are mere shadows of His magnificence.

But we should strive to be like Him and to create as He does. To make a new song is a godly act. And surely to repeat ourselves intentionally is inherently wrong. This principle has application, if we dare, far beyond the making of music or the arts. It is a powerful rationale against cloning, for example. Most Christians oppose it intuitively. But one reason against this kind of creating is that it creates in exactly the opposite way of God. It is not neutral; it is actually anti-God. For God has never created two living creatures identically. And cloning seeks to do this very thing. It is against God's nature, and therefore it is sin. It demonstrates the fall in us that we are attracted to this kind of invention. All we can do is ape Him, making poor replicas of what He makes new.

God's creative energy is never exhausted. It is inevitable, for example, that His work in us is ongoing. One of the most logical concepts in the Bible is the regeneration of the Christian, as described in Ephesians 4:22-24. We find Christ and He begins to remake us, continuing His creative work. Read these verses with this understanding: "You were taught, with regard to your former way of life," (that's the invisible ink) "to put off your old self, which is being corrupted by its deceitful desires; to be made new in the attitude of your minds;" (that's getting a brand new notebook full of blank pages) "and to put on the new self, created to be like God" (a Being who is expansively creating in orderly freedom) "in true righteousness and holiness" (obeying the law of love).

> If God's creative energy is infinite and divine, ours, although finite, is nevertheless His gift to us.

It All Begins in Childhood and Continues Through Life

If God's creative energy is infinite and divine, ours, although finite, is nevertheless His gift to us. As young children our desire to create is undeniable. Think back once more to those days in school sitting at your desk with a nice clean page before you. If the lecture was stimulating, you covered the page with notes. But if the teacher wasn't interesting, you simply covered it with little musings from your own mind. You picked up your pen and proceeded to draw shapes, covering the edges, turning words into pictures, drawing faces staring back up at you. You couldn't bear for the page to be left blank, untampered with, unchanged by your personal touch. We have a need to create,

> It may seem presumptive to describe simple doodling as "God within you," but that is what it is; it is the expression of God's creative nature at work in you.

and we gravitate to the blank page intuitively. It may seem presumptive to describe simple doodling as "God within you," but that is what it is; it is the expression of God's creative nature at work in you. You long to leave a mark on the world, changing it to reflect the fact that you were here. It's a good desire. Let it bear fruit in you.

Consider Your Entire Life an Easel Upon Which to Paint

The fact that the secular world is in general more creatively productive than the community of faith is not because we lack talent. Talent, in fact, has an inexorable tendency to go where it is rewarded, and a great many people from our community happily work in the society at large. But within creative expressions of faith, we suffer greatly from a false and self-imposed lack of freedom. We limit our creative impulses to a narrow part of life, and in many cases to what happens on a stage or in a book. Take the time—now, if possible—to consider your whole life a creative platform. Consider your relationships—individually, name by name—as a palette upon which to express love creatively. Consider your speech and dress and home equivalent arenas to the stage or playing an instrument for expression of your individuality. Don't be reticent to celebrate your individuality because of the fear that it is self-aggrandizing; your uniqueness gives testimony to the creativity of the One who made you, and expressing it gives Him glory.

The next time you sit to create, consider your script. Embrace what is positive, and make an effort to move past what is negative. Open yourself up to saying what you are afraid of and writing what you long to express. Let your creative soul be set free.

1. Leland Ryken, editor, *The Christian Imagination: Essays on Literature and the Arts* (Grand Rapids, Michigan: Baker Book House).

CHAPTER 5

The Christian in Secular Music
By Marty Roe

For Steven [Curtis Chapman], being involved in Christian music has been a great experience. But I've also maintained that the world needs more Christians who are a part of the entertainment industry as a whole and are impacting that world with their beliefs.

My name is Marty Roe, and I'm a Christian. Like most people, I have a job, and mine is singing country music. I try my best to do that to the glory of God in the same way that a teacher or a plumber or a carpenter would. I respect the talented people that make Christian music their life and livelihood, and I listen to their music with appreciation. But I've found that being a Christian in the mainstream of the entertainment industry is a great challenge and a wonderful opportunity to be a witness for Christ. There are challenges that are peculiar to this life, but if God calls you to it then I believe you can successfully navigate them.

I grew up in a Christian home, which to a large extent has made me the man I am. Zane and Roberta Roe, my father and mother, made sure I was in church every Sunday, and that was where I learned to sing—a capella, mostly, because we were members of the Church of Christ. The music of the church became a part of my life and it stays with me to this day. But country music was also a part of my life from the very beginning; my grandfather had a country jamboree every week at his house, which was a little bit of history that's unfortunately fading away in these days of mass entertainment. The band was made up of my cousins and an uncle, and sometimes more than 200 people would come to hear us play. I got up to sing at a very young age and fell in love with performing. To me it wasn't a conflict with church; it made perfect sense to me that I could sing sacred music while at worship and country music for the pure joy of singing and entertaining.

Eventually I went out on my own, playing guitar and singing at banquets and proms in my area. I remember my first paycheck: It was $50, which was quite a bit of money at that time. I also remember thinking how great it would be if I could make a living doing something I loved so much.

> The Bible says that we are to do whatever we do unto the Lord, and that means that I dedicate myself to doing great entertainment under the authority and inspiration of Him.

Because I was already interested in country music, I decided to come to Nashville for college. Although I majored in management and business, I was still able to study music with great teachers at David Lipscomb University. But the real benefit of being at school in Nashville was the opportunity to get my feet wet in the country music scene. I was able to work at the Opryland theme park, which has been the proving ground for a lot of successful people in the music business. It was great performing experience, but it was also significant for a much more important reason: It was there I met Jimmy Olander and Dan Truman, and together we founded Diamond Rio. We worked in a country music show there for a year together and became close friends. It was inevitable that when Diamond Rio formed we would all three be a part of it.

Diamond Rio has gone through some personnel changes over the years, and we eventually added Brian Prout, Gene Johnson, and Dana Williams. The six of us have enjoyed a great deal of success, and I firmly believe that God has had His hand on our work. I hope that my experience can help encourage you to seek God in what He wants you to do with your musical talent, whether it is in Christian music or any other musical venue.

Entertainment and Ministry

I draw a distinction between ministry and entertainment, and for me a country music concert is clearly the latter. I don't expect ministry from a country concert, and I don't attempt to offer it. My job as a country music entertainer is to entertain, in exactly the same way my father's job was to be a teacher. I don't see a difference there. The Bible says that we are to do whatever we do unto the Lord, and that means that I dedicate myself to doing great entertainment under the authority and inspiration of Him. It doesn't mean I preach during a concert; that's not an appropriate venue. People have paid money to hear their favorite songs, and we try to deliver great performances of those songs.

Even though I'm a Christian, I made a conscious decision not to go into Christian music. I've had a lot of interesting conversations about this, and some of the best have been with my good friend Steven Curtis Chapman. Years ago he and I worked together in a show at Opryland, and we used to debate the whole Christian/secular thing fairly often. We're still friends to this day, and we understand the decision that each of us has made, and the fact that it's right for us as individuals. For Steven, being involved in Christian music has been a great experience. But I've also maintained that the world needs more Christians who are a part of the entertainment industry as a whole and are impacting that world with their beliefs. As a part of Diamond Rio, I've had that opportunity—something people in Christian music, no matter how popular, rarely get. Through the positive message of our songs and the image we present, the Christian point of view gets to be a part of the mainstream.

Band Identity

Every band must have an identity. If you think about it, you can quickly define any truly popular band, regardless of musical genre. The Rolling Stones, Garth Brooks, Whitney Houston—all of them fill a definable niche in the marketplace. They know who they are, and more importantly, their fans know who they are. It's really no different in Christian music, except that every Christian band defines itself as distinctively Christian in addition to its musical identity. In pop or country, that's obviously not the case. Being in country music means that although you might be a Christian, it isn't the main identifying mark of your band.

Diamond Rio has found its identity in our music. We focus on our vocal ability, great harmonies, and striving for a higher level of musicality than some country bands. Lyrically, we're known for doing positive songs, especially in the area of relationships. These aren't songs that are about God per se; rather, they present a Christian point of view about life. For example, when we're singing about love we don't sing about having affairs. Instead, we focus on the positive aspects of sticking it out and staying together. We don't say, "Jesus says not to divorce." We reinforce the Christian view in a subtler way. You have to decide which way to communicate is right for you. Both are valid.

It's no surprise that the way a band or artist looks is another important part of how it will be defined. A lot of money is spent on this in pop and country, and for good reason—for better or worse, appearance has a lot to do with success. Appearance alone isn't a substitute for talent, but all things being equal, an appealing look is a powerful plus for an artist. In country music right now, for example, there is a tremendous emphasis on sex appeal. It seems as if new artists are getting younger and more overtly sexual every year. If you're interested in that market, you have to understand those pressures and need to have made some personal decisions about how far you're willing to go in that direction. Everything will be easier if you define yourself from the beginning rather than have to change your mind later.

Diamond Rio doesn't go for a lot of hype in the way we dress—it's just not who we are as people. We're more comfortable than flashy. We take the trouble to look our best and we understand the way we look matters. But we don't play a racy show or try to work our fans up with a fantasy.

In today's market, music videos play a huge role in building not only public awareness about a group, but also in defining that group's image. There are times when difficult decisions have to be made in making videos, particularly if the song is about romantic love, which it usually is. For example, it's almost inevitable that the singer will have to appear with some kind of actress who represents the love interest in the song. Diamond Rio had a hit single named, "Love a Little Stronger," in which just this situation occurred. It was awkward for me to do, and I did draw some lines about how much affection the couple would show in the video. I wanted to make sure that nothing was gratuitous. But the principle of appearing with a model or actress is certainly acceptable to me, in the same way that Christians appear in films that dramatically represent fictional relationships.

The most important thing I did was to show the finished video to my wife with the clear understanding that if she was uncomfortable with the scene I would cut it. I made this clear to the video producers from the beginning, which was my obligation in fairness to them. The video came out extremely well and the song was a strong hit for us.

> I don't expect everyone that works for or with Diamond Rio to be a Christian. I do expect them to be respectful of what our band stands for and to behave accordingly.

Like it or not, a band's identity will always be defined to a large extent by its lead singer. What I mean is this: If you're the lead singer in a band, people are going to want to talk to you and interviewers will naturally gravitate toward you more than the others. The answer you personally give to questions will become the answer for the whole band. If you're working with people who aren't Christians, you have the potential for a lot of dilemmas there. If you're asked a question about faith and give a certain response that others in the band don't agree with, you have a possible conflict. In my case, God surely brought the right people around me because what could have become a minefield has been relatively easy to manage. In Diamond Rio, these issues were talked out very frankly among the band members so that we all understood how to handle certain things. Some of these talks were a little uncomfortable, but it was important for everyone to be honest. Just because some of the people in the band weren't Christian didn't mean their opinions didn't need to be treated with respect. We had made a mutual decision to go into business together, and that meant listening and reaching decisions with which everyone could live.

In the early days of the group I was a bit hesitant to make a strong Christian stand publicly simply because of my obligation to represent everyone in the band. This is an obligation anyone in business can encounter, not just in music. If you're the president of a corporation or even the president of the United States you have to represent all the people, which can get tricky. I never compromised my beliefs, but I would sometimes hesitate to make strong Christian statements to the media simply on the basis that I was speaking for the band. Then a wonderful thing happened. After continuing to talk about it, the rest of the guys in the band gave me the freedom to be more forthcoming about my faith in interviews. It was in keeping with our overall philosophy: be real. So after that point, I just say what I think and try not to worry about it so much. I'm very fortunate because the tolerance that the guys in the band show me to be who I am is probably greater than a lot of people would find in most business situations—and sometimes more than you will find in a church environment.

Business Relationships

Remember that other members of your band aren't the only people with whom you might be in business. As a recording artist, you also have a vital relationship with your record company. In my case, once again God watched over Diamond Rio because at Arista we have been supported in our positive stance on certain issues. This isn't something we take lightly; it has a real cost that everyone must be willing to bear.

I don't expect everyone who works for or with Diamond Rio to be a Christian. I do expect them to be respectful of what our band stands for and to behave accordingly. We look for integrity and a successful track record in our business relationships, not simply a statement of faith. Our management team understands us and doesn't put us into compromising situations. We're very involved with what they do, and they send us a weekly memo detailing everything they do to promote the band. That way we can make sure that nothing is happening with which we would be uncomfortable. Obviously there are people at our record company who aren't Christians. Frankly I don't expect them all to be; I would prefer to work with competent, creative professionals in that capacity rather than give them a test of faith. I've been in meetings with Arista in which we were seeking songs for a new album. Hit songs are the lifeblood of the record business, and they are the basis for any successful career. More than once a song has been pitched to us that had all the earmarks of a strong hit,

122 Getting Started in Christian Music

but had lyrical content that I felt was inappropriate for a Christian to be singing. At this point you really find out how important your own faith is, and how real your relationships are with band members and record company alike. Remember that these lyrics might be something with which the nonbelievers in the band have less problem. They are being asked to turn down a major career boost based on the convictions of someone else, which is asking a lot. The record company, as well, is watching the potential for a lot of money vanish. But I can honestly say that Diamond Rio has traversed these problems well; in every case, the band and the record company supported potentially costly decisions in order to remain respectful of the Christian faith that some of us had.

It's hard to succinctly describe the philosophy we use to decide if a song meets our standards or not. But country music, like most popular music, is mostly about love. Today the idea of love has been made completely sexual, and there's an obvious temptation to play into that with our songs. My philosophy is this: Love, by definition, must be well-intentioned. Otherwise, it's not love. So when we sing about love, you'll find the intentions to be good.

If you go to a Diamond Rio concert you'll hear this theme running through our hits. And on a nightly basis I'll have someone ask me after a concert, "Are you guys believers?" That shows me that the thread of real love—not what passes for it in a lot of music these days—is running through our music.

Being a Christian doesn't just have the potential to cost you in finding hit songs. Simply being positive can greatly impact you in the area of public relations. Getting on television can be important for an artist, especially when a new album is being released. The publicity that comes from getting to do your new single to a national audience can be critical in jump-starting the success of an album. So public relations specialists work hard to get their clients booked on the most-watched programs. The competition can be intense because the stakes are high.

Improving Performance
By Stephen Clapp

Confidence is the single factor most responsible for successful performance. That's true for the football quarterback, the tennis player, and the musician. If you're looking at yourself while you toss the tennis ball, counting the seconds until the racquet connects, you won't hit an ace—or at least not consistently. The rhythm of the swing has to be so automatic that your mind is blank, and your body follows through with an automatic response.

Musicians who perform after insufficient preparation are doomed to dialogue with unwanted inner voices, creating doubts and inhibiting the flow. Confidence, on the other hand, is the result of being able to say to those voices, "Be quiet! I've done that shift/leap a thousand times and have performed the whole piece successfully half-a-dozen times for an audience. I know it will be fine today." The first part of that statement comes from extensive practicing; the second is the result of preparing the performance. There is a difference between these two.

Practicing applies a secure instrumental or vocal technique to the demands of particular sequences of notes in each new piece. Careful thought and repetition transform new material into a fluent series of motions and sounds. One great run-through lets you know that you can play the piece well when you're relaxed and thinking clearly. But the dependability goes out the window when the thinking breaks down. And—have you noticed?—when you're standing on stage, there's an excellent chance that you won't be thinking very clearly!

That's when the preparation for performance takes over. Tape-recording numerous trial performances with audiences of family, friends, church members, or nursing home residents will acclimate you to the straight-through, nonstop experience of performing. Listening to the tape will guide you to practice away distracting flaws and ineffective phrases, resulting in ever more effective musical expression in successive performances.

Artistic excellence is seldom communicated when the performer's mind is distracted by uncertainties. In tennis, fluent, automatic motions allow the mind to respond to higher stimuli—returning the ball and the freedom to play creatively! In music, that higher stimulus is a spiritual essence—God's gift of music—which the artist wishes to communicate with an audience. When one's mind is at rest, spirit and emotion come through. True communication brings nourishment and joy to both listeners and performers.

May this be your frequent experience!

Stephen Clapp is dean of the Julliard School in New York.

Although Diamond Rio is a very successful band that has been honored with three consecutive CMA Group of the Year awards— itself an accomplishment worth publicizing—it has sometimes been difficult to get booked on the biggest talk shows. At first we were perplexed by this; why were less well-known, less successful groups getting the time, while we weren't? Finally we hired a consultant to track down the reason. We learned in short order what the problem was: We were considered "too clean," and therefore boring by the producers of these television programs. What they wanted, we learned, was an angle—a bit of gossip or drama with which they could base the interview. Simply to be good people just wasn't interesting enough. In response, our PR consultant grilled us to try to find some indiscretion in our pasts to use to our advantage. Was there any past drug abuse? Affairs? Horrible childhood? They wanted to find something to attract audience interest—a hook. But the fact is that we're all pretty normal guys who don't have any more than the usual crud in our lives. We simply weren't willing to manufacture something that wasn't real just so we could get on television or a magazine cover. As a result, we don't get the press coverage that we might. Diamond Rio chose to respond to this problem in a very direct way. Rather than change who we are, we decided to become more passionate about what we believe in. I believe people enjoy seeing passion, and we have become more outspoken and passionate about what's important to us.

Another area where being a Christian can cost you is in product endorsements. This is an increasingly important concern for acts who are touring, because putting on a great concert is a very expensive proposition. As a result, more and more artists seek tour sponsorships. In country music, alcoholic beverages and cigarettes play a large role. Diamond Rio doesn't participate with those kind of sponsors, and we don't participate in events sponsored by that type of company. There have been occasions that we have found out after the fact that an event at which we played was sponsored by a beer company, but with the number of contracts we play it's not always possible to know in advance. Where possible, we are willing to say no to jobs that involve alcohol or cigarette sponsorship.

There are a lot of Christians who feel social drinking is fine, and I don't argue with them. I don't object to alcohol sponsorship on the basis of whether or not social drinking is acceptable for a Christian; I object because having endorsed the product, I don't feel I can make such fine distinctions. You can't endorse a product by degrees. You either endorse it or you don't. In our society drinking still carries a negative connotation in some circles, and I don't want to cloud the issue by bringing the image of Diamond Rio into business with a beer company. Right or wrong, a lot of people will perceive that as a serious inconsistency, and in order to avoid that perception we are willing to say no.

Home and Church Life

Being on the road means that your relationships are inevitably going to be affected. You have to face certain realities about travel. If you're gone from home for weeks or months at a time there's a price to be paid. For a Christian, the two key relationships are family and church, and in my experience, a lot of road work is hard on both of them. Any artist, Christian or otherwise, needs to understand how to handle the length of time you're going to be out of town.

In country music, the weekend is the key work time. I'm normally out every weekend and return home on Sunday. As a result, a regular church life on that day is very difficult. I have to admit that for a while I let that slide and it was unhealthy. But since about '93 I've been getting into the Word more regularly, as well as using devotional materials like *My Utmost for His Highest*. But studying and reading alone don't meet the need for fellowship with other believers. For that, I attend a regular Tuesday night Bible study that

> The debate about Christian and secular music has gone on for a long time, and I believe it comes down to this: Do what God is calling you to do.

meets in our home. This group is a kind of cell group from our church, where six couples meet and we focus on our spiritual lives. We pray for and encourage each other. There are even times where we confess our sins, which I think is important and best not done in a large congregation. I'll be honest here and say that there are times I hesitate to bare my soul because of my position; I don't want to put pressure on the others in the group to keep a secret about someone who has a public profile. But fortunately these couples have known each other for a long time—long before Diamond Rio was well known. So I can depend on these friendships to be real.

Some people wonder why traveling artists don't take their families along; wouldn't that solve a lot of problems? But the fact is that being on the road is a real burden and the only thing that makes it worthwhile is getting to perform. Traveling without that pleasure isn't really desirable after the initial glamour wears off. My family has better things to do than follow me around with no real purpose to the trip. It's important to our family that my wife and children have a normal life. My wife is active in our church and is able to take the kids every Sunday and Wednesday. She teaches a pottery class there as well. Those kind of fulfilling things just wouldn't be possible if they traveled with me on a regular basis. The life of my family doesn't revolve around my career.

The Bottom Line

The debate about Christian and secular music has gone on for a long time, and I believe it comes down to this: Do what God is calling you to do. Don't assume that just because you're a Christian that you have to be in Christian music; we definitely need more Christians who are willing to undertake the challenge of impacting the world for Christ through the entertainment industry. But this isn't a challenge for everyone; there are very real dangers with which you may have to contend. If your career takes off, the power of fame can spin you around and go straight to your head. If you fail, you can become cynical and negative. The important thing is to be the greatest singer, writer, and performer you can be and to do it all for the glory of God—no matter where you find your audience. Commit your way to God, and follow Him wherever He leads.

Marty Roe is the lead singer for Diamond Rio, four-time winner of the Country Music Association's "Vocal Group of the Year" award. Each of Diamond Rio's six recordings have been certified gold or platinum, and in 1998 they became the first band in 14 years to be inducted into the Grand Ole Opry.

A History of Contemporary Christian Music
By Dr. Patrick Kavanaugh

As the twenty-first century unfolds its music to an ever-growing audience, let us consider the "test of time" which governs all of music history. At any given time, much of the music that is popular will soon fade away, while other works—often ignored at first—may rise to lasting endurance. Obviously, what is contemporary Christian music in 2000 will not seem very contemporary in 2949!

Part 1:
2,000 Years of Christian Music

Historic Roots of Sacred Music: Three Streams

In my book, *The Music of Angels; Sacred Music from Gregorian Chant to Christian Rock* (Loyola Press, 1999), I evoke an image of a long, flowing river to depict the history of Christian music. After a time the river divides into two streams and still later one of these streams further divides, creating a third. It is out of this "third stream" of sacred music that contemporary Christian music has its true roots.

What exactly is the "third stream" of sacred music? To answer this, let us first consider the differences between the first stream and the second.

The First Stream

Christian music was first organized after Constantine converted to Christianity in the fourth century. Before that time, the persecuted Christians sang a wide variety of monophonic music based on Greek and Hebrew influences. But with the triumph of the church, a large body of chant was created which congregations throughout Christendom sang to worship God. Later however, through the Middle and Renaissance ages, composers experimenting with new ideas created music that grew more and more complicated. Soon the illiterate congregations could not handle the newer music and, thus, became spectators at church, while trained choirs sang this more complex choral music. All this constituted the "first stream" of sacred music and reigned supreme in the church for the first 1,500 years of its existence. Still later, this tradition would embrace the immense world of classical music and all its masterpieces of sacred music.

The Second Stream

Martin Luther and the Reformers appeared in the sixteenth century and Christian music changed dramatically. Among other things, Luther wanted everyone to sing at church so that the congregation might stop being merely an audience at high church services. A huge body of new, uncomplicated music for congregations was developed, which we have called the second stream of sacred music. Meanwhile, the first stream continued, with composers creating music for professional performers who played before audiences—as is the case throughout the history of classical music.

One of the most important differences between the first stream and the second was that the first stream set up a performer-audience situation (that is, a soloist or ensemble was "on stage" while an audience or congregation listened) and the second stream obliterated this "performer-audience" condition, allowing everyone to participate, so that no one remained a passive spectator.

Obviously, the music of the second stream had to be kept simple enough to be sung by nonmusicians. This "popular" type of sacred music gave rise to the wonderful heritage of hymnology and congregational singing which is still in Christian churches today. But what happens when this "popular" type of sacred music is sung by a soloist, with an "audience" listening? This is exactly what the "third stream" of sacred music is.

The Third Stream

For the first three centuries after the Reformation, the "performer-audience" situation was reserved for the world of classical music, while the church congregations always sang together from their many new hymns. Luther, Watts, Wesley, and the other great hymnwriters of those days composed for the congregation, not for solo performers. It was not until the nineteenth century that soloists began to be employed in the realm of popular sacred music. The solo format may have seemed "classical," but the music was definitely popular and immediately accessible to everyone—with or without musical training or appreciation.

Thus began the performer (solo or ensemble) tradition of popular sacred music. This "third stream" began in the obscurity of camp meetings and revival services and has now grown to create a multi-million dollar entertainment industry.

PART 2:
FORERUNNERS OF CONTEMPORARY CHRISTIAN MUSIC: GOSPEL MUSIC

The Confusion of Names in This New "Gospel" Music

Before we begin this journey, something must be noted concerning the confusing terminology which has evolved within popular Christian music. When "gospel music" began, it was all simply called gospel music. Each performer was expected to have his or her own style and to be versatile enough to perform different kinds of songs without difficulty.

But by the end of the twentieth century, there were so many sub-branches and sub-sub-branches that almost every new song seemed to have a new branch all its own. At any given time in music history, there are many sub-branches which are useful at the time but are long since forgotten a century later. In the same way, many labels used today will not be remembered long into the future, unless they expand, flourish, and later germinate into other long-term branches. In the meantime, who can tell?

We will not split hairs regarding this or that definition or minuscule sub-division. The role of the music historian is to discern the major events and trends, connecting them to show the ongoing march of musical progress. We will focus on the basic large directions that popular sacred music has taken in the twentieth century: gospel music, then its largest sub-branch, contemporary Christian music.

Of course, part of the problem lies in the wonderful practice of contemporary performers to make music in many different styles. The same person might write a praise chorus for church congregations to sing while also giving personal performances of Christian rock in a performer-audience situation. While such versatility enhances the performances of talented artists, it creates a confusing tangle of music history!

The Gospel in Black and White

The birth of gospel music is a fascinating topic, because it took place exactly opposite to the way that most things occur throughout music history. Usually a certain type of music would begin to surface, gradually expand, and then eventually split into two or more smaller parts. But one might say that the birth of gospel music occurred in two different places, then gradually came together to form something even larger.

I am referring to what is often called "white gospel" and "black gospel." The nineteenth century saw the beginnings of both types, sometimes almost simultaneously, but usually unnoticed by the other. Because of the deplorable prejudice and enmity between the races in America, few African-Americans knew the music of the white churches and even fewer whites knew the music of the black churches.

> Although there still exists evidence of bigotry in society, gospel music has often led the way in the breaking down of racial barriers.

Yet both were initiating a new musical genre. Some musical differences existed, but both sides had the same musical concept: popular music to be sung, not just by the congregation in worship services, but by soloists for the "spiritual entertainment" of a listening audience.

It was not until the twentieth century that members of the two races began to appreciate the other's musical genius. Through the decades, whites slowly began to listen and learn from black artists, and vice versa. By the end of the century, much of the musical prejudice had thankfully disappeared: Music written and performed by a member of one race is routinely played in churches of predominantly the other race. Although there still exists evidence of bigotry in society, gospel music has often led the way in the breaking down of racial barriers.

What is musically interesting is how the music of each race has now influenced that of the other. Musicians have interacted, borrowed, and imitated one another, actually bringing the two sides closer together. In many ways, their musics are now so intermingled that it is sometimes difficult to tell the "white gospel" and "black gospel" apart. They have come together at last, and their combination has now matured to the point that it has spawned new and fascinating sub-streams.

The Early Roots of Gospel Music

As we have already seen, the original concept of popular sacred music was congregational—music that everyone could sing in praise to God. But some people sing better than others! Obviously, in a given congregation those members who were born with excellent voices will come to the forefront. Perhaps then they may band together with other excellent singers to create popular music with a special degree of distinction.

The Fisk Jubilee Singers, a group of very gifted singers from Fisk University in Nashville, Tennessee, was one of the first groups to organize in this manner. In an effort to raise money for the school, these superb African-American singers toured the country in 1871, singing popular spirituals to admiring audiences everywhere. They were the first in a long line of gospel choirs which continue to be popular today.

Meanwhile, Philip Phillips (1834-95) was emerging as the first national popular solo singer in white gospel music. Phillips eventually gave thousands of "services of sacred song." This seems commonplace today but was such a novelty in 1875 that when Phillips gave an international singing tour, he wrote the story of it in a popular book, *Song Pilgrimage Round the World.* How astonished this humble singer might have been if he realized what he had started, with hundreds of Christian entertainers touring globally today.

Many traveling evangelists, both white and black, began to use vocal soloists as an addition to the congregational music which also accompanied their meetings. One of the nineteenth century's greatest teams was the evangelist D.L. Moody and his musical associate, Ira David Sankey (1840-1908), who led massive congregations in hymn singing. But it must also be mentioned that his practice of occasionally singing a solo song or two was soon widely imitated.

The great evangelist Billy Sunday conducted his huge meetings traveling with the songleader Homer Alvan Rodeheaver (1880-1955). Rodeheaver would punctuate the congregation singing with his own instrumental solos. He later published gospel hymns, becoming an early leader in the field. Ultimately his company was absorbed by Jarrell McCracken's then-new company, Word. Word was quickly established as the largest firm in Christian music recording and publishing, and remains an industry leader today.

This "evangelist-soloist" tradition was continued throughout the second half of the twentieth century by the crusades of Billy Graham. His general practice was to use one man to lead the congregational singing—usually the multi-talented musician Cliff Barrows—and save his star singer for the dramatic solo songs which preceded the sermon. For many years, this was the bass-baritone George Beverly Shea, but Graham has also used Ethel Waters and dozens of others.

While this evangelist-soloist tradition was beginning, many other "firsts" were happening in the growing world of gospel music, particularly from the many black churches of America. Charles Albert Tindley (1851-1933), born of slave parents, wrote a number of gospel songs, including the well-known "We'll Understand It Better By and By." In 1919, Lucy C. Campbell wrote the first of her many gospel hymns, "Something Within Me." And in 1923, Paramount Records recorded its first black gospel singer, Hurd Fairfax.

Gospel Pearls, printed by the National Baptist Convention in 1921, was one of the first publications to feature the newer gospel songs. Slowly moving from the country churches into the large cities, gospel music was beginning to happen everywhere. But its efforts were sporadic and disjointed for lack of effective musical leadership. This would soon change with the work of an amazing musician, Thomas A. Dorsey (1899-1993).

The Father of Black Gospel Music

Dorsey's long life spanned most of the twentieth century, and his contributions to gospel music included more than 800 songs. The manner in which he became involved is almost prophetic, in that it foreshadowed the struggles of many future musicians in this field. While still in his teens, Dorsey was such a noted ragtime and blues musician that he accompanied famous singers of his day, such as "Ma" Rainey and Bessie Smith.

He was deeply moved while attending a meeting of the National Baptist Convention and hearing the songs of Charles Tindley. After a struggle between whether to work in secular music or gospel, Dorsey finally opted for the latter. Many churches shunned his jazzy blues style, and his beginnings in gospel music were discouraging. At one point he, "borrowed five dollars and sent out five hundred copies of my song, 'If You See My Savior,' to churches throughout the country… It was three years before I got a single order. I felt like going back to the blues."

But Dorsey never stopped. By 1929 he had devoted himself exclusively to gospel music, and in 1932 he organized the Gospel Singers Convention in Chicago, Illinois. The next two decades were spent touring the United States with talented Christian singers and propagating his spirited gospel music songs—which would eventually find acceptance and imitation. Some of his best known compositions are "There'll Be Peace in the Valley for Me" and "Precious Lord, Take My Hand."

In 1938 Rosetta Tharpe recorded the first gospel record to sell one million copies.

Thomas Dorsey was one of the first of a long line of modern Christian musicians whose music was condemned as "the devil's music" by much of the church. By blending sacred text with what the churchmen considered "secular style" of blues and jazz, Dorsey was considered a renegade. His answer has inspired many musicians of later generations: "When I realized how hard some folks were fighting the gospel idea, I was determined to carry the banner."

Rise of the Great Soloists

By the 1930s, gospel music was beginning to develop into a true entertainment medium. Those who had previously sung only in their local church began to sing in more prestigious venues. The major singers and vocal groups started using managers and made a good living, actually being paid to sing gospel music. In fact, in 1938 Rosetta Tharpe recorded the first gospel record to sell one million copies.

Perhaps the greatest gospel singer of this age was Mahalia Jackson (1911-1972). She was born in New Orleans, Louisiana, where she began singing at a very early age. While only 16, she moved to Chicago and joined the Greater Salem Baptist Church Choir. Jackson's strong contralto voice soon singled her out as a soloist and thus began her career, making her first recording in 1934. Eight different recordings sold over one million copies, and her vocal sound was copied by many blues and jazz artists. "I Can Put my Trust in Jesus," "Move on Up a Little Higher," "When I Wake Up in Glory," and "I Believe," were some of the songs she made famous.

If Thomas Dorsey was "the Father of Gospel Music," then James Cleveland (1931-1991) was surely a prince in his court. Indeed, young Cleveland got his first taste of the gospel style while at Chicago's Pilgrim Baptist Church where Dorsey was the music director. His was not the smooth sound of a typical soloist, but his rough voice nonetheless kept audiences in rapt attention. In his lifetime he recorded 54 albums, including such best-sellers as "Jesus is the Best Thing," "Lord Help Me," "I Stood on the Banks," and "Peace, Be Still." Cleveland still found time to pastor churches—such as Detroit's Prayer Tabernacle and the Cornerstone Institutional Baptist Church in Los Angeles, and to found the Gospel Music Workshop of America.

Another great name in gospel music was Clara Ward (1924-1973). Like Mahalia Jackson, she began singing early, joining her first choir when she was only 5 years old. Although she had a wonderful voice and sang with her mother and sister as well as with huge choirs, her finest contribution was her compositional gift. She wrote more than 200 songs, including such well-known pieces as "Come in the Prayer Room," "How I Got Over," "Prince of Peace," and "Packing Up."

Meanwhile, predominantly white southern gospel was forging ahead thanks to the efforts of men like James D. Vaughn. His innovations in music, ministry, and business still influence the industry today. A visionary music publisher, he was writing songs and publishing them in a songbook entitled *Onward and Upward* before the turn of the century. Over the next two decades he published a series of cloth and paperback songbooks, publicizing them with trips to singing conventions.

Eventually he teamed with his brother Charles and some friends to form the Vaughn Quartet. During the next 20 years, he would pay to have a series of quartets travel in his name—at one time contracting as many as 16 paid quartets to travel to singing conventions and churches across the South on the Vaughn payroll.

Always an innovator, Vaughn looked for new ways to spread his music and the fortunes of his company. He was interested in technology, and as early as 1921 had several of his Vaughn Quartets make 78-RPM recordings. With genuine prescience he anticipated the growth of Christian radio, opening a station in Lawrenceburg, Tennessee. Nightly programming featured a variety of gospel music entertainment from quartet and trio singing to piano and orchestra instrumentals.

Quartets, Ensembles, and Performing Choirs

As we have seen, the "third stream" of performed popular sacred music evolved from the "second stream" of congregational singing.

Therefore it should not surprise us to find that a large portion of gospel music's exponents were not solo artists, but ensembles. From the smallest groups to the massed choirs, gospel music has often been a "group art."

The earliest group, the Fisk Jubilee Singers, inspired many churches in the African-American communities to promote large gospel choirs, and by the 1930s some of these were involved in making recordings. Two of the best of these were the Gospel Light Jubilee Singers and the Roberta Martin Singers. The latter group recorded into the 1950s, producing such hits as "Where Can I Go?" and "Only a Look." Other well-liked large groups included the Argo Singers, the Drinkard Singers, and the Ward Singers—which centered around the soloist Clara Ward. By the end of the century, large mass gospel choirs would be found in almost every major city in America.

Another popular idiom, in both black and white gospel styles, was the vocal quartet. In general, the black groups were more upbeat and unconventional, whereas the white quartets tended toward a more traditional approach. The names of these groups often demonstrate a rather flamboyant style: the Swan Silvertones, the Sensational Nightingales, Wings Over Jordan, the Dixie Hummingbirds, the Souls Stirrers, and the Mighty Clouds of Joy. Most of the famous quartets were exclusively male, while a few were exclusively female, such as the Caravans, the Davis Sisters, and the Harmonettes.

Later in the century, especially within the white gospel categories, we find quartets becoming quintets, sextets, septets, or more. A few key examples are the Florida Boys, the Kingsmen, the Telestials, the Statesmen, and the Imperials. It is not uncommon to have a gospel music group from within a single family (or with several in the group from the same family) as in the case of the Speer Family, the Thrasher Brothers, the Happy Goodman Family, and the Blackwood Brothers.

For each of the groups mentioned here, there were hundreds of lesser-known groups trying to "get a break," to "make it big" in the

> For a gospel artist to release a new album, many thousands of dollars are spent in such nonmusical items as cover design, photography, news releases, and advanced publicity.

gospel music scene. Again we see a major difference between the second and third streams of sacred music. Within the second stream of congregational music there is little competition. Most church choirs simply sang for their own church and no one else. Yet the performers of the third stream are much less parochial. Their impact was national and even international, so the competition between different groups and artists appealing to the same market was irrepressible.

Relationships to Secular Music

Tough competition is just one parallel which gospel music has with the secular popular music of the day. Another is marketing. When a young singer sings a solo in the church choir, at best he or she may get a line in the Sunday bulletin or a mention from the pastor. For a gospel artist to release a new album, many thousands of dollars are spent in such nonmusical items as cover design, photography, news releases, and advanced publicity.

One of the hallmarks of gospel singers is that of touring, just like their secular counterparts. When the Fisk Jubilee Singers toured in 1871, they were trying to raise money for the Fisk University. When a gospel artist tours today, much money is also raised, but it goes to cover myriad tour-related expenses. Unlike the free performances of the musician who traveled with the big-name evangelist, the ticket prices of today's gospel artists can be as high as any secular performance.

Ultimately, there are many similarities between gospel artists and popular secular performers, and this should not surprise us. For instance, from a musical point of view there has never been any major

differences between sacred classical music and secular classical
pieces. A Mozart Mass and a
Mozart opera sound quite similar;
only the words are very different.
The same is true with regard to
the musical aspects of hymns
versus that of secular choruses.

> Ultimately there are many
> similarities between gospel
> artists and popular secular
> performers, and this
> should not surprise us.

These similarities are doubtless the reason that so many artists
have successfully done both gospel music and music of the secular
world. Not only have many gospel artists performed nongospel
songs, but many typical secular artists have worked in the gospel
field with remarkable ease. These include such names as Sam Cooke,
Aretha Franklin, Ray Charles, and Elvis Presley—who recorded a
number of successful gospel albums—to name but a few.

Churches Move from Hymns to "Praise Choruses"

While gospel music continued to grow, the middle of the twentieth century saw a related development in church music, moving
from the traditional hymns to contemporary "praise choruses."
Virtually every denomination began to print its own hymnal, most of
which contained many of the same songs, often with edited text to
reflect the spiritual convictions of the specific denominations.

Certainly some of the church's finest hymnwriters worked
between 1900 and 1940. These include the conventional type of
hymnwriters (composing the text only) such as Elisha A. Hoffman
(1839-1929) ("Leaning on the Everlasting Arms"), Jessie Pounds
(1861-1921) ("I Know That My Redeemer Liveth") and Johnson
Oatman, Jr. (1856-1922) ("Count Your Blessings"). Yet we also begin to
find the newer breed which composed both words and music: James
M. Black (1856-1938) ("When the Roll Is Called Up Yonder"), George

Bennard (1873-1958) ("The Old Rugged Cross"), C. Austin Miles (1868-1946) ("In the Garden"), and Alfred H. Ackley (1887-1960) ("He Lives").

But the 1940s began a new form of popular hymn whose acceptance has made it a genre in itself, the "praise chorus." These simple melodies are often only four lines long, or at best employ a refrain-verse alternation form. The simplicity of these songs remind one of the camp meetings of earlier days and are closely related to the gospel songs of the nineteenth century.

One of the first successful composers of praise choruses was John W. Peterson. Sometimes he would write both the words and the music, as is the case with "No One Understands Like Jesus," "Shepherd of Love," "Heaven Came Down," and "It Took a Miracle." Yet some of his best-known musical efforts used texts written by others, such as "Surely Goodness and Mercy Shall Follow Me" (text adapted from Psalm 23 by Alfred B. Smith) and "So I Send You" (text by Margaret Clarkson).

Two of the best-known creators of praise-oriented music are Bill and Gloria Gaither. This talented couple from the Midwest—who not only compose, but also perform and record their music—began to write choruses in the 1960s and were soon the best known in their field. Their style might be called "the middle of the road"—not too folksy, not too sophisticated. Some of their best-known songs include "Because He Lives," "He Touched Me," "Jesus, We Just Want to Thank You," "There's Something About That Name," "Let's Just Praise the Lord," "I Will Serve Thee," "His Name is Life," "We Are So Blessed," "Gentle Shepherd," "The King Is Coming," "Come Holy Spirit," "Something Beautiful," and "The Family of God."

The last half of the twentieth century has produced hundreds (thousands?!) of praise-oriented composers who continue to produce thousands (millions?!) of songs. Some of the best known are Jimmy

Owens ("Clap Your Hands"), Kurt Kaiser ("Pass It On"), Ralph Carmichael ("He's Everything to Me"), Ken Medema ("Lord, Listen to Your Children Praying"), Jack Hayford ("Majesty"), Naida Hearn ("Jesus, Name Above All Names"), Michael O'Shields ("I Will Call Upon the Lord"), and Ken Lafferty ("Seek Ye First").

If you listen to many of the songs listed above, you will immediately notice that we are a long way from Wesleyan hymns. We're even a long way from Fanny Crosby hymns. There are various musical subtleties to define the actual differences in melody, harmony, and rhythm. But for the layman, an easy way to analyze the growing differences is to notice the evolution of the principle accompanying instruments: from organ to piano to guitar to synthesizer.

An Explosion of Gospel Arts

In the last half of the twentieth century, two fundamental developments have transformed the gospel music genre into an impressive industry. The first is its subdividing into so many categories (especially contemporary Christian music)—more about this subdividing in a moment. The second is the huge explosion of new artists.

Doubtless, many of the newer gospel artists will not be remembered for very long, but others will have a significant, lasting effect on their branch of sacred music. As is often noted when discussing modern classical composers, the "test of time" will eventually show who will last and who will not. But there are some gospel artists who have already made such an impact as to be noted. Since we will later look at artists within contemporary Christian music and other streams, the musicians to be mentioned are those who have stayed in the more traditional gospel genre.

Shirley Caesar has been one of gospel music's most influential female vocalists. To some degree, she followed in the traditions of Mahalia Jackson and Clara Ward, but she also found her own powerful style which has been greatly imitated. Starting her career at the age of

10, she was known as "Baby Shirley" and toured the Southern states before joining the Caravans, an exclusively female gospel group. Once she launched her solo career, she was awarded many honors and gold records, as well as becoming the first female black singer to win a Grammy award.

An important last name to remember within the gospel music world is Hawkins. Walter and Tramaine Hawkins led a musical family which set many standards in the side of gospel which is often called "Soul Gospel Music," showing its relation to soul music. Their albums contained the musical skills of many different family members, and one in particular—Edwin Hawkins—became nationally known in secular music circles as well with his recording of "O Happy Day."

We have already seen how many families have played a prevalent role in gospel music. Still another important one was Buck and Dottie Rambo, with their daughter Reba. Their style was more southern gospel, even country, but their many albums were united by a fascinating distinction: All of their hundreds of songs were written by Dottie Rambo. Reba, after singing for years with her parents, launched her own successful career with a more contemporary sound—strongly influenced by a stint of singing with Andrae Crouch.

Thus we come to the musician who has had the most significant influence on late twentieth-century gospel music, Andrae Crouch. His father was a "boot-leggin' street preacher" and after he started a church in Los Angeles, that church's youth choir became Andrae's musical laboratory. Like many popular artists, his life was soon a combination of writing gospel songs and performing them. For years he worked with a touring band, Andrae Crouch and the Disciples, but he had an extensive solo career as well as becoming a pastor himself.

Perhaps the reason Crouch has had such an impact is his ability to appeal to both white and black audiences. More than any other musician, he has brought those two worlds of gospel music together, reaching out without a musical bias. He once explained, "I have one question when I write a new song: 'Does it reach you?' I feel the feedback from an audience if the song is working. I know what is real. That's what I get from being raised in the church, before those congregations."

> One thing is certain: [Gospel music] is not a genre for just whites or just blacks; gospel music has merged the two and found an appeal to everyone.

There continues to be many new and talented gospel music singers, who will doubtless have a powerful influence on future performers. From the innovative sounds of such artists as The Martins to the more R&B-influenced music of BeBe and CeCe Winans, the gospel music industry is constantly being updated without forgetting its genuine roots. One thing is certain: It is not a genre for just whites or just blacks; gospel music has merged the two and found an appeal to everyone.

Later Divisions of Gospel Music

As we have seen, the original division of gospel music was simply black and white. Yet now we recognize many new subdivisions, and more are rapidly being added. One of the best indicators of these trends can be seen in the different categories of the "Dove Awards," an annual event which recognizes the best achievements in gospel music.

Let us examine the additions made in the Dove Awards from 1969 to 1999. (We will focus only on the purely musical categories, and skip such nonmusical varieties as "Disk Jockey of the Year" and "Record Album Cover Art.") In 1969, the basic categories were:

Gospel Song of the Year

Gospel Instrumentalist

Gospel Record Album of the Year

Male Gospel Group

Gospel Songwriter of the Year

Male Gospel Soloist

Mixed Gospel Group

Female Gospel Soloist

Only 30 years later, the list has grown considerably:

Song of the Year

Songwriter of the Year

Male Vocalist of the Year

Female Vocalist of the Year

Group of the Year

Artist of the Year

New Artist of the Year

Traditional Gospel Recorded Song of the Year

Contemporary Gospel Recorded Song of the Year

Pop/Contemporary Recorded Song of the Year

Inspirational Recorded Song of the Year

Southern Gospel Recorded Song of the Year

Country Recorded Song of the Year

Urban Recorded Song of the Year

Rap/Hip Hop Song of the Year

Alternative/Modern Rock Recorded Song of the Year

Metal/Hard Rock Recorded Song of the Year

Rock Recorded Song of the Year

Traditional Gospel Recorded Album of the Year

Contemporary Gospel Recorded Album of the Year

Pop/Contemporary Recorded Album of the Year

Inspirational Recorded Album of the Year

Southern Gospel Recorded Album of the Year

Country Recorded Album of the Year

Urban Recorded Album of the Year

Rap/Hip Hop Album of the Year
Alternative/Modern Rock Recorded Album of the Year
Metal/Hard Rock Recorded Album of the Year
Rock Recorded Album of the Year
Instrumental Album of the Year
Praise and Worship Album of the Year
Children's Music Album of the Year
Special Event Album of the Year
Musical of the Year
Youth Musical of the Year
Choral Collection of the Year
Producer of the Year
Short Form Music Video of the Year
Long Form Music Video of the Year

What Has Happened? Several Things

Obviously, there are many natural additions which can be easily explained. Such things as choral collections, praise and worship, and producers were around in 1969, but no one had yet thought to include them. Music videos were yet to be invented. Presumably someone later thought of musical of the year and then youth musical of the year.

Many others are subdivisions of the original concept. Traditional gospel moves to inspirational gospel which moves to contemporary gospel which moves to pop/contemporary gospel. Some classifications, such as southern gospel and country gospel, are noticeably related. And as soon as rock music was included, it spread

> Of all the different genres within modern gospel music, this last one—which we call contemporary Christian music—has had the most profound impact.

to include such categories as metal/hard rock, alternative/ modern rock, urban, and rap/hip hop.

Of all the different genres within modern gospel music, this last one—which we call contemporary Christian music—has had the most profound impact. Its repercussions are now to be examined.

PART THREE:
CONTEMPORARY CHRISTIAN MUSIC—
THE CONCEPT

Let us now examine one of the fastest-growing—and perhaps, the most unexpectedly popular—forms of sacred music in history. As we begin, it is important to note the unexpected nature of contemporary Christian music's remarkable development. For if you were alive in 1955 or so, you would probably never have imagined the tremendous success of "Christian rock 'n' roll."

Why is this? Primarily because of two factors which preceded the era of the '50s: First, popular Christian music had largely stayed within the more conservative forms of music and had been historically more adult-oriented than youth-oriented. And, second, rock 'n' roll, especially the most recent variants which were then emerging, was definitively youth-oriented and very nonconservative. If someone would have suggested the idea of "Christian rock 'n' roll," one would presumably have thought that it could never succeed on a large scale. At best you might have imagined a fringe movement, but nothing like what would quickly develop.

By the end of the twentieth century, contemporary Christian music would be so popular that secular recording companies would compete to negotiate deals in order to purchase Christian labels and gain an instant market share in this growing industry. What was at first shocking and then controversial became accepted and commonplace within mainstream Christianity. Although the twentieth century has produced artists within Christian country music, Christian jazz, and Christian folk music, nothing has grown at the same rate as contemporary Christian music.

The Jesus Music of the '60s

Where did this begin? As is the case throughout most of musical history, the beginnings of new ages and genres of music are not easy to pinpoint. Some consider contemporary Christian music an outgrowth of the earlier gospel music. Others argue that it is simply a Christian remaking of secular rock music. But most informed devotees agree that this movement emerged from that peculiar decade in America—the 1960s.

Many factors came together to make the '60s one of the most tempestuous in modern history. The confusing carnage of the Vietnam War, the "God is Dead" movement, the political assassinations, the pressure of the space race, the spread of mind-bending drugs, the fear of nuclear war, the flowering of hippiedom and violent protests, and many other chaos-agitating factors made this a time of great disillusionment among young people. Anti-establishment demonstrations were on every college campus, and the suspicion of conventional institutions became the norm.

Two of the most portentous phenomena which were encouraged by this seedbed of turbulence were the rapid growth of secular rock music and the "Jesus Movement."

Of course, the first development had already begun with such rock 'n' rollers as Buddy Holly, Elvis Presley, and dozens of other stars and groups which appeared in the years following World War II. But in the 1960s, the unprecedented rise of the Beatles accelerated the rise of many similar groups. The anti-war, anti-establishment situation gave them abundant material and an easy audience. By 1965, rock music was a billion-dollar industry that could not be ignored by the world. Nevertheless, most of it could not be understood, accepted, or appreciated by the Christian church.

Yet at the same time as these worldly upheavals, a great spiritual revival was rapidly spreading. This was especially notable among young people. Thousands who had given up on both the establishment and the drug culture became hungry for truth and reality. Many who had long since abandoned the "dead" churches of their parents now began to read the New Testament for themselves. Prayer groups dotted hundreds of college campuses, and it became cool for kids to "try Jesus."

What were these ex-druggies and flower-children to sing within their new-found Christianity? For those used to the driving beat of such rock groups as Steppenwolf or Cream, singing Fanny Crosby's "Blessed Assurance" must have sounded like music from another world—which, in a manner of speaking, it was. Developments in rock music had hastened so quickly that the distance between it and most church hymns was almost as far as what missionaries encounter in foreign cultures.

What to do? Of course, to many church leaders the answer was manifest: have nothing to do with rock music and learn the hymns. Like the early church fathers, they tried to draw a strong dichotomy between the music of the world and that of the church. And like the church fathers, they would eventually see this dichotomy blurred as styles from both sides began to influence one another.

Larry Norman

One of the first radical innovators was Larry Norman. Although his musical contributions were considerable, he modestly stated, "I never invented Christian rock because the blacks invented it years ago." In this he was wisely aware of the ongoing development of popular Christian music, which, as we have seen, actually began many, many years ago.

Like many of his generation, Norman says he "walked out of church when I was 9 years old. I didn't like the hymns and couldn't stand the hymns anymore." He soon began writing his own songs and formed a rock band called People. Norman's first album, *Upon This Rock,* is still considered by many to be the first complete album of Christian rock music.

Norman continues to have a profound influence on Christian music artists. He is also well known for encouraging the talents of other performers, through his founding of Solid Rock Records and the Street Level Artists Agency. Some of his many memorable songs are "One Way," "I Love You," "Moses," "I Wish We'd All Been Ready," "666," "I Am a Servant," and "UFO."

Early Hippies and Rockers for Jesus

Like their older cousins in traditional gospel music, the Christian music world is composed of as many performers as composers. These are either soloists (usually vocal soloists) or ensembles (that is, bands). Of course, this world also includes everyone from record producers to booking agents, from publicists to tour roadies. But for our purposes, we will stay with the most influential performers and songwriters. From its earliest days, specific "stars" came to the forefront.

One of the first well-known artists was Randy Stonehill, a friend and colleague of Larry Norman. Stonehill aligned himself with more conservative Christian leaders such as Billy Graham. (He even starred in a Billy Graham film, "Born to Run.") Stonehill's lyrics are nonetheless very thoughtful and deal with man's honest doubts as well as his confident faith. His best known songs are "Gone Away" and "Born Twice."

Dallas Holm was among the first young artists to be accepted by many from the traditional gospel music world. In fact, in 1978 he became the first composer other than the celebrated Bill Gaither to win the coveted "Songwriter of the Year" award presented by the

Gospel Music Association. That year he also won the "Male Vocalist" category and his band, Praise, won the "Mixed Gospel Group" award. His best-selling albums include *Rise Again, Nothing But Praise,* and *Tell 'Em Again.*

Conversion to Christianity by a leading secular musician has sometime led to their career continuing in the Christian market. Early examples of these are Barry McGuire and B.J. Thomas. Both of these men had secular hits ("Eve of Destruction" and "Raindrops Keep Falling On My Head") before they came to Christ, and their musical style after conversion is not greatly altered. Instead, the message of the lyrics became powerfully Christ-centered. McGuire's best known albums are *Lighten Up* and *Seeds,* while Thomas' are *Home Where I Belong* and *You Gave Me Love.*

The same conversion/career-change occurred in the life of guitarist Phil Keaggy, one of contemporary Christian music's finest instrumentalists who has inspired many others. Before finding Christ, Keaggy had worked in a number of secular venues, including the popular band Glass Harp. But in 1972 he devoted himself full-time to Christian music, both as a soloist and a highly demanded collaborator. He appears therefore on many albums of other artists, and his own efforts include *Emerging* and *The Master and the Musician.*

Many of these soloists formed their own "back-up groups," and Christian bands of all sorts became more and more popular in the 1970s. One of the first successful groups was a trio of singers (Nelly Greisen, Annie Herring, and Matthew Ward) with the original name, 2nd Chapter of Acts. This group toured extensively through America and Europe, and recorded a number of best-selling albums, including *Footnotes, Mansion Builder,* and *To The Bride.*

The Devil's Music?

Before going any further, there should be some discussion of the controversy surrounding the music usually called CCM—called this

almost universally since publisher John Styll started a popular magazine with that title. Many Christians involved in more traditional
forms of sacred music strongly opposed contemporary Christian
music, especially works by the heavy metal practitioners.

So far we have looked at several of the first artists and groups in
the growing field which would soon be named contemporary
Christian music. By later standards of "rockiness," the musicians
mentioned above may seem rather tame. Yet even from its beginning,
contemporary Christian music has raised controversy and argument.
It has often been labeled "the devil's music" and has unfortunately
been a cause of tension between Christian churches, teachers, and
families. Why is this?

There are as many answers to this question as there are parents
and teenagers, and you've probably already heard them all. Rather
than try to sort all this out—which could not be done in a short time,
perhaps not in a long one either—let us examine the principle objection from a historical point of view.

When contemporary Christian music (among other types of
music) is condemned, it is usually attacked on moral or spiritual
grounds: "It is immoral, or wrong, or harmful, or evil, or even
demonic." To the accuser, such words have much more weight than
simply complaining that: "It is crummy music, or it is musically inferior, or substandard, or mediocre, or just plain awful." Perhaps a
more honest parent might say, "I hate it! I don't know if it's demonic
or not, but I can't stand it!"

One could, of course, state this about many different types of
music—including every music imaginable—and be perfectly valid.
We each have the right to our individual musical opinions, without
getting into the more enigmatic area of spiritual judgments. But of
course, musical opinions come and go, and the corporate opinions of
one age are seldom imitated by the next.

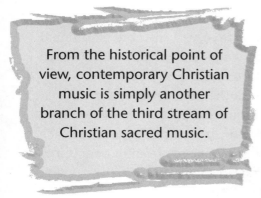

From the historical point of view, contemporary Christian music is simply another branch of the third stream of Christian sacred music.

From the historical point of view, contemporary Christian music is simply another branch of the third stream of Christian sacred music. It may be excellent or dreadful, and it may use a beautiful soprano or a guitar smashed against a huge amplifier. But it is certainly a valid form of Christian music.

The Contemporary Christian Music Industry Arises:
Many New Artists

By the end of the 1970s, there were many Christian recording labels and publishers. Every year brought new artists and bands with their own distinctive sound. Some of the older ones changed with the times and continued, but many were left in the dust, not unlike their counterparts in secular music and entertainment.

Again, as you were warned earlier, one must be flexible in categorizing these new artists. Some are clearly in the rock music vein, others are "lighter" or "middle-of-the-road." There are now so many obscure new sub-branches of contemporary Christian music that to describe them all would be inappropriate here. The artists mentioned are among those who have had the greatest popular impact and influence on other artists.

Keith Green (1953-1982) was a man with a passion for Christ and for walking in holiness. Playing dozens of bars and clubs before he became a Christian, he knew well the corruption of the world. After his dramatic conversion, he wrote and performed songs which implored Christians to turn away from worldliness and backsliding. He was tragically killed in a plane crash, but not before forming the

Last Days Ministries and creating such convincing albums as *No Compromise* and *For Him Who Has Ears to Hear.*

Another very charismatic performer goes by the name Carman—he dropped his last name (Licciardello). He became a Christian while attending a concert by Andrea Crouch and The Disciples, and some of Carman's musical style reflects a modern rendering of Crouch's rhythm and blues. But Carman's lyrics, especially his dramatic brand of spiritual warfare, are very deliberately "in your face." His many albums include *Revival in the Land, Comin' On Strong, The Standard,* and *Carman Live...Radically Saved.* This last album deserves special mention since Carman's live concerts are known for enthusiasm and exhilaration, including dancing from both the stage and throughout the audience.

A very different but equally convincing sound comes from singer-songwriter Steven Curtis Chapman. His youthful enthusiasm and thoughtful lyrics catapulted his career in a very short time. His premiere album, *First Hand,* did not appear until 1987, yet in less than a decade he went to the top of the CCM world with two dozen Dove awards and three Grammy awards. Chapman's style is often called Pop/Rock, and he gives an extended tour following each new album—a custom adopted by many artists.

Another collector of awards (33 Dove awards and five Grammys) is the soprano Sandi Patty. Although she is best known in Christian circles, her powerful voice impresses all who hear it—as evidenced when on July 4, 1986, she sang the "Star Spangled Banner" on national TV and the phone lines at ABC News were jammed for hours with people who wanted to know about this amazing singer. Her many albums include *Songs from the Heart, Make His Praise Glorious,* and *Find it on the Wings.* An indication of the admiration of her vocal style is the peculiar fact that she has sold more than 1.5 million instrumental accompaniment tracks with which aspiring singers may sing along.

One of the top contemporary Christian music artists of the 1980s and 90s was Michael W. Smith. After pulling himself out of the drug culture, he became a very creative songwriter to such singers as Sandi Patty, Larnelle Harris, Kathy Troccoli, and Amy Grant. In fact, Smith was one of the first contemporary Christian music composers since Bill Gaither whose songs have appeared in many mainline hymnbooks. His music is a blend of upbeat contemporary rhythm with a smooth vocal line and interesting harmonies, as exemplified in his ultra-popular song, "O Lord, Our Lord, How Majestic Is Your Name In All the Earth."

Another noted songwriter who has been embraced by both the contemporary Christian music world and included in a number of traditional hymnbooks is Twila Paris. She comes from a family immersed in music and ministry for several generations and her first piano teacher was her father. Her composition is extremely versatile, and her songs range from the progressively innovative to an almost hymnlike adoration. She has recorded many albums and is best known for her solo songs, such as "We Will Glorify the King of Kings," "He is Exalted," and "Hold On."

Of course, there are dozens of other excellent contemporary Christian music soloists and new ones emerging every year. Some are variations on those which have gone before, while others are quite original and imaginative. But few will have the overwhelming impact as that of a young girl from Nashville who wrote her first song at the age of 15 and whose influence has grown every year since.

Amy Grant and the Challenge of Crossover

On November 25, 1960, a baby girl was born to Gloria and Burton Paine Grant who would become a teenage sensation. The release of her first album, simply entitled *Amy Grant,* made her an overnight success. After the resounding sales of the album, *Age to Age,* with its mega-hit

"El Shaddai," Amy Grant became the undisputed queen of contemporary Christian music throughout the 1980s.

But she believed that God wanted her to expand into the secular world instead of just serving within Christian circles. She was not in any way renouncing her deep faith, but simply felt called to reach out beyond the walls of the church. This simple concept—often called "crossover"—had been practiced by classical musicians for centuries but was rather new to the contemporary Christian music world. Predictably, criticism over this decision from Christian fans was soon mobilized.

Her 1985 album, *Unguarded*, was the first to be heavily promoted to the secular audience. Her fans still loved Grant's songs, but were confused by the non-Christian interest. When she released the album *Lead Me On* three years later, many former loyalists were openly hostile. Her biggest "mainstream" or general market success was in 1991, with the best-selling album *Heart In Motion*.

> The entire issue of "crossover" remains a point of debate within contemporary Christian music.

The entire issue of "crossover" remains a point of debate within contemporary Christian music. At the beginning of the movement, Christian artists wanted to greatly contrast themselves to the world and often tried to distance themselves from secular markets. But later, artists have wanted to bring their talents to the "mainstream" audience as well as to their brothers and sisters in the faith. Why would they? What is their motive? The answer depends on who you ask. Some note that the church has always been called to seek the lost and should perpetually endeavor to bring the gospel message to unbelievers. Others murmur that such artists' motivation is less spiritual, only desiring to make greater profits by appealing to larger secular markets.

Christian Folk Music

When the folk singer Judy Collins released her vocals-only version of the hymn "Amazing Grace" in the early 1970s, it was a huge international hit. It combined the sacred and the folk traditions in a popular fashion and emerged about the same time as a new category of soloist: the Christian folk singer. There were, of course, many such singers earlier in the century, but their impact was generally local in scope. Now there would be solo singers of sacred folk music with an international following.

One of the first "Jesus folk singers" was John Fischer. This deep-thinking songwriter became a prophet to the entire Christian music industry. His many albums include *Have You Seen Jesus My Lord, Still Life,* and *The New Covenant.* Fischer has also written nine books and numerous articles which have challenged those involved with any Christian music to stay focused on quality ministry and to avoid the trappings of the "star" business.

Don Francisco was another folk artist who represented the youth of America during the 1970s. Having tried various Eastern philosophies, Francisco turned again to Christ and began writing songs from a biblical viewpoint. Although he recorded 17 albums, his first, *Brother of the Sun*—which contained the song "He's Alive"—remained his most popular. He was at his best in the story-telling song, explaining, "I try to follow the leading of the spirit in presenting the Word of God in contemporary language and song."

As with so many other contemporary artists, secular folk singers have also become believers and then devoted themselves to Christian music. Perhaps the best example is Noel Paul Stookey, who for years was famous as Paul in the folk group Peter, Paul & Mary. His conversion was dramatic and permanent, as he proclaimed, "The old Noel was replaced with the new." He went on to make several Christian albums, including *Something New and Fresh* and *Real to Reel.*

Surely the folk artist who has had the greatest success at appealing to both Catholic and Protestant audiences is John Michael Talbot. After his first two albums, *John Michael Talbot* and *The New Earth,* he underwent a time of spiritual searching. His next album, *The Lord's Supper,* was based on the Catholic Mass and now Talbot's new calling was clear. He continued to make recordings as well as author books, and also founded a new record label (Troubadour for the Lord) and an ecumenical community entitled the Brothers and Sisters of Charity.

We end this section with a versatile musician who is usually categorized within the contemporary Christian music world, but whose roots and writings are in the folk music tradition. Michael Card was working on a masters degree in biblical studies when he wrote his first song, and much of his work is designed to present the power of scripture through music. "My songs are interpretations of the Bible," he says. Card has recorded almost 20 albums, including *The Final Word, Unveiled Hope,* and a children's album, *Come to the Cradle.* Furthermore, he has composed well-known songs for other Christian artists, such as the moving "El Shaddai," made famous by Amy Grant.

Heavy Metal for the Lord:
The Rise of Christian Rock Bands

Some of the most contentious controversies about contemporary Christian music stem from its many bands. The complaints are inevitable. They sound and often look very much like their secular counterparts, many of whom are known for some extremely anti–Christian music and behavior. Yet these "Christian rock bands" have created a loyal following so strong among young people that it might easily be envied by secular groups.

Again, it is quite impossible to give more than a smattering of the Christian bands popular at the end of the century. There are literally hundreds of them, categorizing themselves as rock, metal, alternative, punk, slam, grunge, rap, ska...as it is too early to truly discern which of these smaller categories might sustain itself for long enough to definitely become a new branch, we will not worry much about these specific labels. The bands examined next often perform in several of these categories on a given album. They were selected on the basis of overall impact and influence on other like-minded musicians.

> Surely the most enduring of all the Christian rock bands is Petra, named for the Greek word for rock.

Surely the most enduring of all the Christian rock bands is Petra, named for the Greek word for rock. When it was founded by guitarist Bob Hartman in 1972, probably no one imagined that it would still be together at the end of the century. They have not only recorded over 20 albums—including *More Power to Ya, Not of this World, This Means War!,* and *Wake-Up Call*—but four "greatest hits" albums. They have created their own Bible studies, devotional books, and retreat materials, have won every award possible in their genre, and have sold more than any other Christian band (over 6 million units). Recognized throughout the secular music world as well, they were the first Christian group to be enshrined in the Hard Rock Cafe.

Of course, the personnel and even the musical style of Petra has changed over the years, but their vision of ministry has remained constant. Petra's founder explains, "We want to write our songs to make kids think, to make them see themselves as a Christian as part of something very big, the Body of Christ. Kids have so many influences on their lives now, and probably the hardest thing for a young person is to gain a Christian perspective on the world. We want to help them do that." That motive is echoed by hundreds of similar Christian bands.

The movement called "rap," which propelled the careers of many new secular artists, also found its exponents in contemporary Christian music. One of the best-known Christian groups which incorporate rap into its style is called dcTalk. Its three members (Kevin May, Toby McKeehan, and Michael Tait) created a national sensation with their song, album, and tour called *Jesus Freak*. Its message was simple and unforgettable: "I don't really care if they label me a Jesus Freak." Many of dcTalk's songs creatively explore severe problems within society, especially racism, such as the popular "Colored People." Although the three members come from very different backgrounds, they have effectively forged a musical style that is truly their own.

dcTalk actually helped the next group get started. Three young musicians were attending Kentucky Christian College in the 1980s when they were approached by a fourth who had written a song. Together, they recorded the song, "My God," and formed a new band called Audio Adrenaline. When dcTalk performed at their college, the tape recording was given to one of its members who passed it to their recording label. Soon, Audio Adrenaline's heavy metal/rap sound was heard throughout America, especially through the mega-hit "Big House." Their albums include *Don't Censor Me, Bloom,* and *Some Kind of Zombie.*

Another band which started on a college campus is known as Jars of Clay, the biblical reference being from 2 Corinthians 4:7. In the campus recording studio, several students began experimenting and finally sent a few songs to a contest sponsored by the Gospel Music Association. In 1994, they won their Spotlight competition and their song "Flood" was soon heard on radio stations everywhere, including many secular stations. Their albums, *Jars of Clay* and *Much Afraid,* have many hit songs, including "Love Song for a Savior" and

"Crazy Times." Theirs is one of the most original of the Christian bands, as they blend everything from shades of pop/rock to acoustical folk music.

> The Newsboys may well have set world records for endurance: In 1995 they gave almost 250 concerts, sometimes three in a single day.

America does not have the monopoly on popular Christian bands, as evidenced by the Newsboys from Australia. In the 1990s they became extremely successful with their theatrical performances—wearing quite an assortment of extravagant outfits—and with their distinctively Australian accents. The Newsboys may well have set world records for endurance: In 1995 they gave almost 250 concerts, sometimes three in a single day. Their recordings capture the exuberance of their stage productions and include the albums *Take Me to Your Leader*, *Not Ashamed*, and *Going Public*.

In yet another substream of contemporary Christian music, the Supertones became one of the most well known Christian ska bands. Ska music—with its driving horns and distinctive drumbeat and guitar off-beat emphasis—began in Jamaica in the 1960s and spread in several waves to Europe and America. Since it is usually associated with dance music, it might seem surprising to find it within Christian circles. But the Supertones are leading this new trend, with spirited songs like "Resolution," "Tonight," and "Perseverance of the Saints."

How Grungy Can We Get?

Obviously, there are differences between Christian rock bands and non-Christian rock bands. While the latter often indulges in the grossest of profanity, drugs, violence, and sexual perversion, the

Christian groups sing about Jesus and a biblical lifestyle—including many bold "in your face" lyrics about the need for serious repentance. Furthermore, the vast majority of Christian rock musicians are to be commended for living a life of holiness and selfless ministry. This in itself separates them from the bulk of secular rock stars.

But note that these differences are not musical. Indeed, there are no apparent differences in musical style between Christian and secular artists. There are now Christian bands who are absolutely as grungy, hardcore, underground, heavy metal, alternative, techno, and loud as any of their secular counterparts.

Such groups as The Crucified, Stavesacre, Blindside, Every Day Life, and Skillet represent the current edge; their styles are almost indescribable, but all emphasize a driving drumbeat, harmonic distortion, and very little melodic content. The vocal parts contain at least as much screaming as true singing, and the volume of concerts usually stays above the 100 decibel level. Nevertheless, their lyrics deal with real problems found in the life of young Christians and point to Christ and biblical teachings for the solutions.

It must be admitted that thousands of Christians still ignore or even abhor the music of such groups. Many of the members of such bands have been roundly condemned by their fellow Christians, not because of moral failings, but simply because of the type of music they play. Yet these very bands have been bringing the message of Christ to thousands of youth who might not ever hear it from anyone else within the church.

As the twenty-first century unfolds its music to an ever-growing audience, let us consider the "test of time" which governs all of music history. At any given time, much of the music that is popular will soon fade away, while other works—often ignored at first—may rise to lasting endurance. Obviously, what is contemporary Christian music in 1999 will not seem very contemporary in 2949!

But of course, this process takes many decades, sometimes centuries. Therefore, only time will tell how much the CCM of today (and its various sub-branches) will last into the coming millennium. Until then, "he who has ears to hear, let him hear!"

Recommended Listening

Mahalia Jackson—*I Believe*
James Cleveland—*Trust in God*
The Roberta Martin Singers—*Only a Look*
The Blackwood Brothers—*Sheltered in the Arms of God*
The Imperials—*Heed the Call*
Shirley Caesar—*The Best of Shirley Caesar*
The Rambos—*The Son is Shining*
Andrae Crouch—*Take Me Back*
Larry Norman—*Upon This Rock*
Dallas Holm—*Nothing But Praise*
2nd Chapter of Acts—*To the Bride*
Keith Green—*No Compromise*
Sandi Patty—*Make His Praise Glorious*
Amy Grant—*Age to Age*
Don Francisco—*Brother of the Sun*
John Michael Talbot—*The Lord's Supper*
Michael Card—*Unveiled Hope*
Petra—*More Power to Ya*
dcTalk—*Jesus Freak*
The Supertones—*Supertones Strike Back*
Skillet—*Skillet*

Dr. Patrick Kavanaugh is the executive director of the Christian Performing Artists' Fellowship (Washington, D.C.) and artistic director of the MasterWorks Festival (New York). He is the author of a number of books and is the classical music reviewer for Audio Magazine.

Text adapted from Patrick Kavanaugh's book, *The Music of Angel; Sacred Music from Gregorian Chant to Christian Rock* (Loyola Press, 1999).

The Artist/A&R Director Relationship
By Dan Posthuma

CHAPTER 7

*Record companies actually hope to find young
artists who love music, ministry, and communication with such a passion that they're not
waiting for anybody else to validate them.*

Arrangements and Recordings? Advances and Royalties? Attorneys and Recriminations? Or does A&R actually mean, as one travel-
weary music executive insisted, Airports and Restaurants? Most
young artists have a basic idea of what the marketing person does, or
the responsibilities of the sales team, or how publishing works. But
what about A&R representatives? Do they find talent, or does talent
find them? Do they follow trends, or do they create them? Do they
control marketing, or does marketing dictate to them? Do they care
more about the snare sound in the bridge, or the scriptural reference
for the second verse? And finally, the really big question: "When do
they throw away my demo tape—before or after they listen to it?"

A&R actually stands for "Artists and Repertoire," and it is the
most primary and basic function of a record company. A label's A&R
department is responsible for signing new talent for the company.
After signing, A&R's responsibilities extend to the development of

the artist's spiritual and creative vision, the assembling of the most effective team of songwriters and producers, and the selection of the 10 (or more) great songs needed to make the record. Once recording is finished, the A&R representative works closely with the marketing team and artist management to maximize exposure and sales.

The A&R representative serves as the liaison between artist and record company. When the label needs to communicate with the artist, the A&R rep is that conduit. Simultaneously, the A&R rep needs to be able to communicate the concerns of the artist to the label. As such, A&R balances the needs and wants of both parties—a bit of a trick, and one that requires a person to wear two hats—both business and creative. The A&R rep not only slogs through hundreds of tapes to find songs for the artist, oversees the production of records, and helps develop the live concert, but also works on the logistical details of building a career (touring opportunities, promotional events, Gospel Music Week, radio interviews and such). He must speak an artistic language when necessary, but also keep the bottom line in mind.

A&R people can be as fragile and unpredictable as artists themselves. Most have come from creative backgrounds—producers, session players, songwriters. Because much of their responsibility centers on the recording process, significant studio experience is a major asset. Recording is such a strange and unique experience, capable of bringing out the best and the worst in an artist. It's the A&R person's responsibility to be the artist's guide through it. During those trying times, a good A&R rep is part psychiatrist, part father-confessor, part encourager, and always the big-picture person.

The role of an A&R rep tends to change as a label grows. Most labels are birthed by the vision of a single person—with a focus on a particular type of artist or music genre. Because this effort is creative-driven, it usually begins as a small boutique, or niche company, dedicated to serving the particular needs of its artists and their marketplace. As the label grows, however, its needs change. Inevitably, the roster will expand to include other types of music. Usually the marketing staff will be increased to maximize exposure for their artists. The new marketing people bring their own skills, taste, and vision—potentially changing the direction of the company. As this is occurring, the A&R process tends to become more structured to better serve the label's timetables and projections. For this reason, a younger, smaller label will tend to have a different A&R approach than a more established label.

Large and small labels have their own sets of strengths and weaknesses. Every label wants to be the company with the best pipeline to creativity, with the best ability to nurture it, promote it, merchandise it, and publicize it—in all cases, the objective for artists and the standard of industry success. A reputation such as that gives the label an enormous edge in negotiations that neither money nor persuasion can buy.

Finding Talent

The question most often asked is, "How do A&R people go about finding talent?" As simple as the question is, there are many answers, and each artist's signing has its own unique story.

Although it happens rarely, occasionally an artist is actually "discovered" by a demo tape sent in to the label. The problem with this approach is that many tapes arrive at these companies every day, and the demands of keeping up with the needs of the artists already on a label's roster prevent the staff from giving these tapes a fair listen. That, and certain legal constraints, cause most record companies to decline unsolicited material.

Frequently, aspiring artists will hire a lawyer or publicity agent to "shop" a deal for them. This tends to happen more in the general market than in the Christian industry, but even then, it's often a waste of the artist's money. A more effective approach, though much more difficult for an unknown artist to make happen, is for an established

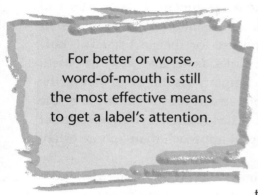

For better or worse, word-of-mouth is still the most effective means to get a label's attention.

manager or music publisher to bring the artist to the attention of a label. The relationship that industry co-workers have with one another can play heavily on a label's decision to pursue an artist. For better or worse, word-of-mouth is still the most effective means to get a label's attention. These existing relationships facilitate the communication that builds confidence and belief in a new artist.

This doesn't happen only through industry channels, however. I first heard about Crystal Lewis in the early '90s, when I was an independent record producer in Los Angeles (this was years before I was able to sign her to Myrrh). In the course of a month or so, at least five people excitedly told me about a Nazarene preacher's daughter who was electrifying huge crowds at Harvest Crusades. Again and again I heard, "She doesn't just sing a song. She makes it explode." At the time, Crystal was signed to an independent Southern California-based record label, and I had heard her name through the normal industry channels, but had honestly not paid much attention.

But when my friends (not just industry colleagues, but personal friends) started saying things like, "I was so moved by Crystal's testimony at my church this weekend" and, "You're not going to believe what she does to this hymn,"—it was then I decided I had to see this girl in concert, and as quickly as possible. Those personal experiences spoke more loudly to me than any label ads or professional publicity. When an A&R person hears about something from people who are already fans, who have no more agenda than sharing something meaningful, that's when they, like anybody else, want to experience it for themselves. It is that "shared experience" that is at the heart of both music and faith.

For new artists, the bottom line is that there are many avenues to the attention of a record company. Some ambitious artists are getting their independent projects played on local stations, and the program directors of those stations are championing this artist back to the record company. Occasionally a signed artist will bring someone new to the label—sometimes having just heard the newcomer open for him in a concert. Often, managers will promote showcases in Nashville enabling the unsigned artist to perform locally, making it easier for as many industry professionals as possible to hear him. Each of these approaches has a success story behind it. But remember: getting the attention of a label doesn't mean you will reach the goal line. The great majority of artists who are successful enough to be heard still remain unsigned, simply because there aren't enough slots at the label to accommodate them.

What Does a Record Company Look for in a New Artist?

Uniqueness

One of the more frustrating things A&R directors face is the similarity of what crosses their desks. Tape after numbing tape, the main identifying characteristic is the press kit, not the music. So the first thing A&R directors look for is a unique sound. Talent is all about individuality. Nothing attracts the attention of a record company like a distinctive and identifying sound—a great voice that comes across in a new way, or a musical approach that sets it apart from others in the marketplace.

Uniqueness plays into another great magnet for attention: authenticity. In my experience, artists who have their own style of expression tend to create from the heart. This singularity can show up in performance, but it can also be in the songwriting. In the happiest of circumstances, it's in both. The artist who writes with new sounds and images and also possesses a unique vocal instrument is the most exciting find a record company can make.

A common mistake of new artists is to make music that is clearly derivative of someone else's work. Record companies receive a great many demo tapes, and all too often it's obvious who that artist was listening to just before they recorded their own project. The vibe, sound, and style of a well-known star comes through the demo loud and clear. That's when you get the "Sheryl Crow sound-alike," or "Amy Grant rip-off," or "Bryan Duncan wanna-be." These young artists haven't taken the time or simply don't have the creativity to develop their own style. That's often an indication of a person who is just enamored with making it big in the industry as opposed to someone who truly has something to say.

Sometimes the lack of uniqueness shows up in a muddled, unfocused demo. This type of artist submits a tape of four different songs in four different musical styles. Being "all things to all people" is not a good approach to creating art. It most often indicates a person intent on showing off their various vocal techniques or how handy they are with their new home demo recording equipment. This is one of the reasons why it's often difficult for trained studio singers, who are experienced in many different vocal styles and techniques, to make the jump into a solo career. Being able to make your voice do anything can actually prevent you from developing your own vocal sound. Many successful artists are technically limited in their vocal ability, but in spite of it—or maybe because of it—they have created a vocal sound that people can identify. That's the real bottom line—not simply being a brilliant singer, but making the connection with an audience.

The Ability to Connect With an Audience

A mentor of mine used to say, "Dan, you have to remember that we aren't just in the music business, we're in the communication business." At the time, this advice seemed a bit odd. I was a 20-year-old bass player who loved blistering guitar lines and rhythm grooves. Years later, I'm still completely captivated by music, but my perspective has changed as I've watched the "how" and "why" of the process of building artistry.

In my early twenties, I started working for the Gaithers as a bass player at Pinebrook, the recording studio they owned and operated. This is when the Gaither's songs were just starting to get national exposure through the Christian musical, "Alleluia." This piece moved me deeply at a personal level, even though the musical idiom was completely foreign to me. I was a Yankee from Michigan who had grown up playing rock 'n' roll and classical music and didn't know a thing about southern gospel. But when I heard "Something Beautiful," it stopped me cold. That simple, plaintive melody, combined with the beautiful and tender words of surrender—that was a song that communicated to me. That's when I began to understand that communication is what it's all about. Consumers don't want to just buy a product, they want to experience a relationship with an artist who can comfort them, challenge them, and inspire them in their walk with God.

> Consumers don't want to just buy product, they want to experience a relationship with an artist who can comfort them, challenge them, and inspire them in their walk with God.

This power of communication that transcends subculture or musical style is what A&R people seek in an artist. A good communicator is someone who understands how to get his message heard. He uses whatever he has at his disposal—a great voice, a powerful song, a hip vibe, a funny story—because he understands that communication is the end. Once an A&R director establishes that an aspiring artist has musical talent, he will then ask, "Does this person have the ability to connect with people? Does she know what is important to the people to whom she is singing? Does she know when something is or isn't working? Besides showing off her great voice, does she have access to a variety of tools to create an impact on an audience?" And, most importantly, "Does this artist really care about leaving these people with something of value?" The people in the seats are in the constant process of voting whether the artist and her message is important to them. What will bring them back next time? Is this person just a good singer, or a good singer *and* a good communicator?

Great communication doesn't have to be profound or heavy. God calls some artists to communicate deep truths or revelations, but others are called simply to celebrate the joy of life and music. Whatever the message is, the best communicators get it across easily and creatively.

It's interesting to note that people who are good communicators on stage are generally good communicators offstage as well. They know how to talk to people and they know how to listen. They almost instinctively find the common ground between themselves and their listeners. They know how to point to the universal truths that are common to us all.

I remember watching Amy Grant when she was coming onto the Christian music scene. She was just out of high school when we started bringing her out on the Gaither tours to do a couple of songs in the second half. Nobody in the audience knew who she was or where she was from. Her voice and musical style were still developing, and she wasn't a seasoned performer by any means. But she knew how to connect with people. She would talk, sing, tell stories about herself, be funny, and over the course of 15 or 20 minutes on stage, she would win over the hearts of that audience. By the end, they were fans. And I noticed it was happening after the concert also—Amy would stand out by the record table, talk directly and honestly to anyone and everyone who came up to her, giving them her full attention. Basically, she gave of herself, just like she did on stage. She would win friends with every conversation. She not only had "star quality," she was honest, believable, and she cared. You wanted to like her.

An Independent's Perspective

By Joey Elwood

Independent labels begin with a narrowly focused group of five to 10 individuals, usually all of the same age, cultural experiences, and musical tastes. As the company grows and becomes successful, there comes a change of focus and sensibilities. Eventually the independent starts to lose touch with the succeeding generation, and some new enterprise quickly moves to fill the void left by the now unresponsive—and probably no longer independent—label. Then all that petty, quasi-Bohemian, "nobody-understands-us" attitude looks pretty silly, because the original company has become the very thing it once scorned.

You would think that someone would, in their transition from independent to major, staff their label (especially the A&R) so that the spirit of each genre and every generation was represented. It would, after all, save the majors from the expense of having to buy whole labels in order to stay competitive with the new and ever-changing tastes in our record world. But nobody does it better, only different.

To keep my anarchist badge, I will state that independent labels always seem to be centered around their A&R efforts, around the music that drew together the small group that founded it. Unfortunately, I have found, and this is only my opinion, major labels seem to be more centered around their marketing efforts. I don't know if this is derived from the leadership level, most of whom come from the marketing or sales side of the business, or the fact that their sophistication in operations leads to the misconception that image really is everything.

Joey Elwood is president of Gotee Records

Musical talent matters tremendously, and it will always be the key that opens doors to record company interest. But the best indicator of an artist with potential for long-term impact is the ability to communicate with people—sincerely, honestly, and with vulnerability.

A Grass-Roots Following

Record companies have a poor record of creating something out of nothing. It happens—rarely—but generally an artist needs to have created as much excitement as possible on the local and regional level to attract the attention of a label. The record company hopes to build on the following an artist has already generated. Many artists will tour extensively within a particular region of the country, or work closely with a particular denomination or church organizational structure. It's in this proving ground that young artists refine and develop their talent. As word-of-mouth grows, they tend to branch out into the bigger churches of the region or start working with other church-related organizations in the area, such as Young Life, Campus Crusade for Christ, Navigators, or possibly some relief organizations such as Compassion or World Vision.

By the time most new artists are signed to a label, they've already recorded one or more custom projects (records that are not affiliated with a label) which they have sold at their concerts. Sometimes these artists will come to the label having already sold thousands of albums to their fan base. These early fans are usually the ardent, loyal fans who are instrumental in creating sales momentum for the artist once they're signed. The record company sees that following as a good indicator that once they give this artist national exposure, success has a chance to follow.

Often artists think they have a following simply because they're working occasionally. But the truth is usually deeper than that. I saw this when I was producing the Bill Gaither Trio concerts. Night after night I would watch eager young artists come up to Bill to ask, "Mr. Gaither, how can I get started in Christian music?"

"Well," he would reply, "are you singing in churches now?"

"Oh, yes," was the usual reply. "I've sung in several of the local churches in my area."

"Well, then, how many of them have asked you to come back?" Far too often, this was followed by dead silence—and the implication was quite clear. An artist may believe he has something uniquely special to give, but do the people feel the same? Being clever or persistent enough to find work is a great start, but building a genuine base of support is something that takes time, commitment, and real ability.

The effort necessary in building grass-roots support shows a label that the artist is performing for the love of ministry and not merely for celebrity. I often encounter artists who are positive that they're called to be the next contemporary Christian star—and are just waiting for the right record label to come to their senses and make it happen. But what record companies actually hope to find are young artists who love music, ministry, and communication with such a passion that they're not waiting for the validation of anyone else. These artists find a way to get in front of people—any people, anywhere—and give of what God has given to them.

The Work Ethic

To quote a friend of mine, "Everyone is born into this world asking the same question: Are there any shortcuts? And the answer is no." There are no shortcuts to getting rich quick, to building a good marriage, to nurturing mature and balanced children, or to building a career in music. It takes a lot of plain, hard work. Self-motivation, a willingness to work, and the drive to succeed are decisive attributes a record company must see before signing a new artist.

Many young artists see only the excitement and glamour of the music, the lights, and the crowds. Often they fail to realize the groundwork that's necessary to build a career. Careers are usually built up over many years of hard work—singing in churches for little or no money, traveling in cars and vans to obscure towns, setting up and tearing down sound systems and equipment, and spending countless hours greeting people, making friends, and getting people exposed to their ministry. After all that they may finally get the attention of a record label.

Once a new artist is signed, these pressures only tend to increase. The schedule demands that a label puts on a new artist can be excruciating, especially early in a career. There is a relatively short window of time during which exposure must be maximized in order to create the kind of momentum needed to push an artist into widespread recognition. When the artist isn't doing concert tours, he needs to be on promotional tours. If he's not doing promotional tours, he needs to be at interviews. When he's not doing interviews, he needs to be recording the next record. And before he records his next record, he needs to be writing songs.

When a label makes the decision to sign an artist, it is committing hundreds of thousands of dollars of capital and staff to break the artist properly. The label needs the assurance that the artist is indeed willing to roll up his sleeves and apply himself in a manner that will lead to the greatest opportunity for success. The attitude of "wouldn't it be fun to be a Christian music star?"

> A good manager coordinates the activities of everyone involved in the artist's career in terms of image, ministry vision, and timetable.

runs out of welcome very quickly. This work is definitely not for the lazy or the faint of heart.

Good Management

Good management is assuming a greater role as the process of breaking artists and maintaining their careers has become more complex. All aspects of an artist's career must work in unison for the greatest chance of success, and making and selling records are just two of the components. Artist management, done well, ensures all aspects of the artist's career are working together with maximum effect. These include not only the record company, but also concert promoters, booking agents, accountants, legal support, and any additional publicity or promotion conducted outside the label. A good manager coordinates the activities of everyone involved in the artist's career in terms of image, ministry vision, and timetable.

Time-management challenges alone can be enormous. For example, the scheduling of the recording and release of a new project is usually planned at least a year in advance. Time must be set aside from touring and other responsibilities for the writing of material, working with producers, and then the recording of the project itself. This will usually come during a period when demand for the artist's time in the areas of promotion and touring is high, and it's the manager's responsibility to balance those demands properly.

Many artists are self-managed in the beginning of their career, and if they have the administrative and organizational skills necessary, this may be workable for a short time. Other artists are essentially managed by the label for the first portion of their career. This, too, can work, but usually on a very short-term basis. As the career becomes more complex, the need for professional management becomes more clear. Established managers will also usually bring with them their relationships with other artists and promoters, which can be very beneficial.

For these reasons, good management in the early phase of an artist's career is viewed as a great advantage by the record label. A talented support team provides the record label with the confidence that aspects of the artist's career not within the label's domain will be handled appropriately.

What Should an Artist Expect from an A&R Director?

Honesty

Remember, A&R is only one aspect of a record company's operations. But when an artist signs with a label, he should be able to expect certain things from his A&R representative. The first of these is honesty. Honesty is an important element in any healthy and productive relationship. Artists should expect responsible feedback from their label, because with much of the record industry built on hype, artists can begin to believe their own press releases. The other side of the coin, however, is that labels are often guilty of attempting to finesse artists into decisions rather than confronting problems directly.

The process of songwriting, for example, is one of the most sensitive areas for genuine feedback between artist and label. Different people look for different things in a song, and while a song is good for one artist, it may not be good for another. An artist will bring a demo to the label, convinced he is playing you the next big hit of his career. There's a tendency to always be "up" around your artists, to slap them on the back and say, "it's perfect." However, the marketplace will vote objectively on that music soon enough, and sales separate the hype from reality. What an artist actually needs is an objective evaluation. A record company does no favors to an artist by being unwilling to criticize a song that misses the mark.

Vocal performance is another sensitive subject. Singing is an intensely personal act, and criticizing someone's voice can be tough sledding. But if an artist brings in a song that asks more of his voice than he can deliver, the A&R representative must somehow find a sensitive way to broach the subject. It may be disconcerting for an artist to hear an honest evaluation of vocal limitations, but it's necessary to go though that process to find the right musical context for each particular voice. Songs requiring vocal pyrotechnics shouldn't be attempted by those who can't sing with the required level of control and range. Conversely, an artist with a light, airy voice probably won't be able to carry a large rock track.

> Honesty is imperative in every area of an artist's career, and with an artist's increasing popularity it can be more difficult to maintain.

Honesty is imperative in every area of an artist's career, and with an artist's increasing popularity it can be more difficult to maintain. Due to other people's careers getting linked to a successful artist, a performer can become insulated, surrounded by those who are eager to flatter. The A&R person's responsibility is to fight through this and, as much as possible, speak the truth with love.

This process of "truth in love" has to be reciprocal. There have been times I needed to be confronted honestly by my artist as to what was really important in a career. As mentioned before, I had kept my eye on Crystal Lewis for several years before being able to sign her to Myrrh. I had watched her totally devastate an audience by sheer vocal expertise and charm. Anxious to build a relationship, I asked her to sing a duet with Bryan Duncan on *Mercy*, the record I was producing for him at the time. That duet allowed me to spend time with her in the studio, earn her trust on a creative and musical level, and finally led to signing her to Myrrh.

Shortly after we finished recording her first Myrrh release, *Beauty for Ashes*, I went to see Crystal at a concert in Southern California. I entered the hall during sound-check, looking around for the beautiful redhead I had just signed to the label. Suddenly a little blonde walked up, wrapped her arms around me, and said, "Hi Dan, what do you think?"

It was Crystal, and her hair wasn't just blonde, it was platinum blonde. For a moment, I couldn't say a word. All I could think of was somewhere, right at this moment, there was a manufacturing plant turning out thousands of *Beauty for Ashes* CDs with a picture of a perky little red head on the front. And then I thought of the grilling that I'd get back at the office and that I had to face the marketing people who had worked very hard for the last six months to get that red head's picture exposed and promoted in every possible way. Being the narcissist that I am, my first response was "How could you do this to me?"

It took some discussion with Crystal before I finally came to realize that the decision to have blonde hair had nothing to do with me, and in fact had little to do with her career at all. It was a personal decision, not a career one. I had to remind myself that she sings and communicates just as well as a blonde as she does as a red head— maybe even better, because in her own way, it was one reminder to herself that she's not allowing her career to totally consume her life choices.

Enthusiasm (Championing the Artist's Vision)

A record label is comprised of many departments and divisions. Besides A&R, there's marketing, which consists of retail promotion, radio promotion, publicity, and touring; there is the sales and distribution division with its field sales team, tele-sales team, national accounts, and specialized markets. There's publishing, which has song-pluggers, studio series soundtracks, and print music. Often there's a general market partner which has its own sales and marketing departments. Then there are the company support divisions of customer services, inventory control, royalties, warehousing, and manufacturing. There are creative services, with album design and video production services. In addition, some record companies also have artist development and touring divisions. For a release to be truly successful, each of these divisions must believe in the artist and the record. The job of building this enthusiasm falls primarily to the A&R director. Working closely with the marketing director, he will try to promote his artist throughout the entire company, keeping people not only informed, but also excited and eager.

Most people who work at record companies do so because they love music. People who work at Christian record companies have the added incentive of believing that God uses Christian music to change lives. The A&R person's responsibility is to keep communicating the artist's music, calling, and spiritual vision to all the company personnel, who in turn generate excitement to consumers.

Focus (Safeguarding the Artist's Vision)

Dozens of people at a record company are involved in building an artist's career. As subjective as music and artistry tend to be, it's inevitable that each of those people will form a slightly different image of an artist. An A&R person must constantly define each artist in order to help all parts of the record company tell the same story. An artist is signed because he has developed a specific image and a certain style which distinguishes him from other artists in the marketplace. The A&R representative is the one person at the record company who constantly strives to keep everyone painting the same picture.

Too often, newly signed artists never have the opportunity to make a second record because the consumer could never really get a handle on who they were in the first place. Is this a church artist, or one called to speak to nonbelievers? An artist for teenagers, or the college crowd? A singer/songwriter, or performance artist? Is he quirky or poetic? Is he intense or good-natured? A thousand details influence these perceptions. The album cover must match the music, the production, the voice, the magazine ads, and the interviews to express the vision.

An artist's only chance at poking through the haze and being noticed is by establishing a clear identity, with all those elements communicating the same message.

The story is told of Peter Frampton, who, back in the '70s, had a small but loyal cult following of fans who viewed him as one of the leading guitar masters of that day. His career was on a fast track and he was gaining notoriety and new fans with each album.

Peter was doing a photo shoot for his upcoming live record and was working in New York with a photographer who had been shooting him all day in various settings and surroundings. Finally, after dozens of rolls of film and hundreds of pictures, the photographer asked him to take his shirt off for a few shots. Peter loudly protested, saying, "Hey, that's just not me, that's not how I want to come across." But he was tired and, in the end, gave in to the photographer for one quick shot before he packed up his stuff and left. Peter later tells the story.

> An artist is signed because he has developed a specific image and a certain style which distinguishes him from other artists in the marketplace.

"The live album didn't need hyping, and yet it got hyped with me on the cover of *Rolling Stone* with my shirt off, which instantly turned off a lot of my musical fans.

"I didn't realize what a split-second photo like that could do. It was only one shot by Scavullo. I let him take just one of me with my shirt off. The rest of the session was normal, you know, with a jacket on and everything.

"But the one with the shirt off was the one they used. It's the one of me that everyone likes to use.

"It just got to the point where the image had totally overridden everything else. Suddenly, I was appealing just to teenage girls. Everyone forgot that I could play the guitar." [1]

Peter Frampton never regained the momentum he had before that incident. One single photo, one that told a different story than everything else in his career, had devastating impact.

While that's an extreme example, it does point to the fact that every single element in how an artist is presented is important, requiring careful thought and monitoring.

Understanding the Artist's Spiritual Vision

An A&R director will spend a considerable amount of time and effort getting to know his artist and to understanding his spiritual foundation. What is his personal testimony of faith? Does he understand who he is in Christ? Does he have a clear sense of His calling on his life? Does he believe in working out that calling within the context of the church (whether ministering to believers or nonbelievers)? And finally, are there spiritual mentors in his life, elders that know him as a person, not merely as an artist? Is he attending a church? Is there a group of Christians committed to pray for him, and who promise to speak directly and honestly to all aspects of his life?

Any of us who have been in this industry for long have gone through the pain of seeing talented and well-meaning artists short-circuit—usually because they are pushed into the limelight without the spiritual foundation or the continuing nourishment enabling them to withstand that kind of pressure. This business of creating stars can be an extremely deceptive and dangerous process, which is why I believe God has placed great responsibility on us to approach this task with the utmost wisdom and discernment.

To gain an understanding of where an artist is coming from spiritually requires time, discussion, and prayer—getting to know the artist's family, friends, minister, and other people who speak into his life. It is often very difficult for a young artist to see beyond the stage lights into the harsh realities of the cost involved in being this type of unique instrument and servant of God. Our responsibility is to support and nurture these artists so they may flourish both spiritually and creatively.

Just as creative development is a process of growing, so too is spiritual development. A relatively recent convert is going to bring to his or her expression of faith an enthusiasm and vitality that can be incredibly effective in his or her particular calling. Likewise, the scholarly wisdom of a longtime student of God's Word can speak in depth to issues important to the church or personal faith. Both of these are vital and important dynamics to the ecumenical diversity of the church, and of Christian music listeners. And I love the fact that both expressions can find their voice in the power of a song.

> It has been said that there are two times in their career that an artist will be open to listening to advice: before they're hot, and after they're not.

Perspective

Perspective is a major challenge on all aspects of an artist's career—including creative perspective. It can elude even A&R reps. I remember Bryan Duncan bringing me the demo of a song on which he'd been working. He said, "Dan, don't you just love it?" Well, on first listen, I did love it. It was hooky, it caught my attention lyrically, and the chorus was memorable. Of course, Bryan could sing anything and make it sound great. Then he said, "Yeah, I just turned the drum machine on and I had the song in fifteen minutes." We listened again, but this time I began to have my doubts.

"Bryan," I said, "it's really catchy but there's not much difference between the verse and the chorus—it's kind of the same chord pattern. And maybe that's not good with this kind of song. Maybe you should put more time into the bridge, and I'm not exactly sure the tempo is right." The more I listened to it, the more I liked it, but the more I started second guessing every little aspect. I brought in Michael Omartian, who was doing some arranging on the record.

"Michael," I said, "I really like this song, but I'm not sure exactly what we should do with it. It is kind of sing-songy and the sections kind of run into each other, and I'm not sure it really goes anywhere."

Michael said, "Dan, this is a great song, you should just leave it the way it is. Don't touch it."

I still wasn't convinced, but I finally just plain gave up, because I couldn't figure out what else should happen to it. Through the whole course of making that album, I was never totally convinced we would actually put the song on the record. We didn't even mix the song until the very end of a week of mixing. Finally, at 3 A.M. on the last day of mixing, I told the engineer, "Well, we've got to get this thing finished, so let's wrap this up before my studio time runs out at 7 this morning." So, instead of taking the usual 12 hours to mix, we mixed this song in four and a half hours, and finally finished the record.

I was shocked when that song was picked as the first radio single, and even more surprised when "Love Takes Time" went to number one on both the AC and CHR radio charts and stayed there for weeks on end. To this day, it remains one of my favorite Bryan Duncan cuts, not only because it is a great song, but because it reminds me how easy it is to lose perspective.

It has been said that there are two times in their career that an artist will be open to listening to advice: before they're hot, and after they're not. One of A&R's most crucial responsibilities is to help the artist keep perspective on his career at all of its stages. The time requirements, the accolades, the time away from home, the money—all of these can impose serious threats to an artist's spiritual and personal well-being. Hopefully, an A&R person can sense when an artist is in need of a sabbatical, spiritual nourishment, or just plain good common-sense counsel.

The music industry is a powerful lure, and it can often distort the world-view of its participants. The A&R person should be one of the voices that reminds the artists that they are not only a singer, but also a father or mother, a friend, a church member—and that to live full, complete, and godly lives, a balance must be struck, even as "professional ministers." I can think of very few professions where the biblical warning, "What good will it be for a man if he gains the whole world yet forfeits his soul?" (Matthew 16:26) is more applicable.

Which is more important: for this artist to make this promotional tour, or be home for his wife's birthday? To keep recording this weekend so the album can release in time for Dove eligibility, or to go on a retreat with his church? To sign autographs at the end of the concert, or to rest his voice for tomorrow's show? There is no right or easy answer for any of these kinds of questions. Ultimately, they rest in the hands of the artist. But the more we can help put these issues in perspective, the better the chance the artist has of fulfilling his calling as a whole person, a complete child of God.

Trust

In the final analysis, the artist and the record company are working towards the same goal—to create impact and to sell records. The constant balancing act between the creative and commercial aspects of that endeavor can be frustrating for both sides, but can also be enormously rewarding. It almost always comes down to one central and primary element: trust.

The artist must ultimately believe that the record company will represent him authentically, to continue to believe if things don't go well for a time, to support each record, and to care deeply about the music. The record company must, in the end, trust that the artist will work hard, listen to advice, stay creatively productive, and turn in albums that can work commercially on radio and in retail outlets.

Building this trust takes time, and there will always be a team of people representing both interests to ensure that things move forward with a single focus. Trust is ultimately earned, and the foundation for long relationships are challenging to build. But once formed, what can be built on that foundation of trust is a career with lasting impact, a platform that truly reflects the mission and calling of a great artist.

Dan Posthuma is vice president of A&R for Myrrh Records, and has more than 20 years of experience in the Christian music industry. He is a Dove award-winning producer, and has been instrumental in the careers of Bryan Duncan, Crystal Lewis, and Fernando Ortega.

1. *For the Record*, Joe Smith.

The Artist/Church Relationship
By Scotty Smith and Steve Green

Our conviction and theme is that every Christian artist, whether of celebrity status or just starting out, is called like every other Christian to be committed to and meaningfully involved with a local expression of the body of Christ.

PART ONE:
A PASTORAL PERSPECTIVE
By Scotty Smith

It has been 30 years since my first collision with the grace of God in Christ. Walking forward to the front of the State Movie Theater in downtown Burlington, North Carolina, in response to a filmed gospel invitation by Billy Graham, little did I realize what more God had in mind for me beyond pardoning all my sins and declaring me righteous in His sight. Until that early spring evening in 1968, life was fun and the future looked great. I was playing keyboards in a local rhythm and blues band, mostly performing for fraternity parties at universities in the Carolinas and Virginia. It was a dream existence for any unredeemed senior in high school. In the upcoming fall I would be a freshman at the University of North Carolina in Chapel Hill, entering pre-pharmacy studies. But March 7, 1968, proved to be the beginning of a redemptive dismantling and restructuring of life as I had known and planned it.

Within six months of becoming a Christian, I realized that God was calling me not to pharmacy but to some form of vocational ministry involving teaching the Bible. I will never forget telling God that I was willing to go into ministry but only on the condition that it would involve neither going to seminary, which I cynically referred to as "cemetery," nor becoming a pastor in a church. Quite frankly, I hated the church. I hated anything that smacked of institutional Christianity. My cry was, "Don't give me theology, give me Jesus!" I thought church was the entity that kept me from the gospel. Why did I discover the love of God in a theater instead of the place where my parents dragged me dutifully all my childhood years? I wanted to move to Switzerland, hang out with Francis Schaeffer, read the Bible, and stay "fired up for Jesus." Who needed church when you could have fellowship with creative, artistic, radical individuals?

Oh, the irony of heaven, God's laughter and sense of humor—the patience, forbearance, and providential dealings of His heart and hand. Here I am, three decades later, a senior pastor of a large denominational church getting ready to go on sabbatical to actually teach in a seminary! For the past 12 years, I have had the privilege of walking with the most creative community of believers to which I have ever been exposed. And to think, they are committed and functioning members, not of a Christian arts council, but of a local church. Like Solomon said, "Men plan but it is God who orders the steps."

I offer this brief vignette of my journey to introduce and give context to the chapter that Steve and I have written. I am a pastor, and Steve is an artist. We have been committed to the same church family and to each other for several years. Together we want to share our thoughts, hearts, and longings concerning the relationship between Christian artists and the local church. This is a topic about which both of us hold deep feelings because it represents the distillation and focus of many of the things that God has been doing in our own lives in recent years.

This chapter has nothing, at least directly, to do with public relations between artists and the church. It isn't about how to work the "church market" or how to behave when giving concerts in ecclesiastical venues. We are not writing to encourage local churches and pastors to embrace contemporary Christian music. Neither are we writing to heal the scarred creative psyche of Christian artists who feel misunderstood and unappreciated by the church. In essence, our conviction and theme is that every Christian artist, whether of celebrity status or just starting out, is called like every other Christian to be committed to and meaningfully involved with a local expression of the body of Christ.

The Scriptures Command Such a Commitment

Even a cursory reading of the Bible affirms that God is redeeming a people for Himself, not just a random assembly of isolated individuals. His people are known as a family, a bride, an army, a temple, the body of Christ, the church of the Lord Jesus. These and many other metaphors in the Scriptures all communicate the corporate dimensions of biblical spirituality. While our salvation is indeed personal, it is not individualistic. There simply is no place for "lone rangers" in the kingdom of God. To forsake the gathering of the brethren, "as some are in the habit of doing," is to incur the rebuke of God Himself (Hebrews 10:25).

In reality we do not technically "join" the church, we are born into it. To become a Christian is to be made a member of the body of Christ. With membership in this new-creation family comes a calling to active participation, growth, and servanthood in the body. This central theme is pronounced throughout the Bible but is seen

> Each Christian is an important part of the body of Christ. We really do need one another. The whole body is greater than the sum of the individual parts.

nowhere more clearly than in Paul's words to the church in Corinth. At the time of Paul's writing, the Corinthians had become a group of congregations suffering from the disease of extreme individualism. The Apostle writes to confront and correct the divisions in the church which were robbing God of His glory.

Consider Paul's main points from 1 Corinthians 12:12-27: By the Holy Spirit God has created one body out of many parts. We are individual believers with a corporate identity. God intends unity with diversity and diversity with unity in every local church. This is to His glory. We are not permitted to isolate ourselves from the rest of the members of the body because of a sense of not belonging or because of feelings of spiritual inferiority. It is God who has arranged the parts of the body as He wants them to be.

We are also not permitted to isolate ourselves from other members of the body from an attitude of elitism or spiritual superiority. God alone has the right to place value on the parts of the body. He decrees that we have equal concern and love for one another in the body and that there be no division among His people.

Each Christian is an important part of the body of Christ. We really do need one another. The whole body is greater than the sum of the individual parts.

The biblical model and mandate, therefore, is that every individual Christian is to find a local expression of the universal body of Christ in which he can fulfill this central calling and cultivate the lifestyle of other-centered living. Each Christian artist should find a local church where he lives, not just to attend, but in which to become a committed and functioning member.

The Calling to Christian Art
Depends on a Life of Community

We should never forget that art itself is a gift of God. None of God's gifts are to be privatized or exploited simply for one's own end. God Himself is the quintessential artist. A Christian artist, therefore, is called by God to be both His servant and a steward of the gift entrusted to him. Art is to be reflective of who we are and directive of who we are to become. Such an important calling depends on the artist's willingness to enter not just his own pain, longings, and journey, but also that of the fellowship of the people of God. He speaks not just to us but also for us.

It is only in community that such a humble attitude can be cultivated. To be committed to walking in close fellowship with other believers in a local church is an important means by which selfishness is exposed and our instinctive proclivity towards self-promotion is arrested. To seek the low place, to choose to be last rather than first, to serve God and people rather than art and a career, to prize being faithful to one's trust more than being successful in the marketplace, these qualities are what it means to be a follower of Jesus in any vocation and certainly one which is qualified by the word, "Christian."

The Needs of the Artist Compel Involvement
in a Healthy Local Church

To pursue excellence in art and forsake one's heart is the essence of foolishness and idolatry. All of us need encouragement and accountability in the things of God. Artists are no exception. Who is shaping our gospel, mind, and lifestyle? To whom do we answer? By whom are we really known? With whom are we praying about our heart and our art? If artists are only fellowshiping with other artists or "industry" people, a very stilted and incomplete view of life and life in the body of Christ is created. These are needs that God addresses in the context of the local church.

You will notice that I emphasize the importance of not simply being in any church, but in a healthy one. Any artist looking for a church home should seek to be under the clear and consistent preaching of the gospel, to be a part of a congregation that is worshiping God in spirit and in truth, and to be under the discipleship and nurture of godly and growing leaders.

What Impedes Artists from Getting Committed and Involved in a Church?

First, we are a part of a hyper-individualized culture, one which encourages each of us to make only utilitarian commitments. "What's in it for me?" tends to qualify one's willingness to be loyal and faithful to anything, including to our Lord. We already have self-centered hearts, but when the basic value of culture is the idolatry of the individual it makes commitment even more difficult. We long to keep our options open. This attitude encourages "church-hopping," going from fellowship to fellowship on the ecclesiastical fast-food circuit.

> When an artist perceives that God is using him and his art an illusion of mistaking giftedness for spiritual maturity is potentially just over the horizon.

Second, the itinerant lifestyle of an artist often mitigates against meaningful involvement in a church family. When you travel and work artist's hours your clock and basic scheduling can offer real challenges. But these challenges are more pebbles than boulders in the road of responsibility and wisdom. Good churches offer worship, fellowship, and discipleship far beyond the old Sunday, 11 A.M. paradigm of yesterday.

Third, the arts subculture often feeds a prima donna attitude making it easy for a Christian artist to isolate and only spend time with other artists. If this attitude represents your heart, I encourage you to re-examine what is feeding and fueling such arrogance. Although on the surface it may sound like someone saying, "because I am not a hand I do not belong to the body," in all reality it may be closer to the eye saying to the hand, "I do not need you!" (1 Corinthians 12). As we have seen, the Scriptures rebuke both of these attitudes.

Fourth, there is also a seductive danger in confusing one's usefulness with one's faithfulness. When an artist perceives that God is using him and his art, an illusion of mistaking giftedness for spiritual maturity is potentially just over the horizon. Sometimes this makes it easy for a Christian artist to subconsciously think, "What does the church have to offer me? I am blessed of God in what I do. Church just doesn't do anything for me." Such thinking is perilous.

Finally, too many artists, like many other Christians in our American evangelical subculture, tend to define "church" simply as any group of Christians with whom they have "fellowship" or meaningful spiritual connecting. Thus, almost any gathering of Christians is labeled "my church." Church may be a neighborhood Bible study, a Young Life Club, praying with one's band members, a discussion group reading the works of C.S. Lewis, or quite simply, "Jesus and me." The fundamental problem with this reasoning is that it ignores the fact that God alone has the right and authority to define and constitute a local church. He does so in and through His Word. There are several elements that will be present in any assembly that biblically can be called a church. These include, among other elements, the ministry of the Word, the sacraments through pastors and elders meeting the biblical qualifications, and church discipline.

A Model:
My Relationship with Steve Green as Pastor and Friend

I am privileged to walk with several artists who have, indeed, committed themselves to the type of meaningful involvement in a local church discussed in this chapter. Steve Green and his family model so much of what I would hope for all artists in this respect.

I'll never forget my first meeting with Steve. As his family was beginning to sense the Lord leading them to join our fellowship, he made an appointment with me, but not to "check us out"—he had wisely already done that. Steve wanted me to know him, his heart, his struggles, his longings. For an hour and a half Steve shared his journey of faith, life, and career with me. It was an incredible afternoon. He entered into our church not wanting to be primarily known as a successful artist needing special treatment. Steve wanted me, as his pastor, to know him as a Christian needing the grace of Christ with a desire to be more fully captured by the love of God. In this posture and attitude, he commends himself as a model to all artists looking for a church home. Start with your own neediness, brokenness, and desire to grow in Christ.

The two main things Steve was looking for that afternoon are the two we share together today—accountability and accessibility. He wants from me accountability both for his art and for his heart. For many years Steve has sought my advice both on the lyrics and the music he has been creating. He understands himself to be a steward not only of his musical talent but also of the countless lives influenced by his concerts and recordings. He is also quite open about the different seasons in his spiritual life, and we talk often about what the Lord is doing in our lives and the mutual need for prayer and changed hearts. An artist is a wise man or woman of God who takes the initiative to get and submit to the accountability we all need to mature in the Lord.

Steve has also requested accessibility with me. Steve was not just looking for a pastor, guru, and mentor. He was looking for a church family. As a member of his ministry board we have regular meeting times. But as his pastor, Steve is not looking for me to always hold his hand. He and his family have entered into the whole body of believers here. He has built

> Throughout our careers we will encounter people briefly and through the power of music leave them with the impression that they know us intimately. The reality is far different.

friendships that are vital. Steve has even restructured his philosophy of touring so as to be at home and in our fellowship as often as possible. But now it's time to let him speak for himself.

PART 2:
CHRISTIAN ARTISTS AND THE LOCAL CHURCH—
AN ARTIST'S PERSPECTIVE
By Steve Green

One of the first questions we ask each other is, "What do you do?" For many people the answer we give to that question will define us. Labels and titles allow people to sum others up into neat packages; we speak of Joe the roofer, Stacy the nurse, or Fred the pastor. But we are far more than our jobs, and for the Christian artist, this is an important realization. Throughout our careers we will encounter people briefly and through the power of music leave them with the impression that they know us intimately. The reality is far different.

But if we are not our job titles, who are we? Scotty has already explained that the foundation of every believer's life is confidence in the certainty of God's gracious work of salvation. It is no small thing to be God's dearly loved sons and daughters. In love, He chose us and determined that we would belong to Him. He drew us to Himself with cords of kindness, making His light shine in our hearts and giving us the knowledge of the glory of God in the face of Christ. Our position in Christ is not based upon any label or upon our performance, but upon His covenant of grace. As Michael Card has sung, "He cannot love us more and will not love us less." Each of us is uniquely created to reflect a facet of His glory that no one else can duplicate. Our names are engraved on the palms of His hands. He knows us intimately and loves us more than we can imagine. God's heart is to fill us with the confidence that we are His forever.

Therefore, before any other title, we are, first and foremost, Christians. With the passing of time, our occupations will change and our marketable talents will diminish, but we are still the Lord's. Regardless of our position or title, God has an eternal purpose for each one of us that reaches across space and time, rendering how others see us as insignificant.

God's Purpose for the Christian Artist

It's easy for me to forget God's primary objective for my life—that I be increasingly conformed to the likeness of Christ. He is far more concerned with my character than with my work; He is more interested that I reflect His nature than my earthly position. But how will He accomplish this molding of my character? What means will He use? God manifests Himself within the community of saints to fulfill the purpose of His kingdom on earth. By the indwelling Holy Spirit and according to His word, He uses the church.

A Story of Healing

One might assume that as a Christian artist, my relationship to the church has been nothing but a lifelong blessing. But in fact it is a relationship in which there were many dysfunctional years, and one which was healed and brought into God's plan through a lot of honest soul-searching. As the son of missionaries in South America, you can well imagine where I was every Sunday and Wednesday. I was expected to be a role model for the other young people. There was not even a discussion about whether or not I would attend the services. If the church doors were open, I was there. But sometime during my teen years my attitude began to change. Burdened by expectation, I began to feel like a POW and the church became my dreaded prison. These feelings were intensely personal and in spite of the fact that my folks were genuinely ministering to those around us. But even though God was working miraculously in the lives of many, my own heart was beginning to harden and I missed the reward of those gatherings. The monotony of always having to attend became a barrier between myself and what God intended for real church fellowship.

Years later, I was invited to travel with TRUTH, a music group made up of young musicians. And travel we did! Try 700 concerts in two years! "Church" during those years came to mean little more than a place to perform. Night after numbing night I mounted the platform to sing for a faceless, applauding crowd. Gradually, I began to feel like a puppet on display. Life became a blur of passing landscape, each day ending with a concert, then off to a host home to answer the same set of questions. Constantly surrounded by people and rarely receiving the spiritual nourishment I so desperately needed, I became more and more introverted. Eventually, I just wanted to be left alone.

By the end of this period of my life, my relationship with the church was deeply damaged. Arriving home after the final TRUTH concert, I didn't attend church regularly for a year. Just stepping into a church building gave me visions of one more fried chicken dinner, and worse, brought back all the pressure of another performance. In the fall of 1983, however, God set about renewing my heart, and things began to change. It was God's will to bring about a sincere love affair between myself and the church, and to accomplish this goal I needed to do serious business about what church meant and who was going to be ruler of my own heart.

The Artist-Church Relationship

By Dan Francis

Any valued relationship demands "mutual submission" in order to establish respect and communication, and this is also true for the artist-church relationship. Think about it: If the relationship is healthy (and it should be), if the goals are similar (and they should be), then artist and church can thrive in doing ministry together. Sadly, this is often not the case.

Let's be honest: Sometimes an artist can feel like the church doesn't support him or her, and the church can feel like artists don't understand its real mission. The artist feels confined (no drums on stage, please) and the church feels cheated (did you just come here for the work?). It's time to bring these two worlds together.

Artist and church must communicate about the goals and expectations of this shared ministry experience. Will this event be a worship experience designed for the believer or is it a seeker event designed for the uninitiated? If it's focused towards the believer, how familiar is the artist with the worship style of this particular church? If it is focused for the unbeliever, how and who will handle the presentation of the gospel?

An amazing thing happens when these simple questions are honestly tackled; a clearly frustrating thing happens when they're ignored or taken for granted. If expectations differ, both church and artist can develop a misconception that becomes a barrier for future opportunities. And ultimately both lose invaluable kingdom opportunities.

Take seriously the admonition to push aside unstated assumptions about what should or shouldn't happen and trade them for clearly defined goals of what will happen. Let both sides be humble and serve, and for the sake of kingdom effectiveness, communicate! The artist will be appropriately utilized, the church will be carefully edified, and the holy Father will be properly identified.

Dan Francis is the pastor of CrossRoads Community Church in Nashville, Tennessee.

Although I had been in music for seven years, not only on the road but working in the studio as well, there was no understanding of a calling or purpose other than to make the best music I could. It was my whole life. I woke up to music, studied it, practiced it, and breathed it. Without realizing it, music had become my idol. I didn't bow down and worship it; rather, I gave it my first love and delivered my talent and gifts to its service. As a result, the church had become little more than a context for my craft. I had no genuine sense of belonging to the body, but rather looked at the body as an audience for my performances. Life had become compartmentalized, and God determined to explode these compartments into the loving relationship He desired me to have. During this time I had the appearance of a relationship with Jesus—enough for an obligatory appearance at Sunday services—but music-making for its own sake had taken hold of me and become my motivation. Because of this isolation from God and His church, a web of sin entangled me and the bondage of fleshly appetites became crip-

pling. But even though I had been effectively hiding my real self from the church, hiding from my family members was more difficult. Able to see through my facade, my older brother confronted me through tears and in this way God in His mercy broke into my prison. The Lord granted repentance and by His grace I came to my senses. For the first time, I entered into genuine relationship with Jesus Christ.

Huge gatherings are emotionally exciting but by definition impersonal. They may give a feeling of closeness and oneness, but they lack the real stuff of which relationships are made.

The light came on and my eyes were opened. I saw the depravity of sin, the amazing mercy of God and experienced forgiveness.

The natural result of my rebirth was a new desire to get together with other believers—not as an audience, but as brothers and sisters. I saw their value—unfathomable in God's eyes—and saw myself as a member in a family with God at its head. The separation of performer and audience was banished; in that inner change, what once had been a burden became a delight. To my wonder, I actually began to anticipate gathering with other believers to hear God's Word and worship the One who had called us out of darkness.

> And this is my prayer: that your love may abound more and more in knowledge and depth of insight, so that you may be able to discern what is best and may be pure and blameless until the day of Christ, filled with the fruit of righteousness that comes through Jesus Christ—to the glory and praise of God.
> —Philippians 1:9-11

For Better or Worse

"And let us not give up meeting together…"

I have been a part of many historic gatherings, from Billy Graham evangelistic crusades around the world to the Promise Keepers sacred assembly of men on the mall in Washington. These thrilling experiences can be the catalyst for spiritual change and serve to spur us on in service to others. But I have come to understand that these spiritual high points cannot sustain the work that God desires to accomplish in our lives. Huge gatherings are emotionally exciting but by definition impersonal. They may give a feeling of closeness and oneness, but they lack the real stuff of which relationships are made. They lack the ongoing commitment to love, the tension of dis-agreements, the blessing of forgiveness, the tears and heartaches, the "doing life" with those who are committed to you with spiritual ambition. Once the meeting is over, everyone gets in their individual cars and goes back to their individual lives. The real, ongoing busi-ness of God only happens in the context of community within the local fellowship of believers. Why is that? It is because God calls us again and again into relationship, first with Himself, and then with those around us. With Christ Himself as our head, we are joined together as one body, connected by the ligaments and sinews that are our brothers and sisters.

The church is also the place where we celebrate milestones and celebrate the sacraments. Scotty baptized my daughter before a con-gregation of witnesses. She gave testimony to her faith in Christ and the church pledged to take part in caring for her spiritual growth. She is being discipled and is growing in grace. The first Sunday of every month, as well as every Wednesday evening, following a Bible study, we share in the Lord's table. It is a sign of the new covenant, a pledge that we partake of the benefits of His redeeming work, and a foretaste of the heavenly banquet of which we look forward. This sacrament is a seal of the intimate union of Christ with His church, and of the many members to one another.

The Mystery of Community: The Word

Although I have a schedule of Bible reading and personal study, I need to sit under the ministry of biblical teaching. How quickly I forget vital truths. How prone I am to wander and lose sight of what really matters. Without fail, as I gather with fellow believers, God reminds, restores, refreshes, and renews. It is not that the services are spectacular or the sermons are always sensa-tional. Rather, it is Scotty's consistent dedication to the proclama-tion of the word that results in a response of worship. God speaks to us through the teaching, and we are compelled to give ourselves afresh to Him.

The Presence of Christ

When we gather in His name, Jesus is there among us. Of course He is already within us (Romans 8:10-12), and the scripture assures us of Christ's presence where even two or three are gathered. But this must never be used as an excuse to have "church" with only a few friends. The danger is in neglecting God's overall design. The church exists for the purpose of corporate worship, evangelism, discipleship, and to be a blessing to the community. These things happen as believers gather together, emerging from their insulated lives to reunite with the body as a whole.

God has instituted systems of authority for our protection. There is no safer place to be than where Christ is honored as the head and where church leaders carry out their callings with humility and reverence. Their authority is God-given. We seek to know the mind of Christ under this authority, as our pastors and elders carry the responsibilities of praying for, encouraging, teaching, and discipling those under their care.

> Popularity is a powerful drug. As Christian artists, there are always those who will remind us of how special we are.

When this protection is in its fullest expression, church members will be enabled to perform an important but often difficult act: confession. Many times, Scotty has ended a service with an invitation to come forward, confess our sins, and receive prayer with an elder. It is as if Jesus were giving the embrace through their arms and speaking words of forgiveness through their lips. Indeed, He is there.

The Safety of Serving

Popularity is a powerful drug. As Christian artists, there are always those who will remind us of how special we are. They will jump at our command and run to satisfy our every whim. It's very easy to begin to expect what is actually the loving service of others. For example, when I started out I traveled with just my family, but now have a road team of dedicated guys. A few years ago I realized that they were out-serving me. Again and again they demonstrated humility by taking care of the mundane and often unpleasant tasks associated with putting on a concert. This was something I had to address, because in our culture it's assumed that serving is for beginners and less-important folks. Once you "arrive," others serve you. But the Apostle Paul shoots down this lie by exhorting us to have the same attitude as that of Christ. Then, in Philippians 2, he details the humility and servant life of Christ. God measures by a completely different standard. He who would be the greatest must become the least. We are not above our Master. The church is the place to serve one another in love. This service goes beyond what we do as artists, extending into every facet of church life. For example, our church nursery was staffed for many years by members of the congregation. Each of us was scheduled to help care for the little ones. It was very beneficial to return from a Saturday concert where I had sung to thousands and then Sunday morning find myself sitting cross-legged on the nursery floor wiping some kid's drool from my shirt.

Nothing Special

If we're not careful, our church relationships can be as unreal as any other. We must guard against that, consistently tearing down walls of artifice and image. For artists, this takes extra effort, because the marketing and glamour associated with being a performer can fool people into thinking we're more than we really are.

Years ago, a young lady approached the stage and looked at me. "You look better from far away," she said. She had been sitting way up in the balcony and when she got close to the platform after the concert and took a closer look, she wasn't that impressed! But in her way she hit on an important truth: We all look better from far away. As a Christian artist, this is especially true; because of an image that is maintained and projected by my record company, you have to get close to me to see my real inconsistencies and weaknesses. A lot of people know very little about me. They see a cover photo, read press releases, and catch far away glimpses from concerts.

People are drawn to mystique. It creates curiosity and excitement. But we must break the bubble and let people see us for who we are, including our faults. It's difficult at first but the payoff is great; there is freedom and reward in taking down the barriers. We are released from the pressure of keeping up an image and then rewarded with genuine relationships where people love us for who we are, not what we appear to be. I need real relationships in my church family to protect me from habitually hiding, habitually lying to myself about who I really am.

The E.F. Hutton Syndrome

When I talk, people listen. During concerts the audience gives me their rapt attention for two hours. During the week, radio stations and magazines ask for interviews and want to know my opinions and insights. After a while it's easy to start thinking that I have a lot to say. The truth is, I need a place where I listen. At my church home I see that much of my apparent importance is actually due to my function and platform. In the listening, I discover a significant truth; there are some very obscure and simple people who have much to say. Their lives and witness speak volumes. Their comments in our Sunday school class are weighty with wisdom. It's sobering to think that although they will never be called for an interview, God reveals the treasures of His heart through these dear saints. An artist who never listens is missing volumes of wisdom that comes through people the world considers small.

An Examined Life

Scotty is pastor to about 4,000 people. I'm amazed at how personally he deals with those entrusted to his care. Still, he cannot be everything to everyone. In fact, he isn't supposed to be. The church body has to be a vital

> To truly serve requires sensitivity to the individual church we are visiting, but one should not assume that service is always simple encouragement.

part of my life. Our Sunday school class provides a needed connection with individuals and a chance to know the details of their lives. Twice a month on Sunday evenings a small group meets at our home for a Bible study. Every week I meet with two men to sustain a relationship of accountability.

I have learned that the tendency to hide and cover my sin only gives the enemy a stronghold. My only hope is in confession and repentance. And not just to God—I can confess to God anytime with perfect security—but also to my brothers in Christ, which requires a special, personal connection. James 5:16 tells us to "confess your sins to each another and pray for each other so that you may be healed." That takes being in safe relationships. Mike Card has told me, "Remember, I'm your friend and I'm on your side no matter how good, bad, or ugly." Every Christian needs that kind of safety—and needs to offer it in return. God has given us all the protection and provision we need clothed in very common threads. It is God's plan for ordinary men and women to meet in the name of Jesus, using their individual gifts to build up and strengthen each member, "until we all reach unity in the faith...and become mature, attaining to the whole measure of the fullness of Christ" (Ephesians 4:13).

212 Getting Started in Christian Music

A Final Note

Much of this chapter has dealt with the relationship between the artist and his home church. But what do we owe the churches at which we sing? This is a different relationship, temporal by its nature and requiring different sensitivities and connections. But even in this, our home church relationship remains key, because the knowledge we are sent out from a place under pastoral authority is a natural encouragement to those whom we serve in other cities.

Once we arrive at a host church the greatest need is humility. Many artists have been insensitive and taken advantage of a local church platform, causing music ministers and pastors to become hesitant to use outside artists. Some pastors actually use the word "pillage" to describe their experience with some high-profile guest artists; it was apparent from the outset that these artists felt no desire to serve the needs of the church body but only saw an opportunity for work. Needless to say, these churches are extremely reluctant to repeat this experience. We must remember that the church is not a place to find money; it is a place to serve, and only then is the workman worthy of his wages.

To truly serve requires sensitivity to the individual church we are visiting, but one should not assume that service is always simple encouragement. There may be times of exhortation as well, and this in particular requires maturity. On what basis may a Christian artist enter a church sanctuary as a guest and exhort, even strongly, a message that God has for that congregation? Only on the prompting of the Holy Spirit, and only when the artist has conducted himself in such a manner as to have gained the credibility to speak out.

We know from Scripture that heaven is our home, and God is our father. We look forward with anticipation to the day in which church becomes something we experience "in spirit and in truth." But until that day, every Christian artist should pursue active relationship with Christ's body on earth, seeking His will under the inspired authority and security of church leadership.

Scotty Smith is senior pastor of Christ Community Church in Franklin, Tennessee, with nearly 4,000 weekly attendance. He has a long-standing ministry with leading Christian artists and serves as adjunct professor of Covenant Theological Seminary.

Steve Green has released 21 recordings, receiving six Dove awards and four Grammy nominations. His 17 No. 1 hits include "People Need the Lord," "The Mission," and "God and God Alone." Steve's touring career has encompassed thousands of performances including "Stand in the Gap," the march on Washington sponsored by Promise Keepers.

Booking and Self-Management
By Brion Connolly

Although you may have a romanticized view of booking, it's actually sales. Make yourself do it. Endure the pain and know that a door will open for you if you are talented, have something to offer, and are persistent.

In these times, we in the contemporary Christian music industry are faced with enormous challenges. Not only do our artists have new opportunities to infiltrate the mainstream, but they also must continue to make fresh and encouraging music for the church. Although these opportunities are compelling, they have simultaneously created a new level of competition for attention in the marketplace.

Within this competition the personal life of the Christian artist remains foremost. Artists tend to make a lasting impact on individual lives and on culture as a whole by maintaining a strong spiritual life, developing talent to the maximum, and by exercising wisdom in the marketplace. Music is a powerful force for change and those who handle it must do so wisely and with noble purpose.

Before you consider a career in Christian music, consider the three purposes of artistry within the church. First, music was created to praise the Creator. Every Christian artist, therefore, should logically be a person of praise. Surely the musically gifted among us should dedicate a portion of their talent and time to this devotion. One simple way to accomplish this is to develop the ability to lead the church in familiar praise and worship choruses. Some artists will be more comfortable with this than others, and obviously certain groups are more performance-oriented than interactive. But the ability to lead praise and worship is a practical help and a mission calling that most artists should develop.

> Don't write in a vacuum; remember that your audience is looking for something to hang on to even after the concert.

Second, music is a powerful tool of exhortation and encouragement. Therefore, in the quest of being truly useful to Christ's church and in the service of His purposes, Christian artists should approach their songwriting and performances as an opportunity to minister. Don't write in a vacuum; remember that your audience is looking for something to hang on to even after the concert.

Third, and closest to the hearts of many performers, music is a personal expression of the soul life of the artist. Elements of the writing will include a personal world-view of life experience from a Christian perspective even when not being evangelistic or pastoral in nature. Each of these three purposes is valid, and each deserves attention in the writing life of the Christian artist.

Self-Management

The developing artist should know that a professional manager probably will not come into the picture until a record deal is secured or pending. This manager will often come recommended by another key industry player, such as a label executive, booking agent, or lawyer. An important question to ask yourself, if you're pursuing management, is this: "Do I have anything to manage?" In other words, a manger doesn't create something from nothing. Artist management is extremely time consuming and offers very little financial reward in the early stages of an artist's career. The new artist must demonstrate to a prospective manager that there is career momentum already in existence, as well as significant potential for growth.

Because of these considerations, most artists begin their careers self-managed. To be self-managed simply means to oversee and execute all the elements of one's own professional activity. It is not unlike the entrepreneur who has to do everything himself when starting a business. You may be called to minister, but to have any degree of success you must run things in a businesslike fashion.

Since there are so many elements to being self-managed, it may be best to see exactly what it is that professional managers do. By incorporating these professional management techniques into your work early on, you can maximize your effectiveness and avoid having to extend your learning curve through trial and error. This approach also has the advantage of teaching the artist the various dimensions of the business world, which will be a tremendous asset further on should he become successful. Look at these responsibilities as an opportunity to sharpen your business skills and gain awareness of how the music industry works.

Let's look at five areas a professional manager will cover in the work-life of a Christian artist, and remember that if you are self-managed, you are responsible for each of them.

Spiritual Companion and Counselor

Don't misunderstand: A manager can never take the place of a church pastor in the life of an artist. But if you think about it, a manager actually has the most day-to-day contact with the artist. Issues of exercising faith in the real world will be more readily discussed with him than by making an appointment for pastoral counseling. It is therefore imperative that the manager be a mature believer who values the standards of Scripture and has a strong, vibrant relationship with the Lord. If you are self-managed, who will take this role for you? An accountability system and a spiritual mentor with whom you have regular contact is essential.

Manager as Strategy Expert

The manager should be a person who has mastered time management. It will be his responsibility to construct timelines with the artist that determine when tasks and accomplishments will take shape. This would include suggestions on time spent for songwriting, rehearsals, and album recording, as well as record release timing and touring strategy. He will also give feedback to bandleaders, principle songwriters, and decision-makers as to how the band should look or sound without attempting to override the final decisions by the group. If the artist and manager are too often at odds about these things, chances are they shouldn't be working together. The key issue here is mutual respect. The artist will have to trust the judgment of a manager regarding business decisions and the manager has to know when to back off when artistic lines are drawn. The good manager will always respect the idea that an artist ultimately has to accomplish that which he thinks the Lord is calling him to with his work. If you are self-managed, find someone with experience who you can trust for independent feedback on these issues. Don't assume that what you're presently doing is your best effort. No matter how artistic you are, you can never actually know what it's like to sit in the audience and watch your own performance.

Manager as Marketing Expert

Great art is never seen or heard without exposure. Bad or uninspired art can only go so far even with a massive marketing campaign, but if you do truly inspired work, the right marketing can push through a lot of doors. This isn't always clear, naturally; the ears of the general public aren't always the most discerning, and there will inevitably be contrived music charting on radio. In the long run, however, truly original and enduring music will make its mark. Conversely, there will always be great music that never makes it to the masses, simply because there wasn't enough capital or marketing smarts behind getting it to a broader audience.

A newcomer to the music business must understand that this pursuit of exposure is highly competitive. Therefore the manager must possess marketing talent and savvy. Most important is initiative. A manager must be the kind of person who gets out of bed ready to work and doesn't worry about punching a clock. He's someone who is constantly trying to make things happen. He must have a daily battle plan and the ability to hit it every morning whether he feels like it or not. If that person is you, fine. If not, you may have to get realistic about partnering with someone who is willing to help out early on. Some people have a natural affinity for this work, a love for people that shines through every contact. Unfortunately, artists don't always fall into this category.

Roy Morgan, one of Christian music's most seasoned and productive concert promoters, developed the career of the Christian comedian Mark Lowry. Roy wakes up every day thinking, "How can I get my artist more exposure today?" You can learn from others and be inspired in this regard. Even if you don't know anyone working in Christian music, find a role model and aspire to emulate his work ethic.

Every great salesman and entrepreneur knows the value of packaging. A good manager will know how to present his artist in the best possible light, creating the best materials for him in the form of an outstanding press kit and a great demo. He will know how to optimize value with photo, video, and audio recording services. He will build synergistic relationships. A developing manager will do well to get recommendations on capable media production people from other more established managers who have developed these contacts.

Obviously, the artist-manager team may not be able to afford the services of established media enti-ties. Don't assume that there's no hope, however. Simply get cre-ative. It's possible that there are other, developing businesses in media that will take a little more effort to track down. These hope-fuls will be more affordable. They too are looking for opportunities to expand their businesses and make their mark. There will always exist this underground of developing-level professionals just one or two steps away from more visible noto-riety. These professionals can experience more widespread success by being involved with an artist who achieves success with a hit song.

> Make it your business to understand how presentation affects outcome. If you manage yourself, you have to learn how to see yourself objectively, the way others encounter you.

Above all, if you don't know anything about marketing, find out about it. Learn from the effective approaches of others. Make it your business to understand how presentation affects outcome. If you manage yourself, you have to learn how to see yourself objectively, the way others encounter you.

Manager as Record Deal Negotiator

This one achievement can successfully set in motion all the other activities of the artist's career. But you should know that even experi-enced managers utilize the services of attorneys with entertainment experience. Typically, the recording contracts will go back and forth between the attorneys of the artist and the label several times. Here, no matter how diligent you may be, the experience of quality legal representation is paramount.

Manager as Life-long Career Strategist

An experienced manager knows how to be a big-picture thinker. While the artist is focused on writing and performing, the manager is dreaming about ways the artist can expand his impact, visibility, and influence. And—shocking as it may be—a truly big-picture manager is even thinking about the time when the demand for his artist begins to wane. Is the artist going to be financially secure when this happens? Is there a retirement plan in place? Are there investments that will protect the artist's income from inevitable downturns? It's extremely wise for even the self-managed artist to realize that through the flush of excitement even a successful career has a life-span. There will be life beyond it, and to prepare well for that time is an essential component of good management.

What is a Manager Typically Paid?

Although you are at this point self-managed, you should understand the basic parameters of management compensation should that need arise. Like everything else in the music business, every deal is subject to negotiation. But generally speaking, depending on how much administrative work the manager's office does on behalf of the artist, a manager can expect to receive between 10 percent and 20 percent of a group's gross earnings, especially if he is also booking dates for the act in lieu of having an agent do it. At the point that this task is delegated to a professional agent the management fee will be adjusted to approximately 10 percent to 15 percent. In return for this fee, artists expect the day-to-day details of their careers to be handled. And, of course, they expect increased work opportunities. If everything flows from the muse artistically, professionally everything flows from live performance. The new artist must work as often as possible, building momentum and establishing a base of fans who will support him when he goes to the next level.

Obviously, there are significant obstacles to booking without the visibility and credibility of a record company, booking agent, and manager. Nevertheless, you should take heart from the fact that people do successfully book themselves without these assets. It can be done. It takes tenacity and commitment. It's also essential for survival; most recording artists derive approximately 80 percent of their gross income from live performance.

Setting Up Your Office

Before you begin booking, you should set up a separate work area or office for this work. Like any business, setting up shop will inevitably require some expense, and a decent computer is probably foremost among these. I'm personally a fan of mobile computers, because when you do begin to travel more frequently, you can bring your work with you. It's probably a good idea to invest in a zip or jazz drive as well to back up your work. You'll be surprised at how much information you can accumulate over time, information that would be extremely difficult to reproduce if lost. Your computer should have, at a minimum, the following software: a contact manager (hopefully integrated with a calendar), a contract generator, a word processor, e-mail, and Internet access.

The market is full of good contact managers. You can customize templates to include the information you find most important. Once you've created your template, you're on your way to building a contact base. Don't forget to include space for a running log of each conversation or written communication you give or receive from the contact. If you're aggressive, it simply won't be possible to hold in your head the contents of various discussions, and you will sometimes find yourself unable to even remember if you've returned calls. There's nothing more embarrassing than calling someone whom you've too recently contacted, or missing a follow-up on a good lead. Use the calendar to set up times to follow up on contacts.

A contract generator will contain a template of your standard performance contract and any versions of it you deem necessary. Your computer must have a decent modem and fax program to send faxes directly from the computer instead of printing them and faxing the paper each time. You should always have a separate phone line for this activity. A good headset will keep your hands free to do other tasks while you are talking on the phone. You will also need a good printer, and a fax machine if your computer lacks the capacity to receive incoming faxes automatically.

Your contract should include much more than the financial agreement you make with a host. It should also spell out all the information about the event itself. For example, your contract should list the time of the show, load in, doors opening, etc. Included with the contract will be your rider, which is simply a document detailing all the technical and logistical information about the date. These include a precise description of any sound and lighting requirements, the number and type of hotel rooms, and how many hands will be necessary for loading equipment in and out. For nationally known groups, these riders can be amusingly complex, and mere expressions of the artists' ego. But even for new artists, it's devastating to leave details such as sound or piano requirements to chance. Get it written down. Once you have the contract and rider agreed to, they are to be signed and returned with a retaining deposit of 10 percent to 20 percent.

> Once you have the contract and rider agreed to, they are to be signed and returned with a retaining deposit of 10 percent to 20 percent.

Information management is crucial to the booking business. The more organized you are the better. Next to selling, managing information is the heart and mind of the booking business. Exercise the "Do It Now" philosophy. Keep all your information organized and updated, and followed up immediately. It will ultimately pay off in terms of greater opportunities and income.

Once you have your office set up comfortably and productively, there are still a few tools of the trade you'll need. First, a good supply of press kits is necessary, especially if you are an unknown or developing artist. The press kit is your only real opportunity to present your music and image to prospective sponsors, so its quality is important. Include a professional black and white photo with band or artist logo and any contact information. Photos are extremely important; for better or worse, a group's image carries a lot of weight, and this creates something of a dilemma for some bands. If, for example, you are in an alternative, youth-oriented band, your photo should reflect this. Consistency of image is paramount. However, that type of image can be alienating to senior pastors who may wish to review the press kits of bands who are hired for performance. There should be an element of circumspection about your group's image, especially if you intend to perform primarily in churches.

Your biography should fit on a single page; don't overwhelm with minute details, but make sure that your package contains hard-hitting highlights of your musical identity, spiritual calling, and performing experience. It's also essential to include on a separate page the recommendations of others—hopefully influential pastors or promoters. Normally, your demo or custom project will be included in the press folder as well. The kit will require mailers that are appropriately sized and protect the contents. Letterhead, pens, filing cabinets—it's all a part of working efficiently. Once you start touring extensively, you might consider a separate post office box from where you can have bills forwarded. Remember, you only have so much energy, and if you use it all doing business there won't be any left for your artistry. The effort you put into organizing your office so that things stay easy will pay off in the long run.

The issue of recording your demo or custom project requires a separate chapter, and is given one in this book. If finances are tight, you may want to consider recording a "history-making" five-song EP, to be followed up by a full, 11-16-song CD later.

Who Do I Call?

Before making your first calls as a developing artist, determine your sphere of influence. Most of your performance opportunities will be within a day's drive of your residence, or about 300 miles in any direction. Become a U.S. geographical expert. Familiarize yourself with the larger and medium size cities in this circle and eventually in the entire United States. A fairly recent world almanac is a good source of this information. Also become a Christian radio station expert. Find out all you can about which stations exist within the circle, which ones play your style of music, and which ones have the most reach and influence in the region. Interestingly, a small number of independent Christian artists have been able to chart their projects in select markets through good music and sheer persistence. If you have a charting song, booking in that specific area will be much easier.

Once you begin the booking process, your most valuable assets are your lead sources. In the church realm, you will need to get hold of, at a minimum, the Baptist and Assembly of God church directories. Otherwise, the yellow pages for all the cities in your circle will suffice. Magazines such as CCM often list influential radio stations and also show where artists perform. It stands to reason that the churches that sponsor concerts already are the most productive to call. Develop the database by church networking. One of the basic rules of selling is to always ask for referrals. Ask anyone you talk with to refer you to others in the area who do concerts. Booking is a little like a treasure hunt; the more information you gather, the closer it will lead you to success.

Although you may have a romanticized view of booking, it's actually sales. Make yourself do it. Endure the pain and know that a door will open for you if you are talented, have something to offer, and are persistent. The Bible says that the hand of the diligent will prosper.

As you continue, you'll inevitably begin to develop relationships. The goal is to make these relationships long term. A successful regional ministry is inevitably the result of repeat bookings, not scattershot single concerts. As you develop these relationships, keep in mind that there are actually two types of audiences in Christian music, and each has a different gatekeeper. If your musical style is geared to a wide age range, you'll be developing relationships with music ministers, associates, and senior pastors. If, however, you're targeting a younger audience, you will work with youth ministers and independent promoters who do youth concerts—sometimes in neutral sites rather than churches.

> The experience of booking yourself will probably be a bubble-bursting, come-down-to-earth-from-that-rockstar-dream experience.

There's a great difference in working with these groups. Compared with a senior pastor, youth ministers tend to be more cutting-edge and evangelistically oriented. They may also be resourceful at fund raising to finance concerts. They also, frankly, may have next to nothing to offer but a place to do a concert. In the early stages, that may well be acceptable for you, especially if you can get your expenses paid. In either instance, be sure to ask them about their track record in doing concerts, how much success they've had with it, and how much they typically pay for an artist to appear.

Once you've established your sphere of influence, you need to make a call plan. Using your lead sources, you must keep in mind objectives for where you want to minister—specific cities, churches, or markets where Christian radio is strong. All of this effort comes together in a professional phone presentation. Take the time to work out how to present yourself effectively. Don't allow yourself to finally reach a great contact and babble uselessly! Write out what you want to say, learn it, and thereby gain the freedom to cover that ground extemporaneously.

Unless you've been involved in sales or marketing prior to this, this will be a new and possibly painful experience for you. It will involve a lot of rejection and subsequently, character building. The experience of booking yourself will probably be a bubble-bursting, come-down-to-earth-from-that-rockstar-dream experience. There will be times you feel like quitting and times when you get some favorable response that fills you with energy and enthusiasm. These feelings of being on a roller-coaster are normal for the sales world. The marketplace is fraught with rejection, but it's necessary to go through the pain of learning how to sell to appreciate the rewards that come with success. Developing resiliency is good for you. I personally believe the main purpose of the marketplace in the eternal scheme of things is to build character.

You can take comfort from the fact that in a sense, even the chairman of the board of a large corporation has to be a good, although admittedly upscale, tele-marketer. Statistically, executives are either on the phone, in a meeting, or on their way to a meeting. In those phone calls they are selling, persuading, and influencing. In spite of your fears, it really isn't going to kill you to be an artist and an entrepreneur. Remember, the most successful artists have always been a combination of both. If you're resistant to this type of activity, face the fear, turn it around in the direction of knowing that it is something that will bring positive direction in your life, and do it. This is going to take you to another level as an individual. It all comes down to calling. If you believe that you're called to this life, and that you are finding work for yourself and your family, you'll push ahead. Go in with a servant and humble attitude, and share your gifts and faith.

When you call, try to get right to the decision-maker. Your first booking calls will be to find out the name of that individual and get a hearing. Always call with a pleasant demeanor, identify yourself and state your purpose quickly. The secretary who answers the phone has the responsibility of guarding the prospect's time, especially at larger churches where there may be a lot going on. Music ministers are inundated with calls from traveling music ministries these days, so you will find that phone diplomacy and persistence will be your key resource.

If the conversation goes well, the prospect will want to know more about you. This is where you ask if they would be open to reviewing a press kit. If so, get thorough mailing information with fax number, e-mail address, and pager number.

> It's probably not a good idea to expect more than $1 per head in a love offering, however. Experience shows that while one person puts $10 in the plate, nine more pass it down.

Make sure to follow up the press kit with another phone contact exactly seven calendar days later. Be prepared—it's certainly possible that this is your point of rejection. If he didn't like the material, ask him why and what you could do to improve it or your ministry. If he does likes it, congratulate yourself—you may be on your way to a booking!

Naturally, at this point the issue of fees is likely to arise. This is the delicate part. As an unknown, you will typically be working for a love offering, hopefully with expenses added on. Be prepared early on in your career for little or no guarantee, or perhaps a small honorarium ($250-$500) versus a love offering (whichever is higher), or ideally, an honorarium plus a love offering. It's probably not a good idea to expect more than $1 per head in a love offering, however. Experience shows that while one person puts $10 in the plate, nine more pass it down.

Discussing fees requires mutual respect. Living on the road is expensive for artists, but sponsors have to stay out of the red as well. The sponsor should not expect to build relationships with artists if they get in over their heads and are tempted to cancel the date, especially inside of 30 days. It is nearly impossible for the artist or the agent to find another sponsor willing to pick up the date on short notice. As always, actions will speak louder than words.

Expenses will normally cover travel, meals, and accommodation. If you are asked to stay in a host home, your response is a personal matter. It's my advice that for most people this isn't a good idea. Politely decline and request that they get you a room. This will give you the privacy that's necessary for sanity, prayer, and preparation. It will also ensure that you have clean quarters as opposed to being asked to sleep on a couch or in a guest room that may be shared by the family dog. If you politely request fair treatment, more often than not you'll get it.

For the new artist, the best booking is usually a full Sunday night concert, with a Sunday morning introduction to the congregation. During this time you will sing a couple of songs and get the recommendation of the pastor for the concert that night. As an unknown, this recommendation is key. If he is enthusiastic and supports your work because he believes in what you're trying to accomplish with your ministry, he'll convey that enthusiasm to his congregation. Remember, he's putting his own credibility on the line, so come through for him!

Just because a date looks financially thin on paper doesn't mean it can't pan out. New artists often overlook the valuable asset of selling merchandise at concerts. This supplement to the fee or love offering can make the difference between survival and disaster. In fact, some well-known artists actually generate more income from merchandise sales than they do in performance fees. Naturally, the more creative you are in marketing this aspect, whether through great-looking packaging or in interesting products that one wouldn't expect, the more successful you're likely to be. If you're performing in churches, there are logistical problems in selling your product. Be considerate and diplomatic when finding the right place for this in a church setting. Always be respective of a church's wishes regarding this issue. Most will recognize it as a viable way for you to supplement your income. Some, however, will be uncomfortable with it. Whatever the case, respect the sponsor. He is the one who has invited you to the venue.

After You Get the Booking

If the artist understands some of the dynamics of concert promotion, it's an asset. Although you will only be at a given venue a short time, the sponsor has considerable responsibilities beforehand. Do what you can to help in this regard. Be ready to send posters, flyers or other items to make promoting the event easier. If it's a paid-ticket event, suggest an incentive program by offering two free passes to any youth minister who brings ten or more people with him. Have group rates. There are a million ways to promote a concert, only limited by your imagination. Try to arrange for call-in interviews with local Christian radio in that area. Send press releases to all local media and have the sponsor follow up with phone calls. You never know who might pick up the story. If one does, offer to send him a full press kit.

Once you've received your signed contract, rider, and deposit, call back four weeks before the date to "advance" it. This is your chance to maintain contact with the sponsor regarding all the details of the concert. It's also, frankly, the moment you're going to find out how professional the people are with whom you're working. Make sure that everything agreed to is moving forward. All too often changes are suggested, usually for the worse. Of course, the worst change of all is when you encounter a softening of enthusiasm for the event, or even a change of heart entirely. See this as a chance to do some troubleshooting. Find out if there's anything you can suggest to get things back on track. If they are clearly interested in canceling, it's definitely best to try to reschedule rather than abandon the date. It's possible that the problems the sponsor is encountering can be overcome with more time. If the cancellation comes within thirty days of the date, however, you have a bigger problem on your hands. There are integrity issues at stake here, as well as logistical ones. It may be possible to renegotiate the terms and save the date, but remember this: If this sponsor changed the deal once on you and you accept it, what will prevent him from doing it again? If you do make a change, fax the new contract immediately and make it clear that if the deposit isn't received by a certain date, the agreement is null and void. No matter what, always take the high road in difficult negotiations. Even if you are being mistreated, handle the situation professionally and courteously.

An absolute worst-case scenario occurs when a sponsor pulls the date when you're on the road, sometimes only a few days beforehand. Prepare yourself; this does happen. If so, you will have to refer to the contract and protect yourself from being taken advantage of. Occasionally these late cancellations have a legitimate purpose, but it's rare. Usually, the promoter has done a poor job and wants the artist to take the hit. Obviously, it's a great help if the artist doesn't have to handle these calls personally. If you can find someone who can handle these scenarios tactfully and effectively, do so.

Each case in booking yourself will be different. You will only know how to best handle these challenging situations by trouble-shooting real-life scenarios and developing into a diplomatic but tactful negotiator. You have to get into the pool to learn how to swim.

In sum, you should have a clear idea of what the goal line looks like when booking yourself. Far too often, even the most rudimentary understanding of concert promotion is lacking. On the one hand, a new artist rarely understands what it takes to put together a successful event. Unfortunately, the other side of the negotiating team, typically comprised of music ministers or youth pastors, is often in the same shape. Remember first and foremost that your goal is not simply to get work. Your goal is to promote a successful event. Simply to work frequently with no real ministry, no people, and the disappointment of knowing that the perception of the event was that it was unsuccessful will rapidly take its toll on your enthusiasm and emotions.

Successful Concert Promotion

Successful concert promotion is, in the end, just good old-fashioned events promotion. It involves four steps. All of them must be performed well to achieve success. If you're self-managed, it will be your responsibility to be involved with each of them.

Coming to Fair Agreement Between Artist and Sponsor

If there is an undercurrent of unfairness on either side, the likelihood is that things will go wrong later on. A concert requires trust and enthusiasm. Fairness, listening, and respecting each other's needs are essential. This is not simply referring to the financial; for example, does the church expect an altar call? Get these things settled in advance.

I have to admit that I have an intense aversion to working with anyone unwilling to put things in writing. Experience has shown me that anyone who asks me to trust them as a brother in the Lord is probably going to be a problem later on. Conversely, people who mean what they say have no objection to making a record of it. It's just logic.

Obtaining an Appropriate Venue for the Event

Far too often artists are booked into venues where they have no real chance of success. Either the venue is too large or too small, has sound characteristics inappropriate for the music, lacks the technical facilities for the artist, or simply can't attract the target audience. For example, there are certain segments of society that are unwilling to go to a church concert. Before you book, think about where you are being asked to perform and make sure that you are a fit.

> Sometimes the silliest problems undermine great opportunities—even down to not being able to find the keys to open the venue at the early hour required for load-in.

Implementing a Strong Promotional Campaign

This is primarily accomplished by building a music minister or youth pastor network (preferably within a 25-to-50-mile radius) who can bring groups to the event. Obviously, being asked to perform in a church for a particular youth group or congregation can work. But experience shows that blockbuster events that take artists to another level usually require the participation of several churches. If you are performing for a youth group, find out if the event is something that can be partnered with other churches—even citywide.

Paying Attention to Detail the Day of the Show

This is huge. All too often the day of the concert turns to chaos because people don't show up to do their jobs, or something breaks down. Make sure you have the resources to execute what you promised, and make sure that the church or other venue can do the same.

Sometimes the silliest problems undermine great opportunities—even down to not being able to find the keys to open the venue at the early hour required for load-in.

Conclusion

Some of you are cringing now, feeling you absolutely cannot do this for yourself. If so, you'll have to find someone to do it for you. This will take a special person, if you aren't earning much income at this point. He will have to catch a vision for your work, have an understanding of the eternal value of concert ministry, and be willing to work as an essentially unpaid volunteer for an unspecified time. He will obviously have to have some other means of support, care deeply about you and your work, and be a salesman who can get on the phone and the Internet and make things happen. One candidate for this would be a college student who may be able to get intern credit. Another might be a homemaker who may be willing to work during the day while kids are in school. The person needs to have drive and be intensely interested in learning about the Christian music business.

If you find outside help, you should expect to pay them at least 10 to 20 percent of the gross income you receive from your live performances, and you will have to pay for the phone bills, promotional items, and other expenses associated with your booking. It may be necessary to give them a private office space. If you are fortunate, you'll find someone who is interested in developing into a professional booking agent in Christian music and they will see you as the artist who will give them the chance to learn the ropes of the business of booking.

> No matter what, always take the high road in difficult negotiations. Even if you are being mistreated, handle the situation professionally and courteously.

No matter what, get out and work. Work everywhere you can, and don't let money be the determining issue. If you have a gift, exercise it and trust God to open doors. Accept victories and defeats with equal grace. If you're faithful to your call, everything else is secondary.

Brion Connolly is a booking agent and consultant with more than three decades experience in the music industry. He has represented artists as diverse as Steven Curtis Chapman and the Supertones. He resides in Nashville with his wife and three children. Contact Brion at: btcspkr@aol.com.

Recording the Independent Project
By Reed Arvin

*An important axiom about the importance of material
is this: NO CAREER SONG—NO CAREER.*

At some point in nearly every musician's life, the desire to record his work begins to grow. There are several reasons for this, some artistic and some practical. A recording is a marker in time, capturing the artist's vision as it exists at that moment. But a recording has another, more practical use: It goes where the artist cannot, reaching into thousands and even millions of homes, representing him, building relationships, inspiring, and connecting. It is impossible to build a substantial musical career without this capacity to be in many places at once. Additionally, the recording, when successful, can be a large source of income to the artist. So inevitably, even independent artists seek to capture their work on CD and tape.

When Should I Do It?

The first question every artist should ask is this: "When should I undertake a recording?" The answer isn't simple. For some people, recording is an ongoing process that never actually finishes. They are constantly recording, making demos of songs, developing their skills, and building a body of work. For others, going into the studio to record is a unique, highly pressurized experience upon which a great deal depends. For people who don't own their own recording equipment, spending time in the studio is just another way of saying, "go through a great deal of money in a remarkably short time." So the decision of when to pull the trigger and actually record is an important one.

Many aspiring artists make the mistake of recording too soon in their careers. They are not fully mature as singers, and where applicable, writers. They rush forward and spend money on a recording only to be quickly dissatisfied. As their writing matures, they long to record again to capture the improvements. But the cost of even independent projects is such that for most people, it can't be undertaken lightly. Be sure that you are willing to freeze in time your gift as it is before beginning the recording process.

One practical answer to the question of when to record is simplicity itself: The time to record an independent project is when it's necessary. You will probably have no difficulty identifying this time when it occurs if you have the ability to be honest with yourself. People will be consistently asking you if you have something to sell after your concerts. You will be playing out fairly frequently, and need something with which to represent yourself to prospective venues. You will want to include a recording with your press kit, or even, when the time is right, to a record company or manager. If you listen to your career, you'll know when it's time.

How Much Should I Spend?

One of the great mistakes many people make is to spend too much money on an independent project in the hope that they will be commercially competitive. Viewing this expenditure as an investment in the future, they spend far more than can be recouped on the actual sales of the record. The ultimate goal is usually to attract the attention of a record company. This is rarely the result. Budgets of most pop records, and even of contemporary Christian music recordings, are well beyond the range of what the average individual can afford. While no one can object in principle to spending for excellence, the prospective artist should not view this expense as likely to return to him in the form of a record contract. In fact, a virtual mantra

> Spending too much on an independent project without the experience to do so wisely can actually result in the obscuring of a great talent.

in the recording industry is, "simple and good is better than complex and mediocre." In other words, spending too much on an independent project without the experience to do so wisely can actually result in the obscuring of a great talent. The wrong type of heavy-handed production, for example, can swamp a delicate voice. Record companies have producers on hand who can bring the necessary production to a project. Above all, like a physician, make sure that you "first do no harm." Nevertheless, some basis for setting a budget must be found.

My belief, after seeing and hearing a great many independent projects, is that any money spent on an independent project should usually make sense on its own level. By this it is meant that the record doesn't have to be signed to a label or be wildly, unrealistically successful in order to have its recording fund justified. The vast majority—and the use of the term "vast" here is quite intentional—of independent projects remain just that: independent. The money spent on them, if considered an investment, must in the end be recouped through the private sales of the artist, whether through direct mail, internet sales, or concerts.

It's frankly unusual for an independent artist to sell more than a couple of thousand units through the sales life of a project. To sell multiples of this, say, six or eight thousand, is a major achievement that will probably create interest among record companies. In fact, it's fair to say that a letter which begins with the statement, "Hi, I'm Joe Smith, and my independent project has sold ten thousand units," will ensure that whoever opens the letter is certain to read on. If there is a CD included, it will probably be played. So in light of the modest sales of most independent projects, be realistic in setting sales goals.

Think about how many times a month you are performing. If it's twice, and you're in front of a total of five hundred people in those two performances, you would be fortunate to sell to 50 of them. Fifty times 12 months would equal 600 units in a year. If you perform more often than that, you can adjust accordingly. The 10 percent figure used in this example is arbitrary; with experience, you will be able to predict what percentage of people who hear you perform will want to purchase your recording. A great deal depends on the venue and time given; if you are singing three songs on Sunday morning, it stands to reason that fewer people will be interested in your recording than if you are able to perform a complete concert on Sunday night. On the other hand, most churches have much lower attendance for their night-time services.

Obviously the personal finances of the artist play a great role in setting a budget, or the circumstances of a benefactor or investor. If you are wealthy and love to spend money on your art, more power to you. But if that isn't the case, don't despair; it's still reasonable to assume that some income can be derived from the sales of the project, and at least some of your money should come back to you. Because the artist acts as record company on an independent project, a substantial profit can be made from direct sales at concerts. It's not unreasonable to make $10 or more per unit, assuming that all the applicable royalties are paid. Remember that whether or not your project is independent, you must pay writer's royalties on all songs. Failure to do so is what law-enforcement agencies like to call stealing.

Hopefully these realities will influence you to hold the line on your recording fund. If, however, in spite of all warnings to the contrary, you insist on spending more than is rational on your project, you should consider the following realities of the marketplace in which you are attempting to compete.

Four Big Ideas

The Market is Hungry for Different

One of the difficulties in marketing music of any kind is how voracious the public is for change. This has not always been the case, and some aesthetes would probably protest that radio continues to be a disappointing melange of sameness. But within certain commercial boundaries, hereafter referred to as "the size of the table," there is a remarkable diversity of musical style and production presently vying for attention in the media today.

Think of the size of the marketplace as a table with dimensions. The center of the table is the safest, least-offensive music. As you move toward the edges, music becomes riskier and more unique. Remember that although the table is large, there are edges, and if you fall off in your quest for being different, you become unsignable. You may garner a certain amount of admiration for your willingness to reinvent the musical wheel, but record companies aren't usually in the business of changing people's tastes. They have learned through painful experience that pushing the envelope must be done with a certain degree of circumspection.

Nevertheless, music at the very center of the table is extremely difficult to sign. If you make pop music, for example, artists such as Celine Dion and Mariah Carey represent the center of the stylistic world: safe, easy to listen to, and with intentional mass appeal. Both of these artists are hugely successful. Why, then, you may wonder, is it more difficult to be signed if you make this type of music? First, because there is a great oversupply of talented singers in the world, and being one of them does little to attract the attention of a record company. Record executives could simply stand in the dark at a typical Broadway audition to find great voices. If you have little to offer beyond a fantastic voice, this should be a reality check; the record business is simply not interested in finding the next great singer. There must be more—much more—to attract the attention of the industry. Second, although artists such as Dion and Carey are talented, they, together with a few others, amply fill this center niche and call into question the need for more of the same. If you make music like they do, you will inevitably be compared with them, and for most singers, this would be an unfavorable comparison. Unless you sing better than they do, singing like they do will make getting signed very difficult.

As you move outward from the center towards the edge, music becomes more inventive and to many, more interesting. It also, to a record company, becomes more signable (with all else being equal). Record companies are in a tireless search for artists who lean toward the edge of the table without falling off; artists who reinvent clichés without offending; artists who have the appeal of something new without alienating. The recent prototype for this artist is surely Alanis Morrissette, whose debut album sold a staggering 28 million units. Perceived as "edgy" and "different," but nevertheless highly listenable, she effectively moved the center of the table. This movement is evidenced by the fact that certain cuts from her first record are now played on the Muzak® system at Wal-Mart. Consider the impact of this carefully; within the space of a single record, what once was considered alternative is now mainstream enough to be Muzak®. So you can see that the center of the table is not stationary; it moves constantly, responding to the forces of immensely successful projects that redefine what is popular.

The Marketplace Is More Disposable Than Ever

One of the most interesting phenomenon in popular music is the extremely short commercial lifetime of recently successful artists. Because of this fact, it has become increasingly difficult to build a long career. Often, the more successful an initial recording is, the more certain it becomes that the next record will be relatively unsuccessful. To many in the record-buying population, as soon as a thing becomes too successful they begin to be suspicious of it. No one—I repeat, no one—is immune from this possibility. Consider the example given above, Alanis Morrissette.

> To many in the record-buying population, as soon as a thing becomes too successful they begin to be suspicious of it.

Although Alanis' debut album was wildly successful, her second was a sales disappointment. Stalled at just over three million, even her record company had to confess surprise at such a precipitous drop. Now this artist and her label face a sobering reality; if history repeats itself (as it often does) her third recording could well be her last and sell on the order of 200,000 units or less. This is not hyperbole; just ask the members of Ace of Base: 9 million, then about 500,000, then 50,000.

Once the decline begins, it is very difficult to stop. This is not to say that it's impossible; some artists go from strength to strength, but they are extremely rare.

There are reasons why putting together a streak of successful albums is so difficult, and they require more explanation than is possible in this chapter. But briefly, the problem begins with the "noise floor" of recorded product flooding the marketplace, quickly pushing out under-performing material. Retail outlets and radio stations, unwilling to waste time on developing slow-selling material with so many new options available, quickly turn to the next project in the hopes of finding the next "big thing." The result of this fickle relationship is that the cost of breaking an artist has become almost obscenely high. To push through this "noise floor" of recorded product requires very high concentrations of attention and money by the record company. The result has been artists selling gold (500,000 units domestically) and still being dropped from the label. The reason is that in order to sell those 500k units, the label may have had to spend a million dollars—still a losing proposition.

This has powerful implications for new artists as they consider their relationship with a label. Because of this short attention span in the marketplace, the internal commitment of record labels to artists has become commensurately shorter. Whereas ten years ago a label had at least a psychological commitment to try two or possibly three releases on an artist, seeking always to break the artist out, now that commitment may only extend to a single attempt. If the first album fails, in many cases there won't be a second record released.

Remember that this has nothing to do with the contractual obligations of the artist to the record company—that is entirely different. Although the label may have signed the artist to five or even seven records, this is always at the option of the label. They are normally under no legal obligation to release that many recordings. So having made one expensive attempt to break an artist, many are unwilling to try again under circumstances in which they believe that radio and retail have voted against the artist's success.

The Days of Conventional Recording Are Ending

By conventional recording, I refer to the time-honored practice of going to an expensive, professional studio, cutting tracks, overdubbing, recording vocals, and mixing. Today even commercially released label projects are often recorded in what are called "project studios," which are smaller, less expensive versions of their older counterparts. Made possible by cheap but surprisingly high-quality digital recording equipment, the cost of making a good-sounding record has fallen dramatically—if the people involved are talented enough to pull it off.

If you have enough talent and commitment, you may consider investing your recording budget in your own studio equipment instead of in time somewhere else. For the price of one or two records it is possible to buy the equipment to record infinitely—a tempting prospect for the long-term artist. But the reality is that few artists have the capacity to suddenly become experts on production and recording. There are a lot of issues facing the engineer and producer that would fall squarely on you, the "hopefully-suddenly-proficient-at-everything-including-digital-technology" guy. Be sure that you are willing to pull energy away from simply being an artist before you make a decision like that. For some, the home studio is a wonderful tool for unleashing their creativity. For at least as many, it is a frustrating waste of money that ends up taking up space next to the exercise machine that's growing cobwebs in the corner.

If you have enough talent and commitment, you may consider investing your recording budget in your own studio equipment instead of in time somewhere else.

No Record Is Successful Without Great Songs

The most perfectly produced record is doomed to failure without great songs. Conversely, a modest and frankly even mediocre record with the right material can win through its faults and connect with an audience.

An example of this was made clear to me when I first moved to Nashville. Like a lot of studio musicians, I paid a certain amount of dues working on "sound-alikes"—records sold on television, mostly in Europe, featuring hit songs "not by the original artists." A typical session involved showing up at the studio, listening to the song chosen for recording, and attempting to duplicate the original performance as closely as possible. This is mind-numbing work that is the musical equivalent of stocking shelves at a grocery store.

One day we were working on an immensely popular song, and as I listened to the recording, I was honestly appalled at how bad the production was. The musicians stared at each other in a sort of disbelief; there was actually a moment in the song where a trombone player makes a false start, coming in a beat early and then catching up with the others. I'd never heard a mistake that glaring on a commercially released recording. This production was so flawed that I tracked down how it was possible; I later learned that the song had been rushed into production as a theme song for a movie. The producers sent this quickie demo to the movie producers for consideration, assuming that they would have the opportunity to do a proper version if they were selected. But whether through scheduling or the unawareness of the movie people, the demo itself was released. I can honestly say it is the worst label recording I've ever heard. I can also honestly say that it won the Oscar for song of the year, sold over a million copies, and made the career of the artist. It proved that a lot of the obsessing that we producers go through to make music perfect is actually for our own amusement.

An important axiom about the importance of material is this:

NO CAREER SONG—NO CAREER

This is as simple as it gets. You can record good songs, but good songs don't make a career. Only a career song has this effect.

The career song is the song that pops into your mind when you hear the name of an artist. I say Billy Joel, you think "Piano Man." I say Sting, you think, "Every Little Thing She Does Is Magic." I say Michael W. Smith, you think "Friends." Career songs are songs that artists will be singing when they cozily relocate to Branson, Missouri, at the age of 50, prepared to rake in the rewards of years of hard touring with slow grazes through the barbecue buffet. These artists may hate to perform these classics, but they know that without them they would never have become popular.

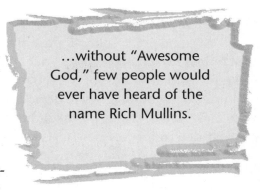

...without "Awesome God," few people would ever have heard of the name Rich Mullins.

I was fortunate enough to produce eight records on a truly brilliant songwriter, Rich Mullins. The first record sold about 33,000 records, which was obviously a disappointment. The second sold even less, which, in these tumultuous times, would have ensured that there never would have been a third. But in those simpler days, we were given a final chance. The next record, which cost very little to produce—less than $39,000—is now approaching gold status, or 500,000 units. What was the difference? The song, "Awesome God." The second album is actually better than the third in many ways. But without "Awesome God," few people would ever have heard of the name Rich Mullins.

If you hope to attract the attention of a label with your independent project, take a hard look at your own writing and see if you're really prepared to move forward. Remember that even talented writers sometimes look beyond themselves if they honestly conclude that there's nothing on the upcoming record that qualifies as "career" status.

The Eight Great Mistakes

At some point you will push through all the obstacles and decide it's time to actually record your project. You have your songs, you know your market, you've set your budget, found a producer and studio, and you're ready to begin. Congratulations! You're now ready to make some serious mistakes that have consistently undermined the most determined of new artists. But the following section can help you avoid them and greatly enhance your chances of being happy with the final result.

Determine Your Best Record

The ultimate vision for any record must begin with the artist. Although a producer can play a strong role, you must know what material is appropriate for your voice, what instrumentation sets your voice in its proper context, and in what style you wish to express yourself. Don't delegate these responsibilities completely; if something feels wrong to you, don't move forward, no matter how much pressure is placed on you. You are the artist, and you carry the weight of creative responsibility.

For some people, this weight lies uneasily. Because of a limited musical vocabulary, they haven't been exposed to much musical diversity and therefore bring little to the table creatively. The record will probably suffer as a result. If you want to record a great record, even on an independent basis, your musicality more than any other single factor will determine its aesthetic success.

One of the most important decisions you'll have to face is whether or not to make a machine record, a record with live musicians, or a hybrid of both. Each choice has powerful implications for your budget and your music.

Most inexpensive recordings are necessarily made in a midi environment, where a programmer "plays" most or all of the instruments on computer-controlled electronic instruments. This can have great advantages to the low-budget project, for several reasons. First, only one person is getting paid most of the time, and second, because money is being spent more slowly, the financial damage from a bad day or even an entire song is greatly reduced. Additionally, computers give producers and programmers minute control over musical ideas, and because there are few microphones involved, the sound quality is generally quite good.

Another reason to record with machines is because of their microscopic ability to create mathematically tight grooves that would be difficult or impossible to achieve with the human error of live musicians. For this reason most dance-oriented tracks are made with machine instruments.

Machine records have significant disadvantages, however, and the aspiring artist should be aware of them. This type of instrumentation is not appropriate for all types of music, in spite of the advances made in their ability to evoke traditional musical expression. A traditional country record, for example, would probably not be a good candidate for a machine rhythm section. Southern gospel would also probably suffer with the limited musical range of machines.

> Ironically, the greatest strength of machine records is also its greatest weakness: It is dependent on the creative input of one or two people.

Ironically, the greatest strength of machine records is also its greatest weakness: It is dependent on the creative input of one or two people. The magical, unforeseen input from a roomful of musicians will never happen with a programmer. You will be dependent on the creative impetus of your programmer, for better or worse.

Many years ago I was producing a Rich Mullins album which contained the track, "Boy Like Me, Man Like You." I was recording at a tracking studio (expensive) with some very fine (also expensive) musicians. After several hours, it was obvious that the track wasn't coming together. The oxygen gradually was sucked from the room as we searched for the ideas that would bring alive what was clearly a brilliant song. Eventually, I called for a break, and the musicians scattered to their beepers.

Except for one. Billy Crockett, a brilliant acoustic guitarist, strummed a rhythm aimlessly on his guitar, his feet up on a chair. As I spoke to the engineer about what I was going to do with the rest of my life since I would obviously never get to produce another record, I heard the strains of Billy's playing softly intrude. The plucking rhythm gradually caught my attention. I pushed down the talk-back button and asked, "What would it be like if you played that rhythm to the chords of Rich's song?" Billy shrugged and began to play. It was instantly obvious that here was the hook upon which to hang the song. I called the musicians back in, and in 45 minutes we had a finished track. The song went to No. 1.

This story should give pause to anyone who dismisses live musicians as unnecessary in a computer age. Without Billy's input, I have no doubt that song would have never become a hit, which it richly deserved. By involving the creativity of several, your record has the chance to grow in unexpected ways. But it would be disingenuous to deny that there is a greater risk to this approach. If, for example, Billy had stood up and got a drink of water, I would have spent a great deal of money and had no usable track at all. You pay your money and you take your choice.

Most records today, for these and other reasons, end up being made with both machines and live musicians. The basic track is sometimes pulled together with machines, with certain parts replaced and added with real players. This retains some of the control of machine records while creating a context for the creativity of other players.

Don't Record Straight Through—Build in Breaks

One of the most subjective acts the human body can perform is the act of hearing. Anyone with experience in the recording studio will tell you that simply going to lunch can make a song sound very different to you than before you left. You can be sitting in the control room, delighted with what you've created, leave to grab a bite to eat, come back, and be appalled to hear that you entirely missed some musical component that now glares back at you. This is because listening changes psychologically and physiologically over time. For this reason, it's imperative that you give yourself time to separate from your project intermittently to gain the perspective that only space can deliver. If you are going to record for 12 days, for example, don't agree to record them consecutively. For most people unused to the recording process, probably three or four days in a row is a good limit to attempt without a break of a day or two. During those breaks, fight the temptation to listen to your project. Then, when your break is finished, sit down with a pad and paper and listen straight through the project a couple of times. Write down everything you hear that needs work. You now have a "to-do" list.

Probably the single most important time to gain perspective is before a mix. It's usually a mistake to go directly from recording to a mix, if for no other reason than the exhaustion that often accompanies the end of a record. You want to be fresh and full of enthusiasm at this crucial point of the process. Try to get a break of a few days before starting.

Don't Record on the Wrong Microphone

Every microphone in the world sounds different from every other microphone, and every make and brand of microphone sounds very different from every other make and brand. These differences are sometimes subtle, but they can also be dramatic. In other words, if you are singing on a microphone that isn't flattering to your voice, you can undermine your vocal performance before it even begins.

A lot of project studios only have one or possibly two vocal microphones. The engineer may lead you to a microphone, smile, and introduce your voice to its worst nightmare. Before you record a thing, you should perform what's known as the microphone shoot-out.

The mic shoot-out is simply a process to find your best microphone. This process can get complicated, but it doesn't have to be. You simply line up three good but different microphones next to each other (any more than this gets too hard to keep straight) and sing a verse and chorus onto tape through each of them. Remember to keep everything else the same; use the same preamp, and don't use an equalizer or compressor at this point. You simply want to hear the microphone. When you've finished, go in and listen to each track. You will probably be surprised by how different you sound. One will probably be a clear winner. If you're not happy with any of them, you may have to keep searching.

If the studio doesn't possess an array of quality vocal mics, don't despair; most large metropolitan areas have services that rent them at surprisingly low cost. Even the most expensive microphones rent for $100 to $150 a day, and usually paying for four days gives you the use of the mic for seven. I believe that even a very inexpensive independent project deserves the $300 to $500 commitment of renting the right microphone for the artist. If the studio says, "Don't worry about it, Amy Grant sang on this one and that ought to be good enough for you," don't buy it. In the first place, they probably never met Amy Grant, and in the second place, one person's great mic can be another's worst. Just because Michael Bolton sings on a certain

> Just because Michael Bolton sings on a certain microphone, that doesn't mean that it wouldn't do you in.

microphone, that doesn't mean that it wouldn't do you in. You can't cheat here, you just have to do the test and find out. The good news is that even the inexperienced person can usually hear the difference and you shouldn't have much trouble picking a winner. If you have a home studio, I still urge you to conduct the shoot-out when you record your vocals. Good microphones to consider are: AKG C-12, Neumann tube U-47, Telefunken 251, Manley Reference Gold, and the Shure SM-7 (for rock).

Don't Wait Until the End Before Recording Your Vocals

One of the most fascinating phenomena in working with artists is their mental relationship with their instrument, the human voice. Many times an artist begins to develop vocal problems as the days for vocal recording approach. It's completely psychological; as soon as the record is finished, they make an instant recovery. But after 15 years in the music business, I've learned to take as much pressure as possible off the artist to sing well on a given day. You should do the same.

Most independent projects are recorded very quickly, and as a result, you may only have a couple of days to sing an entire album's worth of material. Try with all your might to resist this; in fact, set things up so that you can sing at any time the mood strikes you. There are practical ways to achieve this, and the most important is to maintain a separate microphone chain.

The microphone chain consists of the microphone, the preamplifier, the compressor, and the equalizer. I try to keep these components separate from any other processes in the recording. The reason for this sacred consideration is that having them always ready to go means that I can record vocals at any time. When the artist comes in for morning coffee, I'm listening to his voice—even when he's just chatting. If he sounds strong and the schedule can accommodate it, I might say, "Hey, why don't we sing something?" You never know when something magical is going to happen.

There are some professional singers (artists are not necessarily professional singers) who can sing anytime and anywhere. They seem to get stronger the longer they sing. I produced tracks on two records by 4HIM, and I honestly believe that you could wake those guys up at three in the morning, push them up against a wall, put a mic in front of them, and record. They have such superb vocal ability (not just in artistry, but in the physical act of singing as well) that they can sing all day long without tiring. But few artists possess this ability. Many can only sing well for a couple of hours or so, and the producer can usually tell when, as we say, "it's going away." By leaving the chain intact I can usually come back and finish a song later without too much fidgeting with sounds.

But experience has shown me (the hard way) that taking a vocal chain apart and even putting it back together with exactly the same components ensures that the vocal sound won't match. Set your chain up and experience the luxury of singing anytime you like. If a guitar player cancels at the last minute—go sing. If the fiddle player finishes early—go sing. If, in fact, you suddenly feel inspired, go sing no matter what else you're doing.

"Fix It in the Mix" Is a Lie

One of the interesting things about making a record is the truism that anything that bothers you a little bit now will drive you insane later. Because making records is mostly about solving problems, you will tend to obsess on the things you don't like rather than exult in the things you do.

It's human nature, unfortunately. But because we all get fatigued, sooner or later the engineer may tempt you to not fix something that bothers you because he claims he can "fix it in the mix." If there is a background vocal that doesn't end exactly with the lead, for example, he may claim to be able to "duck it" to make it match later.

This is invariably a bad idea. It will save you trouble later, and besides, you'll have to get a new engineer, which you obviously need.

Increasingly, records are mixed by a special kind of engineer who does little besides mix. They develop the particular expertise in mixing that makes them valuable in that process.

> Mix engineers are a strange and exotic breed of creative individual that can make a good record sound great.

Mix engineers are a strange and exotic breed of creative individual that can make a good record sound great. They can also make a mediocre-sounding record sound more passable.

They cannot, in spite of their claims, make a bad-sounding record sound truly good. So it would be a horrible waste of their creative energy to have them spend their time fixing problems instead of dreaming creatively about your project. Fixing buzzes, pops, and hums is a time-consuming, soul-deadening experience that will leave you far from the creative peak you need to do great work. Make sure that the record is as right as you can make it before the mix and then let your mix engineer loose to put the final touches on an already good project.

Because mix engineers routinely work on many projects recorded by many recording engineers, they develop opinions about the work of each. When your mix engineer puts up your project and hears it for the first time, watch his face; if he's excited, then you can know that things are right and he's looking forward to doing what he does: being creative. If he looks concerned, or, heaven forbid, *pained*, then you can know that you're in for a long process that won't be a lot of fun. Get it right on tape in the first place and have a great time taking it to another level in the mix.

Even if you don't have a separate mix engineer, the principle is the same; no matter who mixes, it will kill your creativity if you spend hours fixing problems instead of making music.

Set Your Mix Budget Aside and Make It Sacred

Mixing, as we've discussed, can make or break a record. But you'll find that it's tempting in the recording process to have little conversations with yourself about this process, shortchanging it. For example, imagine that you have decided to mix for four days. This will cost you a certain amount of money. But as you move along, you realize that not everything came out exactly as planned, and in order to fix these problems you are running out of time, money, or both. So you tell yourself, "Well, I suppose we could mix it in three. I mean, we'd have to do more on the last day, but hey, I'll sleep later."

Mixing is important and you've worked too hard to undermine things now with little compromises. You can't mix well when you're exhausted, and you'll stress out your mix engineer by putting too much on him. Fight the temptation to compromise here and keep the mix money separate and untouchable. In order to do this, however, you must follow the next bit of advice.

Budget for Your Mistakes

In the end you're hoping for something magic to happen, and magic is fickle. So it's inevitable that not everything will turn out as you had hoped. That expensive guitar player might turn out to be an expensive waste of money. Or perhaps you now realize, with the track half-finished, that what you really want is 12 background singers chanting your name.

The fact is that mistakes happen and some great ideas come during the process. But if you budget every day down to the *nth* you'll have neither time nor money for any new ideas or catastrophes. The way to avoid this problem (and to keep you from stealing from your mix or recording on a credit card) is to actually budget for these items in advance, even though you don't know what they are when you do it. I usually set aside 10 percent of my budget for this, depending on the project. If I know I'm taking a risky approach, I might increase this number. But I never go below 10 percent. Think of it like this: If I have $150,000 to produce a record, I actually work with $135,000 or less—ensuring that any great but expensive ideas I get later can be paid for without stealing from something else. Even if your budgets are small you should still do this. If you start with $5,000, for example, keep $500 or so aside to fix problems or pay for that extra overdub.

Love Your Gift

This is easy for some and hard for others, but it's essential for everyone. At some point it will dawn on you that when you open your mouth it's going to be recorded forever—that you'll have to live with what happens over the next hour or day or week for the rest of your life, and that can be intimidating. But there is a solution, simple and effective: Love your gift. Love that you can sing. Take enormous, ridiculous pleasure in it. Don't compare yourself with others, or even yourself at some later, more advanced and theoretical date. Just love it the way it is now. If you do, you will hear it on playback. If you don't, you'll hear that, too.

The Last Word

Remember that making a record is a mysterious process. To the dismay of many, a great record can't actually be planned into existence. If you are the type of person who, when things go wrong, falls apart so fast that people get hit by the shrapnel, making a record will be a very frustrating experience. The people who enjoy recording are those who see the process as important, not just the final result. The moments that don't work are seen as the doorways to the things that do finally come together. Making music isn't like making widgets, and you will do your best work if you can let go and turn towards the wildness of the creative process.

Be assured that often during your recording you will be frustrated. Know for certain that you will sometimes feel the desire to start over because nothing you're doing is working. Then smile, and welcome yourself into the wonderful world of art. If you're lucky, you're 10 minutes away from the best musical moment of your life.

SONGWRITERS

Initial Steps to Building a Successful Song
By Margaret Becker

The worst thing you can do is miss an idea. You must have the means to capture both the good and bad melodies, lyrics, and themes that come your way.

Okay—so you're sitting there in your car listening to a radio or a CD and a song jumps out at you in all its brilliance. You stop—heart fully tugged. It sounds familiar, yet somehow new. You know exactly what the lyrics are saying, yet you've never heard it said quite that way. You're scratching your head asking yourself, "How did they think of that?" It's as if the content is so plain and yet unique. You wonder why you didn't think of it first. The inevitable question arises—how did the writer get to that idea?

Welcome to song envy: You've got it. You're not alone. I've been there. Some songwriters leave me speechless with their ability to communicate the deepest human emotions in the simplest terms—and without all the trite, too-familiar language. Often they are speaking of things whose fragrance I recognize but whose exact scent has eluded me. I've wondered where they found the inspiration to put it into such plain terms. The answer is simpler than it should be: They have learned to search for inspiration in everyday life.

Experiences that you and I have everyday are the stuff of which great art is made. There is a logic to this: The best art identifies the common bonds of human experience and expresses it in a way that piques our interest. Often profound art comes to us in a subject that we have considered before, but perhaps not quite in the new light that the writer is offering.

One of the most important writing skills that separates the frustrated from the fluent is the simple act of chronicling and documenting events and feelings. If you can put your observations and thoughts into general words, you can probably put them into more specific words, too. But you can't do anything if you don't preserve them somehow. Thoughts can come as quickly as they go if you don't capture them. Take care of them; they're the building blocks for songs. Learn how to capture them. A great way to do that is through a journal.

Journalizing and Descriptive Writings

Do you keep a journal—a place to write the daily impressions of your life? You should. These sometimes seemingly insignificant scribblings can prove to be valuable building blocks in the creative process. If you chronicle the things that have left an impression on you, you'll find that common themes emerge over the course of months. These themes comprise the feelings and experiences in your life that are meaningful to you. Since you find meaning in them, the chances are good that others will as well. What better place to start when searching for a lyric idea than within your own experiences?

Maybe you're going through a tough time, for example, and someone's kindness reminds you of God's mercy. Record it in your journal. Record how you feel about it…maybe even similar feelings you've had in the past. Then a few weeks later, perhaps you read a book that makes you think of God's infinite care for you. Allow yourself to feel the full scope of that emotion, and then chronicle it.

When you put your journal entries together, you're left with two different angles on mercy (perhaps a verse one and a verse two eventually)—two distinct, moving, life-giving entries. The theme emerges as you chronicle. Without the reference of the journal, you might miss the connections entirely.

These entries don't have to be long. You're not looking to win the Pulitzer. What you want is to keep casting your nets into your daily life to see if any nuggets are brought to the surface.

What If I Have Nothing to Say?

Although I've kept a journal since I was 8 years old, there are still days I have difficulty making a meaningful entry. On those days I approach my journal as a kind of discipline. For example, I might try to describe something familiar, like a sunset, in a way that is fresh. I take my journal with me as I observe the sun going down. As I watch it descend, I begin to jot my thoughts—completely unedited—about what that process looks like to me.

We've all heard about sunsets of brilliant orange and fiery gold. But I try to deliberately steer clear of those words and come up with new impressions that would still have meaning to someone reading the piece. For me, it's a way to get the creative juices flowing without the pressure of the song format. That was the way I began the journey of writing a song called "Say The Name" (included in the tape series).

Discipline

"Say The Name" started as a simple journal entry one evening. I wanted to lay out some goals for myself for the upcoming year. My goals began with the basis for my life—my faith—so it was a natural progression to start with that area when writing. In thinking about that faith, one thing kept coming to my mind: I wanted to make sure that I was being responsible with the name of Jesus. This is how I wrote it in my journal:

Our generation has almost overused and under-defined the name of Jesus. It's sad when my close friends hear that name and respond with images of one dimensional televangelists and fallen Christian personalities. I feel the name has been sullied to this generation, almost denigrated to a dismissable prime-time option. How sad. I want to speak that name only in the most appropriate of circumstances, not as casual reference or chatter, the way some do to fill in the blanks after church conversations that grow stagnant for a moment. I want to protect it and shelter it in my own life within the sphere of influence that I have so that when I do say it, people will see it as sacred, knowing sacredness to me and my abstention for bringing it out for none but the most appropriate of situations—like fine belongings handed down from generation to generation. I will protect that name. Not because I'm ashamed, but because I am proud of it and want to be a priest of sorts of sacredness. I want it out of pop culture with all the other mindless banter and into a sanctuary of responsible expression.

A lot of words! Obviously, I was thinking in broad brush strokes, letting out a stream of thoughts. As we go on, I'll show you the refining and editing process for these thoughts and how they made the transformation. For now though, just know that everything started as a disciplined journal entry that made the transformation from task to true emotion in that first sitting. It was enough to spark a desire to go deeper with the thought.

If you commit to using this journal technique, you can find an endless array of material. Chances are, what is being revealed to you in your writing is also being revealed to many other people in their own lives. Common experiences are the foundation of many strong lyrics, even if they are first written only out of discipline. So keep a journal.

Essays and Content Outlines

Although I had an intriguing journal entry, I still needed to take several steps to create a song. I knew I wanted to address the idea of Christ's name further, but I found myself stumped on how to best express the concept. I wanted to communicate the need to revere and protect the name of Jesus in our culture, not only by imitating His best qualities, but also by adjusting our attitudes to accurately reflect His sacredness to our faith. That idea seemed very complex to express in three and a half minutes with every other line rhyming!

Charlie Peacock, my producer, made a suggestion that changed the way I write altogether. He told me to write an essay about my subject before I started the song. Charlie encouraged me to put aside at least an hour for this exercise. There was a catch though; he didn't want me to edit or fix anything that I wrote. From the moment my fingers hit the computer keyboard, I was to write without editing or re-reading. I agreed, and sat down at the computer. I wrote everything I could think of about the name of Christ, and came up with six pages. I have to admit I found myself going off on a few tangents, like the ones below:

...it's a name that I base my entire existence on. It is the name that is linked to the love of my life—the center of my world. It is the name that exemplifies mercy to me—the most awe-inspiring mercy my heart has known...

...I will speak it, but only when I feel that the moment is up to the task of containing it...only when the ears present will consider its power and dignity...

...otherwise, I will use a descriptive name, like Abba, Father, Provider, my Savior—anything. They will all point to the same Being, but the proper name for my God will be brought out like fine china, set in velvet and fine wood...

I read my essay back upon completion and found that for the first few pages I was meandering, basically restating my journal entries. But the final pages were loaded with phrases and principles that I wanted to express in the song. So I got out a highlighter and marked the particularly poignant passages. This enabled me to construct what I call a "content outline" for my song.

Is Songwriting Prophecy?

By Darrell A. Harris

Sometimes when a publisher asks a young writer to rewrite a song, they meet with the response, "But this is the way God gave it to me." Once the writer has countered critique or suggestions with the claim of divine revelation, it's difficult to have productive dialog.

Dallas Holm attests that whereas he labors over most of his songs, he wrote "Rise Again," in the few minutes it took him to get the words onto paper. Many who have participated in the creative process have experienced this sense of "downloading information" from outside themselves. But even if such experiences would qualify as prophetic, are the resultant songs then exempt from critique? (By the way, to my knowledge, Dallas Holm has never made a prophetic claim for the song I have cited, and the publisher was wise not to ask for a rewrite!)

St. Paul's instruction in 1 Corinthians 14:29 is to "Let the others weigh what is said" by those prophesying (NRSV). While church historians differ as to whether these "others" were believers with the gift of "discernment of spirits," others with prophetic gifts, the elders of the church, or the entire congregation, all acknowledge that there was an evaluation process.

Perhaps our options for evaluating songwriting are not so far removed from the experience of our prophetic forbears. Even if a song qualifies as prophetic, there will always be value in the opinions of other songwriters, publishers, pastors, and Bible teachers, and ultimately in the response from all who eventually hear the song. The principle is still the same, "Iron sharpens iron, and one person sharpens the wits of another" (Proverbs 27:17 NRSV).

Darrell A. Harris co-founded and served as president to Star Song Records from 1976 to 1996. He now serves as chaplain to the Gospel Music Association and the Institute of Worship Studies.

Content Outline

A content outline is constructed as a guide for the thematic progression of a lyric. It's an excellent tool to help you define just what you do—and don't—want to say. It helps you see how realistic it is to include all of your subject in a song. I often have too much material for one song and find myself having to thin things out after I complete this process. A content outline can also help you break through a block on a particular lyric. It forces you to formulate your thoughts before you exhaust yourself with other issues like rhyme and meter.

Here's what the first content outline looked like on "Say The Name" (the title was different at that point too):

The Shelter of _____?

(Jesus)
The Name that moved mountains
to catch my falling tear
the Name that...
(Jesus)

This Name
means more to me
than any words can say
with a love for my soul
that nothing can replace

With all my heart, soul and mind
With all the passion I can find
must/I will Say The Name
with/for all that It has done for me
all that It's become to me
must/I will Say The Name

Both a comfort and a shield to me
a counselor and a...?
(all encompassing? Omnipotent?)

As you can see, it looks almost foolish. There are lots of things that don't make sense, lots of un-poetic couplings, but that is exactly what's supposed to go on here. This is where I allow myself to be free—even to the point of "trash"—in order to further streamline my thoughts. In this example, the second stanza was my idea of a chorus. In the final edit, it actually became the bridge. That alone was worth the exercise, because it needed only a little attention to fit in the final version of the song. It also was the catalyst that allowed me to understand the main expressible point of my song.

Expressible Points

I had many thoughts from my journal and my essay, but when I laid them out in rough song form, I saw that I truly had to pick one aspect of my thought and just focus on it. I tend to be wordy and sometimes try to jam too many ideas into one song. This outline helped me to thin things out and choose the most universal point that I want to communicate.

In this case, I realized that instead of presenting the concept of how I wanted to protect the name of Jesus and restore some of its sacredness, I would be a better communicator if I did it by example in the song itself. I decided to communicate the meaning of Christ's name to myself, and make my point about its overuse by actually avoiding using it. In that way I could illustrate my desire to revere it more completely in my own life.

> Although I've kept a journal since I was 8 years old, there are still days I have difficulty making a meaningful entry.

Emotional Intent: Second Outline

Now I was able to narrow my field of expression and become more specific with my mission. I proceeded to the next step in my outline process. In this outline, I picture the listener hearing my response and I imagine what I want his response to be. I did this with each line of the song, sometimes even down to singular words. I outlined—in rough form again—what emotional expression I had to employ in order to usher the listener into the place of hearing the intent behind the words.

In this case, I walked away from the outline for a day and returned to write a fresh one with this new goal in mind, complete with the emotional intent of each part of the song. I also designed some tools that would allow me to illustrate the intent.

> A content outline is constructed as a guide for the thematic progression of a lyric.

Verse 1:

Emotion: Vulnerable

How precious the name of Jesus is to me. Some hints of its expression in my life*

Chorus:

Say The Name because it is majestic, beautiful, full of meaning and power.
I will say that name.

Verse 2:

Emotion: Vulnerable still, but a humble strength I hope I never forget this truth because of my own stubborn pride or because I am intimidated by others. I will remain faithful.

Chorus:

The same, but now add the actual name of Jesus.*

Bridge:
No matter what, I will say this Name with all my heart and soul appropriately, and with conviction. I will not be ashamed of it.

Chorus:
*Same, with the Name so listener can say it also.**

* Denotes some of the tools I propose to use

I wrote down the emotional content of each verse because sometimes it will affect the adjectives and verbs I choose. In this song, as I attempted to communicate more strength, I chose stronger verbs and more resolute adjectives. This outline was easily gleaned from the essay. In fact, some of the lines that made it into the song came directly from the essay. The essay coupled with the content outline kept me on track, and gave me ample resources for expression during the construction of my lyric.

In sum, writing an essay on your subject is a good way to access your thoughts about the subject. It may seem like a roundabout way to clarify your ideas, but in the end, you'll find that you have more raw material to work with than you would have otherwise. It's actually easier in most cases to find a rhyme word at the end of a well thought-out lyric than it is to build a cohesive lyric around a one-word rhyme. So go for your content first, and worry about rhyme later.

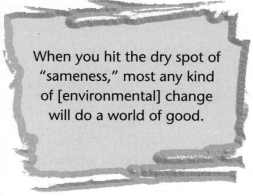

When you hit the dry spot of "sameness," most any kind of [environmental] change will do a world of good.

Environment/Creative Budget

No matter how disciplined you are, sometimes you'll still find yourself bone dry. There are times when I've written in my journal, chronicled things for the sake of writing, written essays about emotional things, and still nothing is leaping out at me. That's when I mix it up a bit. I get in my car. I ride my bike. I go to a record store. I sip Starbucks at Barnes and Noble. I go see a band. I baby-sit my neighbor's kid—anything to change my environment. Environment is a nutrient to creativity. When you hit the dry spot of "sameness," most any kind of change will do a world of good. Something as simple as leaving your house with a laptop can turn it all around. Get out of your usual routine. Go to a coffee shop and see what you can write there. Go to a park and people-watch. Put yourself in some of their shoes...what are their struggles, dreams...hopes? How are theirs similar to yours? How can you address them in a song?

Creativity sparks creativity. Is there an art gallery near you? Go there and study how other artists express themselves. Simpler still, go to a record store and begin to randomly read titles on some of the records. Even title-reading may generate some ideas of your own which you can later expand. Bring your pad and jot notes. Go to the bookstore and do the same. Think of yourself as an impressionable entity with the ability to give unique commentary on everything with which you come in contact. You must "feed the machine" with good stimuli. Be brave. Do things outside of your comfort zone. Create new stimuli in your life. Expose yourself to new environments. It could be the "change" that breaks a song wide open for you.

When I became "stuck" on some lyric ideas for "Say The Name," I went to a small, nearby sanctuary and sat by candlelight for an evening. I was trying to get in touch with the quiet reverence of the building. No doubt many lives had been touched and changed over the years in that tiny space. Though it was old and musty, there was an antiquity there that mirrored the antiquity of the Christian faith. I felt that if I sat there long enough I could feel its power and it would be reminiscent of the time-honored antiquities I was attempting to write about. It worked, and I had some fresh ideas as a result.

Creative Budget

Creative budget comes into play here. Sometimes, in order to feed yourself with things that challenge and inspire, you need a little money. Hence: your creative budget. It doesn't have to be an extravagant sum, just enough to perk you with things both new and familiar. For example, in my home I keep a steady supply of scented candles. I burn them often when I am writing. I even take one with me on the road to make the hotel seem more friendly. Just the smell wafting up from my suitcase puts me at ease. Its familiarity relaxes me and causes a sterile environment to become more friendly. Sometimes it's enough to get me started in my writing process.

I also find that familiar sounds accomplish the same thing. I have a CD of the ocean I play while I'm composing. It doesn't compete with any music that may come to me, and the natural sounds put me at ease.

My writing instruments sit in front of a window so that I can gaze out when I'm trying to mull something over. I used to have them up against a wall because it created more space, but I found the view very antiseptic and inhibiting. There have even been times when I've moved all this gear into the center of my living room so that I wouldn't feel closed in. It looked like a mess to my friends, but it made me feel open and expansive. The blatant disregard for the "normal living room attire," coupled with the added aesthetics made for a good return in creativity.

> Make it a goal of your life to feed yourself with inspiring things.

Listen to music outside of your usual tastes. I have a "new music" budget. It's not huge, just enough to expose me to some new textures every so often. I listen to many different things in an attempt to expand my musical vocabulary. Some of them become favorites, and some go directly to the second-hand store. Through this process, I found World Music—the music of other cultures. I wondered how the Africans expressed what was valuable and passionate to them musically. What about Bulgarians? How would they express their faith, their patriotism, their struggles (the core emotional ingredients of many touching songs)? I don't limit myself here. Sometimes I don't even understand the language, but I understand the emotion (that is one kind of good writing—the kind that bypasses the mind and gets directly to the heart). The more exotic the expression, the more expanded I become and the better communicator I'll eventually be.

Books are another necessary source of material. I've found many passionate spiritual themes from the "mystics," a group of Christian writers who were often persecuted for their unbridled longings for God. Poets and commentators from the mainstream publishing world offer some great inspiration as well. Why not experience through someone else's eyes what it was like to be searching for meaning at the turn of the century in France...or longing for redemption in Germany during WWII? The desire for spiritual connection is the backbone for many meaningful poems throughout recorded history.

These perspectives will help expand and enhance your own experience base. Input of this kind will give you a broader array of tools from which to choose when creating your own work. Inspiration begets inspiration. Make it a goal of your life to feed yourself with inspiring things. Chronicle your thoughts on these inspirations. Write down your immediate response to their impact. Even if it is only one sentence—write it down.

I've found that my first exposure to new creative works by others jump-starts my creativity. When I listen to a CD for the first time, I listen with paper nearby so that I can jot down any thoughts that come to mind. I listen as a student and a dreamer. I want to learn about each artist's techniques of expression. I want to be impacted by their expression, because in many cases, it leads me to expressions of my own.

Tape Recorders

Did you notice the "s," as in "plural" at the end of this title? You need a few tape recorders, and here's why.

Have you ever been driving along in your car, thinking over some brilliant concept, and—wham—it hits you: the perfect melody, or the most clever lyric that you've ever come up with? What do you do? Probably, you lean into the passenger side of the car and begin fumbling through the Burger King napkins in the glove box, looking for anything that would leave an impression on any surface so you can write down your idea. The car swerving—you sweating—it's not a good thing. What if you had a ratty old tape player that you kept handy in the car? Fresh batteries...work tape inserted—you could easily, and without much law-breaking, record your little gems—without causing anyone bodily injury.

I have a few ratty recorders like that: one in my car; another is in my bedstand (I write tear-jerkers in my sleep...only to awaken most times and find that my chorus was built upon rhymes like Reggie and veggie...but who knows? Maybe one day). There's one in my purse—backpack—briefcase—whatever I am toting around at the time. I've found that if I only have one, I tend to forget it quite a bit, and the inspired moments pass without documentation. These are cheap, often garage sale portables, but they do the job. They create an audible memory of my meanderings. I refer to these tapes often and some wind up as songs.

A quick recording like that became the melody for the bridge in "Say The Name." I was stumped as to where to go with that part of the song. One day I took a long drive out in the country, and after a particularly mesmerizing vista, the melody started forming itself. I had my old Radio Shack special on the center console, hoping that the moment might arrive. It did and I was prepared. I sang it into the recorder and presented it to Charlie. We didn't use all of it, but we did use a part.

The worst thing you can do is miss an idea. You must have the means to capture both the good and bad melodies, lyrics, and themes that come your way. If you only carry a pen and paper (which I also recommend), unless you're a "reading" musician who can create manuscript on the back of a napkin, you'll surely miss some of the melodic opportunities that spontaneously come your way.

Get Away from Your Principal Writing Instrument

Do you ever find yourself writing the same song in five different keys? Do you see a lack of diversity in your melodic content? Do you sometimes want to bring a melody to a different place, only to lose direction as you "hunt and peck" for the correct chord on your instrument?

Cut the cord. Break the chain. Get away from your principal writing instrument.

We're all limited by our present knowledge of our instrument. We're bound by our skill level and musical vocabulary. We hear things that we can't present correctly on our instruments, so we leave them for more familiar progressions. This is called stagnation—a major contributor to writer's block.

I was in the airport at 6 A.M., waiting to catch a flight. I had my tape recorder and my notebook in front of me—replete with the deadly "blank page." A man sat down beside me and asked what I was working on. I answered ruefully, "Nothing." I turned to look at my new acquaintance only to find an old friend who was now an A&R vice president at Frontline Records. We wound up talking about melodic writer's block. He challenged me with this: Go to a record store and buy a compilation CD of Rogers and Hammerstein songs. Live, eat, and breathe it. Study the genius of their melodic content. Let it become a part of your tool chest and then write—but not with any instrument at all. Take a tape recorder, maybe some lyrics and go to a secluded place where you can sing unselfconsciously. Construct melodies. Sing everything that comes to your mind. Even if it's only small snippets—sing it out. Don't imagine chords. Don't even address support music, just sing melodies.

The formula he prescribed combined inspiration and uninhibited expression, and it helped me find some of the best melodies that I've ever written. I got away from my limited chordal vocabulary and my voice naturally followed its instinctual leanings.

Some instruments tend to send our melodies in one direction or another. For example, sometimes you'll notice that if the writer is predominantly a guitar player the melodic content will be more simplistic, with less interval movement. That's because the guitar is somewhat of a "drone" instrument: tones that are struck and held out over several measures, often without much variation. On the other hand, piano-based writers tend to write more movement into their melodies because the piano itself lends itself to individual note movement. There are 10 fingers doing many different things, whereas guitar players have generally four fingers moving, if that. Compare Michael W. Smith's melodies with Bruce Springsteen's work. Yes, they are very different stylistically, but how much of that style was just inherent to what felt natural and good to them as musicians?

Playing on an unfamiliar instrument can break you out of ruts.

Playing on an unfamiliar instrument can break you out of ruts. Even though you may find yourself playing the most simple progressions on a new instrument, they'll sound fresh and inspiring because they're being expressed in different textures. Keyboard writers, if you want to challenge yourselves, go to a bass or a guitar. Find little progressions—even if they are just single notes—that are exciting to you. Guitarists, go to keys. You don't have to know how to play, you just have to give yourself over to exploring new textures. Mix it up and get out of what is comfortable to you. When you've secured your melody and have it on tape, you'll be able to go back and fill in the chords. You'll probably find your musical vocabulary will increase as a result of your melodic expansion. If you can't find the proper chords, enlist the talents of a co-writer who can.

New ideas come from these melodic exercises. In the best cases, the melodic content can dictate the emotional content. Once you understand the emotion of a melody, you only have to find the words with which to paint the emotion. It can start with the words. It can start with the melody.

Quote Books

Many award-winning writers don't leave the house without a set of writing tools. Simple and readily available, these tools can open up a whole new world to the lyric-writing process. They can take a predictable song and turn it into a cleverly crafted, fresh one. One of the best tools is a quote book. These generally contain catalogues of themes, and a group of famous quotations about them. From love and war to children and roses, the themes are listed alphabetically with a great many pithy comments readily available. The great commentators of history are in these books. What they have to say on any given subject will surely urge you forward in your own work.

Don't be shy about using these tools; even the very best songwriters use them liberally. On a recent songwriting session with Wayne Kirkpatrick, co-writer of Eric Clapton's huge hit "Change Your World," I was at a loss for direction on how to formulate the body of a lyric. We were writing on love. He brought out his quote book and from those words we found at least seven different directions to pursue on the theme of "the power of love as it is expressed through the believer." Eloquent quotes by the greatest minds inspired us in our own journey. Of course, be careful not to plagiarize these writers. Use their thoughts only as tools to help you formulate your own.

A Thesaurus

For those who don't know, this is a book that lists words and offers alternate words which have similar meanings. Some versions also include words that have opposite meanings, or antonyms. This is a great tool for making a line more descriptive. For example, take the word "love." We've heard it a zillion times in songs. A thesaurus might list related words: passion, yearning, heart, tenderness…and many more. Instead of using the age-old stand-by, "love," you can find something new to throw into your mix. Maybe the new word will spark other associations that will lead you into new directions.

The thesaurus is also helpful when you are trying to continually hint at your theme throughout the song. It enables you to make a list of all the similar yet different words. You can insert them in the lyric throughout your construction process to build a stronger subject foundation. This tool offers word building-blocks quickly and efficiently. I use one on every session I do. It's a must.

I used the thesaurus liberally on "Say The Name." After I finished my previous outline, I began a search for descriptive words that are evocative of my subject, but not overly repetitive. I took key words that I knew I would use in the song and looked them up in the thesaurus for synonyms:

Speak/Say: whisper, talk, converse, utter…

(I chose whisper—it seemed poetic but accessible)

Peace: tranquillity, repose, quiet, truce, calm

(Nothing seemed good here, so I looked up calm)

Calm: quiet, tranquilize, soothe, ease

(Soothe and ease seemed right for the song)

I continued this process for the rest of the key words. Honestly, I probably only used four of all the words I researched, but they turned out to be key words that made my lyric stronger and more cohesive.

> Once I had a rough melody, I started to refine my words, using the old adage, "less is more."

Digging and Editing:

Now that I had my tools, right down to the nails, I could begin constructing the song. Charlie, my co-writer, gave me some of his melodic ideas. I searched for one that would match the emotional intent of my unedited lyric. I found one that was delicate, keyboard-oriented (and very melodic because of that). I began there. Once I had a rough melody, I started to refine my words, using the old adage, "less is more."

Since there was a lot of melodic movement within the song, I resisted the temptation to use too many words in an attempt to "fill in" the melody. The movement of the melody would be interesting enough by itself. My job was to elongate simple words that would sing well over the melodic hills and valleys. I began by plugging in some of the thoughts I'd already assembled. Some were poetic enough to start building upon. From there I filled in the blanks—keeping the intent and finding rhymes. At no point did I sacrifice intent for a rhyming scheme. If a word didn't work, I tried changing the rhyme that preceded the awkward word, instead of jamming in something that diluted the impact of the song. After many hours,

creative environments, writes and rewrites, I finally had it smoothed
out. The final version looked like this:

Say The Name
A more sweeter sounding word
these lips have never said
a gentle Name so beautiful
my heart cannot forget
Just a whisper is enough
to set my soul at ease
just thinking of his Name
brings my heart to peace

Say the Name
Say the Name that soothes the soul
The Name of gentle healing and peace immutable
I'll say the Name that has heard my cry
Seen my tears and wiped them dry
from now until the end of time
I'll say the Name

May I never grow so strong
that my heart cannot be moved
may I never grow so weak
that I fear to speak the truth
I will say this holy Name
no matter who agrees
for no other Name on earth
means so much to me

Say the Name
Say the Name that soothes the soul
The Name of gentle healing and peace immutable
I'll say the Name that has heard my cry
Seen my tears and wiped them dry
from now until the end of time
I'll say the Name

With all the honor I can find
With all my heart my soul my mind
I will say the Name
without defense, without shame
*I will always speak the Name of Jesus**

Say the Name (Jesus)
Say the Name that soothes the soul
The Name of gentle healing and peace immutable
I'll say the Name that has heard my cry
Seen my tears and wiped them dry
from now until the end of time
I'll say the Name [1]

* I deliberately held back the actual name until halfway through the song. It was my only way of expressing my original idea of revering the name by not overusing it. Although I couldn't explain that complicated principle within the three and a half minutes allotted to me, I could illustrate it by withholding it. I didn't talk about it. I just did it.

How All These Tools Ended in a Song

Let's review my journey of writing "Say The Name." The process went like this:

Random writing and expressing

I had no ideas.

I wrote in my journal as a discipline and chose a subject that I eventually wanted to address. It didn't seem inspirational at the time, but rather task-oriented.

I wrote in free-form without any restraints. I discovered that I felt passionately about a subject that revealed itself through this process.

I wrote a full-blown unedited essay on the subject—nonstop, without interruption.

I found useful thoughts that formed "touchstones."

Outlines and refining

I used these "touchstones" to form my first lyrical outline of a song.

I identified the true expressible subject, and did a second outline that was more specific, even down to the emotional picture that I wanted to create with each section.

Tools for construction

I got my thesaurus and assembled my "nails," the words that would keep the theme consistent without allowing it to become redundant. These words would hold the song together in continuity.

I got away from my principal instrument and experimented with melodic content to form an appropriate setting for these words.

Final touches

I took all my existing tools and employed all my "environmental stimuli" and began laboriously assembling and reassembling the pieces of the song puzzle until they fit together in a clear, concise manner.

But What If?

But what if it doesn't work? What if you make many attempts at a subject only to end in frustration? What if your songs begin to resemble each other more than you'd like?

Inevitably, there are days where your blank paper is just that—blank and intimidating. There will always come a time when your seemingly endless number of great ideas vanish into thin air, leaving you feeling uninspired. Writer's block happens. Everyone goes through it. It's not the end of some creative river—that's the good news. It is correctable and probably fairly easily correctable too. That's the best news. In those instances, cut yourself a break. Give yourself some room.

Allow yourself to create for the sake of creating only—not for any other purpose. You will probably find the change cathartic.

Sometimes my writing gets gummed up with sameness. Lyrically, I find myself addressing the same subject over and over in different formats. This isn't so bad when it's something as vast as God and all His attributes, but when it's something like a particular "hurt" or a "desire to get away from it all," or a long list of others, it can get tiresome.

In these instances I find myself trying to somehow get the expression out of my system and I use every musical format granted me to do it...searching for the one that will enable others to see my point of view. Of course the truth is that sometimes it's not necessary for others to see that point of view. Sometimes there are expressions that are only for me—my healing, my journey, my metamorphosis. Instead of letting these impulses dominate my writing, I've learned over time to give them form immediately. In other words, I've learned to indulge myself.

If I want to write a song about the recent death of a loved one, I just let it come out in the exact form it needs, instead of searching for a way to turn it into a commercial statement, knowing that it is only for me and most certainly not a waste of energy. It's simply a creative journey meant to relieve me. Sometimes I do a whole body of work like that just to get the juices going. I write in the full knowledge that these songs aren't for public consumption. They don't have to be three and a half minutes long with a happy ending. They can be angry or sad or searching or bleak or a polka for that matter. They are only for me, for my personal growth. I find I'm better for expressing them, and I'm settled in for the next wave of writing. When I've fed my own need, I can slide more easily into the box of creative boundaries necessary for writing works in a more commercial format. It can work the same for you—when you hit a dry spot, abandon all the rules and write whatever you want. Let your creativity go without edit. Let your expression find its voice. Siphon it up and once it's flowing you can control the process for the more disciplined side of things.

> Remember: Writer's block haunts every writer. It's not fatal.

So Get Started Writing!

Everything I've mentioned will breathe some new life into your dry spots. Pick a few of the suggestions and try them out. Remember: Writer's block haunts every writer. It's not fatal. Just be free with yourself and nurture your creativity through these times. Your artistic side needs inspiring stimuli and it's your job to provide as much of it as you can.

Don't edit yourself too much during these periods. Get your expressions out, then edit when you have exhausted the subject.

And above all: Keep that journal and watch the progression of your life unfold in its pages.

Margaret Becker has released eight solo records on the Sparrow label. She has received four Grammy nominations, three Dove awards, and 12 No.1 singles. Her collected essays, *With New Eyes,* is published by Harvest House.

Poetic Devices
By Robert Sterling

*I am confident that, like all worthwhile creative
endeavors, writing a song is simply an opportunity for the writer to get a little closer to God.*

The Christian Songwriter's Pitfall:
Sunday School Lessons That Rhyme

As a songwriting instructor for the Academy of Gospel Music
Arts, I am frequently in the position of giving face-to-face song critiques in a room full of amateur Christian songwriters. By and large,
it's a fun and educational experience. Everyone is there to learn and
most everyone has a good attitude about accepting honest construc-
tive criticism. I certainly admire the writers' courage to allow a perfect
stranger to criticize their baby in front of a small crowd. I try not to
hurt anyone's feelings and, so far, nobody's threatened me with
bodily harm. During these sessions, time and again I come across
songs that can best be described as "Sunday school lessons that
rhyme." The lyrics are truthful, theologically sound, and sometimes
they make a worthy point. But they lack art. Short of a simple rhyme
scheme, they are void of poetry. Not a single picture graces their

lines. They may be long on truth, but they are short on beauty. Regardless of their theological soundness, and difficult as it is say, they are bad lyrics.

We are all made in the image of our Creator. Those of us who would mirror His image in the craft of songwriting should work as hard at being inventive and original as we do at being biblically sound. The lack of creativity in Christian songwriting often results in music that falls on deaf ears rather than songs that connect with the audience. A good songwriter has a command of the language and intimately understands the tools of the trade. Primary among those tools are poetic devices. Over time, the dedicated writer internalizes their capabilities so that they become a natural extension of his creativity. Like a master chef, the writer carefully spices lyrics with metaphor and simile, turning an average song into a gourmet dish. These touches of poetry don't draw attention to themselves, but the song is better for their presence. Because cleverness is no substitute for content, a good writer doesn't force "poetry" into songs. Instead, he works to incorporate these devices naturally, confident the result will be a more effective and more powerful song—not another Sunday school lesson that rhymes.

> A clearly structured rhyme scheme defines the framework of a song, creating an aural road map which makes the song easier to follow.

Why Rhyme?

There may be a strong urge to skip ahead past this segment on rhyme; after all, everybody knows about rhyme. It's old hat. Just another observation from the "Encyclopedia of Things That Are Painfully Obvious," right? But surprisingly, many beginning and even intermediate-level songwriters display an apparent lack of understanding, let alone mastery, of the creative use of rhyme in their writing. So any discussion of poetic devices must begin with the one device that is most commonly used and abused—rhyme.

Any honest examination of the great songs of the day will reveal a healthy dose of rhyme. Like a hammer in a carpenter's toolbox, rhyme is one of the basic tools that every good songwriter must know how to wield accurately and efficiently. Otherwise, the result will be shoddy workmanship—a song that doesn't hold up. Rhyme acts as a song's verbal adhesive, bonding words to one another in the listener's ear, connecting lyrics across the span of a verse or chorus.

A clearly structured rhyme scheme defines the framework of a song, creating an aural road map which makes the song easier to follow. And because rhyme is the repetition of key sounds in a lyric, rhyme also makes the song easier to remember. The childish rhymes of nursery songs may seem overly simplistic to adult ears, but there is no denying that those little verses are memorable. Decades may pass, but no one ever forgets the words to "Mary Had a Little Lamb." Effective use of rhyme holds the listener's attention and creates a sense of expectancy for the rhyme he knows is coming. A good song-writer understands that rhyme is pleasing, even comforting, to the ear. Finally, musical phrases that parallel one another often cry out for words that do the same. To ignore the rhyming demands of the melody is to weaken the power of the song.

A Songwriter's Definition of Rhyme

My well-worn paperback Webster's dictionary defines rhyme very simply as the "agreement in the terminal sounds of words." This definition, however, allows for the inclusion of homonyms, which songwriters, as a rule, should avoid. A homonym, sometimes called an "identity," is two words which are spelled differently but sound the same (see and sea). When used as rhymes in a song,

290 Getting Started in Christian Music

homonyms tend to sound dull and lifeless. (I know this to be a fact because I have made this error myself in an otherwise good song, and it bothers me every time I hear it.) So, in our pursuit to become better songwriters, I will rely upon Sheila Davis' more specific definition of rhyme from her wonderful book, *The Craft of Lyric Writing* (a book every serious student of songwriting should own). Davis defines rhyme as two or more words which contain "the same final accented vowel and consonant sounds and a different consonant preceding that vowel" (p. 185). That means "peal" and "steal" do rhyme, but "repeal" and "appeal" do not. Why? Because the final accented sounds of "repeal" and "appeal" create an identity, not a rhyme. Got it? Good. Let's keep moving.

The Basics of Rhyme

Rhyme, as I'm sure we all know, mostly appears at the ends of lines. There are three common types of this end-line rhyme, and they are exactly what their names suggest them to be. The first, single rhyme, is also called masculine rhyme. This involves rhyming single syllables (scheme/dream; snow/grow), or the final syllable in multi-syllable words. (amazed/appraised) The second is double rhyme, also known as feminine rhyme. It occurs when the last two syllables of words agree, and the stress is on the first of the two syllables. (traded/faded; cheaper/keeper; date you/hate you) Finally, triple rhyme is (you guessed it) the rhyming of the last three syllables of words (Havana/banana). It, like double rhyme, is often created by rhyming phrases, not just single words (call again/fall again).

Not all rhyme occurs at the end of the line. A rhyme that spices up the inside of a line is known as internal rhyme (As I was falling I kept calling out to you). If two rhyming words are adjacent to one another in a line, that is called contiguous rhyme (the great state of Texas). In the hands of a skilled lyricist, both internal rhyme and contiguous rhyme can offer a sort of "bonus" for the listener.

The Quest for Perfection

Perhaps the biggest question surrounding the use of rhyme today is whether rhyme should always be perfect rhyme, or whether it's OK to settle for an imperfect rhyme. Understand that for decades the standard for rhyme was quite simple—all rhymes were perfect. Absolutely, dead-on perfect. End of argument. All the great craftsmen of Tin Pan Alley implicitly understood that the only way to rhyme was with a perfect rhyme. Anything less was laziness or simply bad songwriting. As a result, the writer wishing to rhyme the word "love" was pretty much limited to a handful of choices— "dove," "glove," "shove," and "above." Perfect rhyme is still the standard in theater music. However, in today's pop music, perfect rhyme is not always the only appropriate solution. It can be sterile and predictable. And, as we've seen with the word "love," perfect rhyme can also be very limiting in word choices, even hindering the message the writer may want to convey. Sometimes an imperfect rhyme can be the perfect solution to a writer's dilemma. Imperfect rhyme, also called slant rhyme, near rhyme, and false rhyme, is an "almost perfect" rhyme. Close, but not exact. With imperfect rhyme, the writer's choices are often increased dramatically. Consider our "love" rhyme again. Now the writer has at least another dozen or so options to choose from—words like "rough" and "enough," and maybe even "flood," and "bug," and "tub." None of them are as strong as a perfect rhyme, but all are possible substitutes (although I struggle to imagine why anyone would write a song that would rhyme "love" and "bug"). A word of caution regarding imperfect rhyme to any

> Predictable rhymes will telegraph the lyrics ahead, telling the listener exactly what's coming and spoil any surprises in the song.

writer who genuinely wishes to grow in their craft: Don't settle for an imperfect rhyme simply because it was easy. That's not good writing. That's laziness.

Rhyme Tips

Finally, regarding rhyme, here are 10 tips that will help you make the most of your rhymes. Try using these tips as a checklist. They may help you determine if you are utilizing rhyme in a creative way, or just settling for the same tired old rhymes you used in your last three songs.

1. Rhyme the important stuff. Rhyme naturally draws attention to the rhyming words, so choose to rhyme words that reinforce the song's message or atmosphere. If you rhyme unimportant words, you're telling the listener that you've written an unimportant song.
2. Save the stronger, more creative rhyme line for the second half of the rhyme. Make the listener wait for that great rhyming line. They will appreciate the payoff more that way.
3. Avoid predictable rhymes. Don't you just hate it when someone guesses your line before it even happens? Predictable rhymes will telegraph the lyrics ahead, telling the listener exactly what's coming and spoil any surprises in the song. Double and triple rhymes have a greater tendency to do this than single rhymes.
4. Avoid rhyming slang words. Slang words date stamp your work. Just ask anybody who ever rhymed the word "rad" in their song. There's a time and a place for trendy words. Trendy language has an immediacy to it, and can often be used for comic effect. But remember that all trends eventually fade away, and you may find yourself rewriting your trendy song six months down the road.
5. Vary the color of rhymes within a song. Using only one kind of rhyme can be boring. Mix up the use of single, double, and triple rhymes. Or try slipping an internal rhyme in somewhere. Also,

overusing the same rhyme vowel can become tedious. If every rhyme in your first verse is a single rhyme using the "ee" vowel, the listener may never make it to your second verse.

6. Rhyme "naturally." A classic problem of beginner writers is inverting words in a phrase to force a rhyme ("go to Him, he will"). I lovingly call this "Yoda speak," named after the little green creature in the "Star Wars" movies that spoke in awkward, sometimes backward phrases. Better to simply write the words the way people actually speak today, and look for a new rhyme, if necessary. Also related to this problem among Christian songwriters is what I call "hymn talk." This is the use of archaic language to make a rhyme work. For example, if you used the word "thou" to rhyme with "now," you have committed the sin of "hymn talk." That might have worked for Fanny J. Crosby, but it won't work for you.

7. When you're stuck for a rhyme, try rephrasing the line. Sometimes you can say the same thing another way and open up new rhyming possibilities. For example, the line "Because it always ends up that way" can be rephrased to "Because that's how it always ends," and suddenly you have a new rhyming word without changing the essential message.

8. Don't settle for sloppy rhyme. Even imperfect rhymes shouldn't be weak. Rather than settle, dig a little deeper. You may find something terrific.

9. Get a good rhyming dictionary and a thesaurus. These books are not crutches, they are tools which you can use to "jump-start" your thinking processes and open up new avenues of words from which to choose.

10. Every now and then—don't rhyme. That's right. After this entire discussion, remember that sometimes little or even no rhyme can be very effective if it is done purposefully and with solid craftsmanship.

More Sound Effects (Repetition, Repetition, Repetition)

In addition to rhyme, the serious songwriter also carries a few other sound-effect tricks in his toolbox. Like rhyme, these devices all involve repetition of sounds. However, because these effects are rarely featured so prominently as rhyme, their effect is generally less obvious and more subtle to the listener.

Alliteration (Repeating Consonants)

Alliteration is simply the rapid repetition of consecutive consonants in a line of lyrics. (The underlined letters in the previous sentence are a hint: They are alliteration. Get it?) Effective alliteration calls for subtlety (unlike my previous heavy-handed sentence). Also, excessive alliteration can sound silly (as does my previous heavy-handed sentence). An excellent example of subtle alliteration is found in the opening lyric to the song "Via Dolorosa," by Niles Borop and Billy Sprague: *Down the Via Dolorosa in Jerusalem that day...*[1]

The repeated "d" consonant in the line doesn't jump out at you. It quietly reinforces the power of the lyric by making the words flow more smoothly.

Assonance (Repeating Vowels)

Assonance is the repetition of stressed vowel sounds in neighboring words in a lyric. Probably more subtle in its effect than alliteration, assonance can add to the atmosphere and the warmth of a line. Greg Nelson and Phil McHugh used assonance very well in the title/hook line of their popular song, "People Need the Lord." As that lyric is gently repeated in the chorus, the "ee" sound in "people" and in "need" adds to the warmth of the song. (And to further strengthen the effect musically, the melody notes on those two syllables are the same pitch.)

Anaphora (Repeating Words)

Anaphora is the repetition of a word or phrase at the beginning of successive lines in a song. This effect is probably more obvious than alliteration and assonance, and is often suggested by a melody which repeats itself at the beginning of successive lines. Anaphora is a great tool for the writer to establish a feeling of familiarity, and make a lyric quickly memorable. Used well, it can strengthen a song's structure and focus the direction of a lyric. In the first verse of the socially conscious song, "How Long Will Be Too Long?" by Wayne Kirkpatrick, Amy Grant, and Michael W. Smith, we see a terrific example of anaphora as it focuses the lyric's message and drives the song forward to the chorus.

> Great lyricists understand that lyric pictures, painted with creative figurative language, make the words of a song leap to life in the listener's ear.

Tell me, how long will we grovel at the feet of wealth and power?
Tell me, how long will we bow down to the golden calf?
Tell me now, how long will be too long?
Tell me, how long will we curtsy to the whims of new religion?
Oh, how long will we water down the truth 'til truth is no more?
How long will be too long? [2]

Figures of Speech (High School English Class Revisited)

"A picture is worth a thousand words" is a trite but true piece of wisdom, and one that might seem a bit out of place in a discussion about lyric writing. After all, lyric writing is all about words, right? Yes and no. Great lyricists understand that lyric pictures, painted with creative figurative language, make the words of a song leap to life in the listener's ear. A single well-placed lyric picture can instantly set a mood, create a believable character, or shed new insight on the subject at hand. Experienced lyricists employ these devices instinctively. They understand the power of pictures in their songs.

Of course, nothing in the following discussion on figures of speech will be news to those of you who paid attention in sophomore English class in high school. That's when everyone was, at least in theory, learning about metaphors and similes and other riveting minutia like that. The problem is most of us were concerned with more important stuff...such as "Is my face gonna clear up before the weekend?" and "Who do you think was better—the Beatles or the Stones?" So, for the benefit of the majority, let's take a brief ride in the "Way Back Machine" and revisit some vaguely familiar territory, and perhaps discover in the process that you can actually use something you learned in high school for fun and profit.

Metaphor

A metaphor is a direct comparison of two things that are essentially unlike one another. The lyricist simply finds a piece of common ground between two dissimilar things and creates a verbal equation. In doing so, the writer expands the meaning of the object that is being compared. When Paul Simon sang, "I am a rock. I am an island," he was using metaphor and expanding the meaning of his own human condition. In reality, he is neither a rock nor an island. But isn't that a much better way to say "I am a hard and lonely person who requires no one else in my life"? It certainly sings better.

The first verse of Bruce Carroll's hit song "Breaking the Law of Love" demonstrates how effectively a metaphor can crystallize the message of a lyric. The first two lines of the song take aim at the contradictions in the singer's spiritual life. The third line drives the point home with an artful metaphor, equating his life's version of righteousness with garbage and lies. *Lord, I'm laying down this life of contradictions, All the Sunday resolutions and the Monday rationales. 'Cause my righteousness is filthy rags and fiction. When I'm talking love and charity and living something else.*[3]

Sometimes a metaphor is contained in a song more as concept, and not stated directly. In the brilliantly crafted lyric of "Luck Be A Lady" from the musical "Guys and Dolls," Frank Loesser maintained the comparison of a gambler's good fortune to the whims of a well-heeled female throughout the song. In my own song, "God Is With Us," made popular by Point of Grace, I made the repeated, but never directly stated, comparison of a rushing river to the difficulties of life that threaten to sweep us away from a relationship with God. In the '80s hit "Broken Wings" by Mr. Mister, the writers make the comparison of a wounded romance to the broken wings of a bird.

Simile

A simile is a comparison of two things using the word "like," "as," or "than." Much like the metaphor, it compares unlike things and, in doing so, expands meaning. Think of simile as the first cousin to the metaphor. A good listener (and all good songwriters are good listeners) will hear similes occurring

> A good listener (and all good songwriters are good listeners) will hear similes occurring naturally in the conversations of their funniest and most colorful friends.

naturally in the conversations of their funniest and most colorful friends. For some people, it's a natural way of talking, so pay attention. "She's sweet as honey." "He's nuttier than a fruitcake." "That's as crazy as a screen door on a submarine." You've heard them all.

For a simile to be effective, it must ring of the truth. Jim Croce sang to us that Leroy Brown was "meaner than a junkyard dog." Nobody would've bought the record if he had said a junkyard cat. Donald Fagen, in the song "Ruby Baby," tells us he's never going to give up on his unrequited love with the clever simile, "Like a ghost I'm gonna haunt you." In other words, he'll always be hanging around. In the song "God Only Knows," I described a young girl's sadness by saying her "tears still fall like summer rain." There's a gentle melancholy attitude in that line that felt truthful to me. And no matter how clever or artful the simile, it needs to be truthful.

Personification

Personification is the simple trick of giving human qualities to inanimate objects. The writer paints the picture by breathing life into something that is lifeless. "The walls laughed at me," "the whispering breeze," "a weeping midnight moon." These are examples of personification.

Occasionally, in a dramatic first-person point-of-view, the singer can become the inanimate object that is being personified. Barry Manilow sang to the entire world that "I am music, and I write the songs," and Bruce Johnston, who actually penned the tune, made a gazillion dollars.

Synecdoche

Synecdoche (pronounced sin-EK-doh-kee) is a counterpart to metaphor and simile. While they expand meaning, synecdoche contracts the meaning by reducing the image of something to one significant characteristic or part, substituting the specific for the general. For example, if I wanted to say that an angry dog met me at the front door, using synecdoche I could write, "A fierce growl answered the doorbell." I reduced the dog to a single identifying trait and reduced the front door to the sound of a doorbell. In the pop hit, "You May Be Right," Billy Joel reduced his entire chaotic neighborhood (perhaps his whole life) picturesquely with the metaphorical phrase, "I've been stranded in the combat zone." For those of us who choose to face the challenge of writing songs that refer to an all-powerful and ever-present God, synecdoche is our friend. Think about it. Every time we refer to God as "Father," or to Jesus as "spotless lamb," we are reducing Him to a single attribute, which makes it possible for our finite little brains to deal with the infinite Creator of the universe, if only for a moment.

Metonymy

Like synecdoche, metonymy is another device that reduces meaning. It does so by representing the subject with an appropriate symbol. So, when one uses the phrase "from the cradle to the grave," metonymy is employed three times. First it represents birth with the symbol of a cradle, and then represents death with the picture of the grave. Finally, the two metonyms join together to symbolize the entirety of life. Because metonyms are symbols, they show rather than tell. As a result, they are particularly economical, using just a few words to say much. In his song "Face the Fire," singer-song-writer Dan Fogelberg wrote the line, "The demon is free," to symbolize the spreading danger of the nuclear poison that was leaking into the waters surrounding Three Mile Island. In the second verse of the song "One Love," Brent Bourgeois places three metonyms to good use.

I want to face eternity with Your loving guarantee

(symbol for promise of salvation)

You've already paved the way...

You sent Your Son to save the day

I can't imagine what I'd do without my daily bread from You

(symbol for God's sustenance)

Your sweet manna from above,

(symbol for God's love freely given)

filling up my heart. [4]

Irony

Irony is the method of making a point by emphasizing the opposite of what you mean. The most pervasive form of irony in today's culture is sarcasm, which is generally blunt and often hurtful. That is

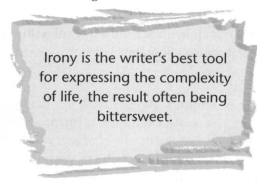

Irony is the writer's best tool for expressing the complexity of life, the result often being bittersweet.

not what we're talking about here. Irony is the writer's best tool for expressing the complexity of life, the result often being bittersweet. Remember the O. Henry story, "The Gift of the Magi." A young husband and wife, poor but much in love, each sought to secretly purchase a special Christmas gift for the other. The husband sold his most prized possession, a gold pocket watch, to buy a set of combs for his wife's long beautiful hair. At the same time, the wife cut off her hair and sold it to a wigmaker to buy her husband a chain for his watch. Sad, isn't it? And yet, their love for one another became richer for their mutual self-sacrifice. That's irony.

Of all the poetic devices, irony is probably the most difficult to express. It requires an intimate understanding of the truth that it carries and generally needs to be delivered in a subtle fashion. Like metaphor, irony can be assigned to a single line in a song, or it can embody the entire lyric. Here are three basic types of irony that a songwriter should understand:

Understatement treats something significant in a casual manner. To say that Microsoft CEO Bill Gates has a little money set aside for a rainy day is an understatement of colossal proportions. In the song "Living for the City," Stevie Wonder underplayed the surroundings of a boy raised in the abject poverty of a ghetto with the lyric, "surrounded by four walls that ain't so pretty."

Hyperbole is the opposite extreme—an extravagant overstatement. Again let me refer to a song by Dan Fogelberg—his romantic ballad "Longer Than." He sings to his lover that "longer than there've been fishes in the ocean...I've been in love with you." That's a long time. That's hyperbole.

Paradox is a self-contradictory statement which is somehow still true. For example, I can say with all honesty that "the more I learn, the less I know," because I've discovered that greater knowledge always leads to a greater awareness of how much more I have yet to learn. In their song "She's Leaving Home," Lennon and McCartney told us, "She's leaving home after living alone for so many years." How can someone live at home and still live alone? Anyone who has ever lived in a home where communication has failed completely understands the truth of that paradox.

Characterization

Characterization is the creation of convincing characters in a song. This might involve only a line or two in a lyric, or it might weave through the entire song as a story. Perhaps more than any other group of writers, country songwriters know the value of this device as they create vivid characters who come to life in their music. Songs like "The Gambler" and "A Boy Named Sue" are character-driven songs that rode the top of the country charts and put their writers in the Songwriters Hall of Fame. On Bruce Carroll's best-selling gospel record, *Sometimes Miracles Hide*, there is hardly a song without some sort of colorful character woven into the lyric. Here's just one example of many from that project, in a song called "Highway of Life." In four short lines we meet a man, come to care about who he is, and wonder what will happen to him.

> *He's driving eighteen wheels, dodging automobiles*
> *He's got a picture on the dash of his cab*
> *Too many years on the road and now his family's all grown*
> *And they really don't remember much about Dad.* [5]

Of course, country songwriters don't have the exclusive rights to characterization. Billy Joel has told his fans the stories of the Piano

Man, Brenda and Eddie, the Big Shot, and Anthony and Mama Leone. Lennon and McCartney gave us Eleanor Rigby and Father McKenzie. Sting sang to us about an Englishman in New York. Donald Fagen introduced us to the Night Fly. And Paul Simon humored us with a song about a guy called Al. We remember these songs because we can remember the characters in them.

How Colorful Is Your Lyric?

Poetic language is colorful language. As a movie filmed in Technicolor is generally more stimulating to the eyes than one shot in black-and-white, a colorful lyric is more interesting to the ears than one that is lyrically "black-and-white." A song that perhaps has a metaphor or two, a creative rhyme pattern, or some subtle irony is going to be more intriguing than a song with no word pictures, no believable characters, and a worn-out, overly-repetitious rhyme scheme. I am not saying that every lyric you write should be burdened with heavy metaphors and strained by acrobatic rhymes. A little can go a long way. Still, you may want to examine your writing for these devices to see if you are writing colorful songs.

Here is a simple exercise that I have borrowed from Molly-Ann Leikin's book, *How To Write A Hit Song.* Get yourself a box of crayons or colored pencils. Assign a color to each of the different poetic devices and to each of the different types of rhyme. (Blue for metaphor, red for irony, green for single rhyme, orange for internal rhyme—you get the picture.) Now grab a crayon and go through one of your lyrics and circle each occurrence of these poetic devices with the assigned color. When you're finished, you'll have a pretty good visual answer to the question, "How colorful is your lyric?" If you've used three or four or more colors—terrific! But if your lyric is a monochromatic picture, a coat of only one color, the desperate demonstration of a lone crayon, then chances are you need to do some rewriting.

Conclusion

Those of us who desire to create music for the sake of the kingdom need to always be about the business of improving our craft. We are to be reading plays and books, studying the art of writing, enlarging our vocabulary, and expanding our creative horizons. How can we claim to know personally the Creator of all there is and not strive to be the most creative of His children? Sadly, all too often when the Father entrusts us with a song we are tempted to settle for that brief moment of inspiration, proudly claiming, "God gave it to me," and believe that's the end of it. Those who stop there, at that intersection where God gives His gift of music, are missing out on the best part—the continuing joy of toiling side by side with our Lord until the song is the best that it can be. You see, I believe that writing a song is not so much about penning another hit tune for the kingdom. No, the Lord of the universe certainly doesn't need our help creating music. Instead, I am confident that, like all worthwhile creative endeavors, writing a song is simply an opportunity for the writer to get a little closer to God.

Robert Sterling is a Dove award-winning record producer, composer, and songwriter. Many of Sterling's songs have made it to the top of the Christian radio charts. In addition, his choral compositions have been published by Word Music, Belwin Mills, Shawnee Press, Genovox Music, and Meadowgreen Music.

Writing Is Rewriting
By Joel Lindsey

It's not enough for lyrics to be accurate—they must be relevant. After you have read over your lyric, ask yourself, "so what?" Have you given your listener a reason to care about your subject matter?

I heard a story once about a famous sculptor who had created an astoundingly beautiful statue of a horse. Everyone was amazed at the intense detail of his work and asked how he could possibly have carved such a masterpiece. "Simple," he stated. "I take a slab of granite and then chisel away everything that doesn't look like a horse." Hmmm.

When I begin the rewriting process, I am always at a loss. "The song is complete," I tell myself. "How can I possibly jump back in and make it something it's not?" It always takes a while, but inevitably I begin to visualize what I had hoped the song would be and then how it actually did turn out. When I compare, I usually find that I got off course somewhere. If I can take my raw song (my granite, if you will) and envision it in its desired setting, I can usually approach the rewrite a little easier. Then it's just a matter of chipping away at what doesn't "look" like my original idea. For example, if I'm writing a song for a baritone soloist to sing in a church choir Easter program, I actually try to imagine the performance and the audience. What elements should be present here? What type of melody would be most appropriate? Of course, in order to visualize the setting you have to be familiar with it. If necessary, I'll go back and listen to other musicals the choir has performed. I would take into consideration the abilities of the singers, the attitudes and mindset of the congregation. Obviously if I am writing a song for a talented singer like Sandi Patty to sing, then I can use a broader range than if I were writing one for me to sing! And if I can picture Sandi standing on a stage singing my song to her audience, then I know the genre and the parameters in which I'm working.

I wrote a song once with Regie Hamm that Point of Grace recorded called "Life, Love and Other Mysteries." The original second verse went like this:

I cannot reason with men in defiance
Or try to explain all the mysteries of science
'Cause I'm just a child in the face of these giants
But I've got a sling and a stone.[1]

I really like the fourth line. I thought it was cool and artsy even though, to be honest, the coolness of the metaphor doesn't really add any meaning to the song. Even now, I'm not quite sure what I meant when I wrote it!

When Point of Grace became interested in the song they called and asked for a couple of rewrites, including that fourth line. Their comment was, "it just doesn't sound like us." After swallowing my pride a little, I stopped and took a good look at it and realized that what they were saying was true. The line didn't "look" like Point of Grace. Since I definitely wanted them to record the song, I needed to think about their style, their audience, their message. Picturing them performing the song, I realized that the line was more masculine, more figurative than what would seem natural for them. The line eventually became "but I never face them alone." It was a little more straightforward and literal than the original line, but it served them much better. Now, if I had been writing the song for another artist, or for another purpose, the line could well have turned out differently.

Point of Grace, like most artists, have always been gracious when asking for any changes and take the time to let songwriters know how appreciative they are of their work. This is not always the case, however. Sometimes artists will take it upon themselves to make changes in the studio and to then inform the writer later, sometimes even asking for writing credit. This should never happen. This song belongs to the creator and the owner (usually the writer and publisher), and any changes should be made at their sole discretion.

Inspiration and the Call to Excellence

There are those writers who feel that rewriting is totally out of the question—that their original stream-of-consciousness song is just as God intended it to be. While I do not doubt that God has the ability to drop complete, perfectly crafted songs into our laps at His whim and will, I believe the majority of the time He provides us the inspiration and leaves us to our devices to create something that will bring honor to Him. Just as a pastor studies for his Sunday morning sermon, meticulously writing and erasing, researching Scripture, looking for study guides for the illustrations that will not only relay his message but also be palatable to the ears of his congregation, I also believe the songwriter owes it to his listener (and, of course, to God) to use the best tools he has to create a work that's challenging, enlightening, and also entertaining. "Study to show thyself approved of God, a workman that need not be ashamed"(2 Timothy 2:15 KJV).

> Often, the big question is not how to rewrite a song, but how to know when to rewrite.

Rewriting: The Process

Often, the big question is not how to rewrite a song, but how to know when to rewrite. It's important to get ego out of the way and develop habits that better serve the song. Remember, the purpose is to communicate.

If we're willing to listen, our instincts can be the most effective tool in gauging when a song still needs work. I remember playing songs for publishers and hoping they wouldn't notice a line or two that my instinct told me wasn't as strong as the rest of the song—they caught it every time. Be hard on yourself. If your instinct tells you a line is weak, trust that, because others will notice it as well.

It's imperative to find someone who will give you an honest and objective critique. This doesn't have to be a publisher, although if you have access to one willing to work with you, it's clearly the ideal. But it could be a competent minister of music, a college professor, or even a friend who shares your interest in music. Such a person can be invaluable to your craft. But remember, it must be someone who can listen with objectivity and feels free to be honest. I would never ask my mother, for example, to critique something I have written—she likes everything I write! Once you have found this person, try to keep in mind that their critiques are simply their opinions. Listen to their critiques carefully, ponder them with an open mind, then decide if you agree or disagree. Only you can make that decision.

If you're observant, you'll certainly discover songs that just don't evoke the response in others that you intended. If the listener is confused, unmoved, or even worse, uninterested in what you've written, try to breathe new life into it. Start off by looking at the basic idea. I have actually written entire songs and then decided that the idea itself just wasn't interesting enough. One of the problems with writing Christian music is that the subject matter can feel somewhat limited. It seems that we're writing the same themes over and over:

1. Praise songs about God's goodness.

2. Songs dealing with hurt and healing.

3. Songs about sin and redemption.

4. Songs about spreading God's Word.

These are all wonderful things to write about—sustaining song-writers for generations—but as songwriters, we must find new ways to get the message across. This can be done either lyrically or musically, but there has to be something different about the idea to make it worth pursuing. Salvation, for example, has been written about so many times, but we still feel the need to express it. If we can find a new expression or write it in a new musical style that has not been heard with this type of idea, then perhaps we can give the listener a reason to keep listening. Remember, this is the age of channel-surfing Americans. The typical attention-span is very short, so if our basic idea is not compelling, the chances are that our song won't be.

After you're sure that you've got an original idea on your hands, check out the structure of the song. Do the verses match up structurally—same number of lines, same length of lines, same placement of the rhymes? The structure of a song affects the flow and how the listener emotionally identifies with it. Sometimes this is so subconscious that the listener may not even be able to tell you why he doesn't connect with a song—he just knows he doesn't. Maybe the song needs a bridge to take it someplace new either musically or lyrically. Or maybe you've structured the song so that it doesn't have a chorus and it really needs one. As always, the key is communication, so we should use any tools available to communicate the message on our minds.

Christian music requires that the lyrics receive special care. I suggest reading them out loud to yourself and then to others without the distraction of the music, so you can get a real idea for what you are conveying. If there are questions about scriptural correctness, do the necessary research with your Bible and concordance. Also, don't be afraid to talk to a pastor or a teacher if there are any areas of uncertainty.

It's not enough for lyrics to be accurate—they must be relevant. After you have read over your lyric, ask yourself, "so what?" Have you given your listener a reason to care about your subject matter? I heard a song once about what kind of rocks were in the road on the Via Dolorosa. This would have been fine if it related to anything of a spiritual or even a historical significance, but no connection was ever made. Every song doesn't have to have a heavy, deep subject, but every song should at least be relevant.

With the spiritual questions of the song decided, we're ready to move on to craft issues. Is the lyric well written? Is it interesting? Is it clever? Can the listener hear the lyric and see the song? Have you made good use of word pictures? Instead of saying, "her eyes were blue" try saying something like, "her eyes were bluer than the sky in early springtime." Now we get the picture a little more clearly that her eyes were really blue!

I wrote a song once about going to see an old friend. It went like this:

Verse:
She met me on the front porch of her tiny white brick home
it was good to see her old familiar smile
I knew her health was failing and I knew she lived alone
So I thought I'd stop and visit for a while.
Oh, we talked about the weather—it would be an early fall
Then she showed me all the pictures of her grandkids on the wall.
Then I stood and said, "I have to leave"
She smiled and said "I know"
But her eyes filled up with tears as she said,
"Please—before you go—
Let's talk about home some
I'm getting lonesome...."[2]

After I read this to a friend of mine she said, "I can smell the old wallpaper and the coffee brewing." That was a tremendous compliment! The wallpaper and the coffee were nowhere to be found in the lyric, but the listener was taken emotionally to a place where her imagination could kick in. Make your lyrics visual. Paint pictures with your words. Don't be afraid to use metaphors to get your point across. I'll never forget hearing Susan Ashton sing "Down On My Knees" for the first time and hearing Wayne Kirkpatrick's line "I've got one hand on the table and one in the cookie jar." What a great metaphor to describe the human condition. Not only did that song touch me in a real, emotional way, it also opened up the world of metaphors to my writing. When I've got a song that just seems too ordinary, I scope out the lyric and see if it's possible to use a metaphor somewhere in it.

Melody

Probably the single most-common flaw that I see in inexperienced writers is that their melodies sound dated. It is extremely important to stay current on musical styles. It seems that styles change so often that it's hard to keep up. I'm not suggesting, however, that you be unoriginal or that you try to emulate someone else. I'm just saying you should be aware. I live near a huge Tower Record Store with listening centers stocked with the latest music. I make an effort to go at least every couple of months and spend an hour or two keeping myself informed. I'm also constantly changing the stations on my car radio in an effort to hear the latest.

> Probably the single most common flaw that I see in inexperienced writers is that their melodies sound dated.

Melodies should be, above all else, memorable. To hear a melody once and find yourself singing it for the rest of the day is a great compliment to that writer. Many times when I'm writing a song I'll write

312 Getting Started in Christian Music

lyrics to a "dummy" melody. In other words, I plan to go back and change the melody later—I'm just trying to get the lyrics down. The reason for this is that I want to spend time with it—I want to try to find some interesting progressions or melody licks.

When examining your melodies, keep in mind that your verse melody should set up the chorus melody. Nine out of 10 times, the chorus should be melodically higher than the verses to give it a bit of a punch. If you have a bridge, you'll want to break away from anything that you've done in both the chorus and the verse and go someplace totally different. Changing to a different key going into or out of a bridge can be a great place to start. This will, hopefully, get you into a different mindset.

> Keeping a melody within a 10-note range is a fairly good measuring stick for making it universally accessible.

Ask yourself, also, if the melody is truly singable. If you have written a song with a three-octave range, few people will be able to sing it. If you are writing for yourself to sing it, and you have that three-octave range, go for it! But you should know that the song will have little life beyond your own performance of it. Keeping a melody to just over an octave range is a fairly good measuring stick for making it universally accessible.

If your melody still seems lifeless, play around with the intervals and the phrasing. Some of my best melodies are those that I have stumbled onto during the rewriting process when, usually out of frustration, I am willing to try anything and will fall into something wonderful.

If the melody is set but something's still missing, try reharmonizing, or changing the chords underneath it. This is sometimes as simple as changing a bass note, or adding a ninth, or a suspension. Try different things!

Rewriting as Co-writing

Try as we may, sometimes it's hard to take a song that you've already lived with and disregard what's been written to come up with something new. Sometimes you just need to get away from it for a while and then come back to it later. At other times you need to just plow through and force yourself to try alternatives to what you've already written. If you've done all of these things and you still don't have the song you need to have, it might be time to enlist the help of a co-writer. I realize that sometimes it's hard to find someone who shares your vision of the song, but if you are willing to seek that person out, then it will be worth your while.

The first thing you should do is to get the business out of the way. If you simply need a couple of lines rewritten, offer your co-writer a percentage of the song that you think is fair. Typically, a song is split 50/50 between the music and the lyrics, so if you just need help rewriting the music offer your co-writer 25 percent, half of the music share. Be fair to yourself and also to them. But it is important to have an understanding upfront and to then adhere to that.

Sometimes you're forced into rewriting. Several years ago I wrote a song that I was really proud of only to discover that I had accidentally plagiarized the melody to Billy Joel's song "And So It Goes." I spent weeks trying to get that melody out of my head and to write a new one, but I just couldn't shake it. I really loved the lyric and didn't feel like I could just trash the whole song, so I called a co-writer friend of mine and told him of my dilemma (but not which song I had "lifted") and together we came up with a melody that fit the lyric perfectly but was nothing like the original melody.

Writing As Rewriting
Billy Sprague

Sing along with me! You know the tune!

"City sidewalks, busy sidewalks dressed in holiday cheer / And on every street corner you hear / Tinkle bells. Tinkle bells. / It's Christmas time in the city."

What's the matter? Don't like the original version? That's what it was until Ray Evans and Jay Livingston took their new Christmas smash hit home to their wives the day they wrote it. Jay's wife was shocked. "Tinkle" didn't just sound wrong. It implied somewhere someone making yellow snow. Not exactly what the great song-writers intended. So, the next day, what else? Rewrite. Aren't you glad? Strike that. Aren't you relieved? See what a little rewriting can do?

What do you think of the following statement by Nicolas Boileau in his L'Art Poetique? "What is conceived well is expressed clearly, / And the words to say it with arrive with ease." First, what lousy spellers those French are. Hey, Nick, it's "poetic." Second, is that statement a. arrogant, b. naive, or c. a crock? Have you ever written with someone who on every occasion spills, with ease, brilliant, moving, commer-cially viable lyrics and music directly from their mouth onto the world stage and into their bank account? If so, please introduce me. However, most good and great writers I am familiar with wrestle with their creations until they are good or great. Certainly there are times when music or words simply pour out and may be better left alone. But many of those messes should be hosed down by the delete key.

With your permission, Nick, may I offer a rewrite? "Conceive well. Express well. Fashion your words like silver bells." Why? Until they ring most clear and true, mon amis. (Options: Chase your meaning like a gazelle? Don't settle for any mademoiselle?)

We should all do well to heed these words of Franklin P. Adams in *Half A Loaf*. "Having imagination, it takes you an hour to write a paragraph that, if you were unimaginative, would take you only a minute." (I wonder how long it took him to come up with that?)

Please, dear songwriter, take the extra time to rewrite. Those of us who are listening thank you.

Billy Sprague is an award-winning artist, songwriter, and purveyor of whimsy.

As your writing develops, you may find that you excel more as a lyricist or as a music writer. Don't feel that this makes you any less a writer than someone who does both. Hal and Marilyn Bergman are two of pop music's most enduring writers and neither of them profess to be melody writers. They are smart enough to team up with people like Marvin Hamlisch or Burt Bacharach to create wonderfully classic songs. If you can be objective with yourself about what your strengths and your weaknesses are, you can go about the business of finding co-writers who will accent and enhance your talents with theirs.

> If you can be objective with yourself about what your strengths and your weaknesses are, you can go about the business of finding co-writers who will accent and enhance your talents with theirs.

Conflict and Tension

There is a wonderful tool that can be used to make both melodies and lyrics much more effective, and it is what I call conflict. In its simplest form, conflict can be the question and answer aspect of a song. This is often reflected in opposites:

hate/love
pain/relief
thirst/rain
sorrow/joy
hot/cold
minor chords/major chords
hurt/healing
problem/solution

The most common use of conflict in a song is simply to present a question or problem in the verses and then give the answer or resolution in the chorus. There's a good reason why this is the most common use of conflict—it works! It is most effective when both music and lyrics reflect the conflict. Remember the movie *The Wizard of Oz* when Dorothy steps out of the house and the film goes from black-and-white to color? This is the effect we want conflict to give us. Don't be afraid to show us the extremes. Just like with any good book or movie, we want to feel moved.

When I wrote "You Set Me Free" for Sandi Patti, I wanted so hard to write a 100 percent positive song—nothing negative at all. After much frustration, I realized that to fully appreciate anything positive such as freedom or forgiveness, you must first realize the feeling of captivity or failure. So I actually trashed my original verses and started over.

The first verse contains the conflict:

There've been times in my life you've opened doors
They weren't what I was hoping for
So I walked right by them, I didn't even try them
There've been dreams I forgot and dreams I let die
Unnoticed sunsets in front of my eyes
I just couldn't see them—I thought I didn't need them.
Sure there are things I'd do different and yet
But grace gives me days where I simply forget...

Now, here comes the release of that conflict in the chorus:

You set me free to run through fields of laughter
And to sing as though I have no yesterdays
You set me free from my befores and afters
From a debt I know I'll never pay
Father, you father me ever so patiently
You give me wings to fly
When you set me free.

When the release comes in the chorus, it's not only lyrical—it's also musical. The verse and the channel (or pre-chorus) are full of tension in the form of minor chords and suspensions, but when the chorus kicks in, it's major chords all the way! The listener can actually feel the emotional release that the singer wants to convey. By using these "negative" images and musical atmospheres, the end result comes across much more powerfully, thus the tension and the release of conflict.

Prosody

The rewriting process is the perfect time to review prosody, the relationship between the words and the music. Prosody is difficult to describe but great songs invariably use it well. When it's working, the "music" of the words will feel entirely in sync with the "music" of the melody. It might surprise you to think that words have music, but they do; poets have often described their words in terms of melody, even when no actual music was ever contemplated. It all comes down to a match of emphasis in tone and feeling. For example, if the lyrics speak of suffering, the music shouldn't be happy and joyful; it should reflect and support the lyric in dark tones and chords. This goes beyond harmonic concerns; it can be done with phrasing as well. Think of the Supremes classic, "Stop In the Name of Love." What happens to the music when the lyrics say "Stop"? Right—it stops. This is a great example of prosody. Think also of the classic song "Climb Every Mountain"—what happens melodically on the hook-line? It goes up (or climbs) the scale. Even the sounds of the words themselves contribute to a consistent attitude. There are times that the word "gravel" would be right where "stones" wouldn't; stones is a harder, more immediate word, gravel more brooding and dark. That's the art of pulling everything together to make a song as effective as possible. If you're not looking at your words and music as two elements that have to fit together perfectly, you're missing a subconscious element that

318 Getting Started in Christian Music

impacts the listener as much as any overt lyric or musical choice ever will.

One of my favorite examples of a classic use of prosody is in the old southern gospel song "Stepping On the Clouds." In the chorus, there's a line that says "I'm going higher…higher…higher…stepping on the clouds." Every time they say the word "higher" the melody goes up a third. At that point, some of those great old southern gospel showmen would use the opportunity to modulate to a new key taking it even "higher." Of course, you can overdo that kind of thing; be careful your use of a technique doesn't end up feeling like a cliché. Some types of music give you more latitude on that kind of thing than others.

"Dream Big" is a song I wrote with Willie Davis that was recorded by The Martins. The song is about the unlimited possibilities that lie in the life of a believer. The original music was slow and the melody sounded confined; not a match at all for the title. It bothered me for a long time and I really didn't know just how to fix it. Finally, I was on vacation and I was standing in the ocean chest-deep in water looking out over the horizon, feeling a little awed by the bigness of the ocean and its Creator. I started singing the song out loud, getting caught up in the moment, and I realized that prosody is what was missing. By taking out a few suspensions and making a few melodic twists, the song came alive. By the way, a change of environment never hurts the writing process, so I now want to take a vacation every time I need to do a rewrite.

I believe that anything is possible
If we understand who Jesus is
I believe there's nothing that can stop us
If we learn to dream like Jesus did
So don't limit your ambition
To what's commonly defined

God has a special heart
For those who walk outside the lines
Don't be afraid to spread your wings and fly
It doesn't hurt to try
If you're gonna dream...

Dream big—it's the Lord's desire for you to
Dream big—in everything you say and do
You'll see your greatest dream come true
'Cause all of Heaven is dreaming big for you.[3]

One of the most important elements of prosody that will subconsciously undermine the listener's enjoyment is an uncreative use of rhyme. Part of my rewriting process always includes scoping out my rhyme scheme and making sure that I haven't succumbed to every phrase ending in the same vowel sound or some other trite approach. I look hard for any telegraphed rhymes or other pitfalls in my rhyme scheme. I want to include inner rhymes where appropriate to subtly bring the listener inside the "melody" of my lyric. Notice the inner rhymes in the chorus of "Wherever You Are":

Wherever you are, wherever you're going
God is right there beside you seeing and knowing
Wherever you go He already knows
What lies ahead and what's behind
And you'll always find He's never too far
From wherever you are.[4]

The end rhymes (going/knowing, far/are) are obviously essential. But the inner rhymes (go/knows, behind/find) do more for the flow than even the strongest end rhyme could.

Universality

> ...if we cannot only make our audience hear the lyrics but see them as well, we can convey our message on a much more dramatic, thus effective, scale.

I heard a country song several years ago called "I Saw It All On the Radio." This is exactly what we want our listeners to feel. Since the goal of every songwriter should be to express or communicate an idea or an emotion, if we cannot only make our audience hear the lyrics but see them as well, we can convey our message on a much more dramatic, thus effective, scale. This is where your imagination kicks in. If letters and phone calls are an effective meter of a song's effectiveness, then my most successful song ever is "Life is Hard (God Is Good)" that I wrote with Pam Thum. Instead of describing any one specific pain, we put the listener into a place where we've all been, so that everyone could relate to it.

You turn the key
Close the door behind you
Drop your bags on the floor
You reach for the light
But there's darkness deep inside
And you can't take it anymore
'Cause sometimes living takes the life out of you
But sometimes living is all you can do.
Life is hard, the world is cold
We're barely young and then we're old
But every falling tear is always understood
Yes, Life is hard—but God is good[5]

I wish I could say we knew what we were doing when we wrote this, but the truth is we stumbled into it. Looking back I realize that what we did was to paint the lyric in such a way that if you were a middle-aged housewife bored and disillusioned with your marriage or a college student stressed about exams or an AIDS victim or a businessman tired of the rat race you could relate to this song. Instead of telling you what the pain was, we simply described the environment of the pain. I honestly believe the picture of bags being dropped on the floor is the one picture that made this song something that so many people could understand.

If All Else Fails

Sometimes rewriting means cutting. A rule of thumb is that if your song seems even a little bit long to you it almost certainly is too long. After all, nobody is going to be as interested as you are. If you have a long lyric and it seems like it just takes forever to get through, put every word to the test of relevancy. Make sure that nothing is included that isn't essential. Look at the form itself; surprisingly often you can actually cut an entire verse and leave the message of a song completely intact. Inexperienced songwriters often repeat and embellish ideas needlessly. Worse, they often paste together many pictures or ideas that don't all point in a single direction. Whenever you detect that your point is being made with too many words or more than one point is being made, get out the knife.

Do the Work—No Excuses

Taking an ordinary song and making it a great song is not easy. Rewriting requires patience, diligence, imagination, and sheer determination. I'm reminded of a line in the movie *A League of Their Own* about the women's baseball team. One of the players storms off of the field and screams "I quit—it's too hard!" The priceless response of the coach (Tom Hanks) is, "It's too hard? Of course, it's too hard—if it were easy everyone would do it!"

If you really feel that you have a great song inside of you—find a way to get it onto paper or a tape. Don't give up if it takes a while. There are no rules about how long it should take to write a song. Just remember—great songs aren't written; they're rewritten!

Joel Lindsey is a Grammy and Dove award-winning songwriter, and has been nominated for GMA's "Songwriter of the Year." Lindsey has written for Larnelle Harris, Gaither Vocal Band, Point of Grace, Clay Crosse, and many others. In 1998 he had more than 50 cuts, including "Come On In" for the Martins and "You Set Me Free" for Sandi Patty.

The Songwriter/Publisher Relationship
By Don Cason

Since Christian music is such a "message-conscious" music, it requires more than just a talented person singing a good song—it requires an intelligent artist who is able to communicate deep thoughts, concepts, and ideas.

So you write Christian music, and you feel it may be time to determine whether or not songwriting will be a hobby or a vocation. If you're serious about your writing and believe that your songs have some potential beyond your personal enjoyment, then it's time to learn about the music publishing business.

If you're anything like most developing songwriters, you write songs because it's fun and because you have some talent in this area. But through my years of experience in the Christian music industry, I have come to learn that the really good songwriters write out of a passion to seek for truth and express it in ways that others can't. This passion and inner drive are essential because becoming a great song-writer is difficult. Why do you write songs? Maybe you find your answer in one of these:

Some write because songs "are just in them." It seems as though an expression just wells up inside from divine inspiration and then flows from the heart as if God was writing Himself, using you as His vehicle for communication.

Some songwriters write because they feel a strong desire to strengthen others in the faith. The songs these writers compose may challenge people to a deeper spiritual walk or they may be expressions that encourage corporate or individual worship.

Some songwriters write because they feel an urge to express what they themselves are feeling—as if to create an opportunity for looking into their journey in ways in which another listener may identify. In this case, the songs might be written about any aspect of life, but they are generally couched in some larger, spiritual or moral perspective about that particular life experience.

Some songwriters write out of specific needs—the need to lead a church congregation or Bible study group, or the need to perform at an upcoming concert. In this case, the song is born out of practical considerations.

> Often, the commercial life of a song is dictated by the reason it was created.

In each of these cases, the songwriter is driven to express something—perhaps it's God's own Word, encouragement to another, a statement of feelings, or an expression to fit a particular moment. These distinctions are important because the motivation for songs generally points toward different outlets. Each type of song tends to find a natural home in a particular publishing venue. The sooner you find out where you fit in, the better able you'll be to locate a productive relationship for your artistic endeavor.

Often, the commercial life of a song is dictated by the reason it was created. Some songs are so personal that they never find their way out of one's diary or notebook; some are meant to be shared in congregation; some are meant to have commercial success, maybe even national or international exposure. Each individual song that you write will have a life of its own. By knowing first your reason for writing and second the potential life that a particular song may have, the more capable you will be of identifying the type of help that will send you and your songs on their way. Providing that help is where a music publisher may come in.

What Is a Christian Music Publisher?

Before going any further, let's consider a couple of terms: "Christian music" and "publisher." First, what is Christian music? For the purpose of this chapter, the term "Christian music" encompasses all musical styles, whether contemporary Christian music (CCM), gospel, alternative, praise and worship, choral, congregational, that transport a Christian or Christian-theme message. Don't get caught up in the terminology because the intent is to include all musical styles in "Christian music" unless one is specified.

Next, what does it mean to publish? Most dictionaries offer two meanings for this word: to produce or release literature, musical scores, recordings, art, or other intellectual property for sale to the public; and to make something generally known. This first definition takes into account the creation and production of a manuscript or a piece of product that is made available to a user, and the second definition implies the promotion or publicizing of something. In music publishing, that something is a song.

By definition, music publishers set out to accomplish both of those things—to produce and release products using songs and to promote or publicize a song. It's the daily business of music publishers to complete these two tasks. Consider these areas of activity:

Publishers Are Creative

- Help writers refine their songs
- Search for places or projects where songs can be promoted
- Create demonstration recordings of songs
- Plug or pitch songs to prospective users
- Stimulate creativity in writers

- Stretch and challenge writers
- Look for collaborators and create co-writing opportunities

Publishers Provide Practical Support

- Direct and build a songwriter's career
- Provide opportunities for writers to network
- Provide comfortable places for writers to work
- Help writers stay organized
- Provide royalty advances and other benefits that allow writers to stay focused on the creative process

Publishers Protect the Rights of Songs

- Register copyrights in songs to ensure worldwide protection
- License the use of and collect royalties for songs
- Register songs with the Performing Rights Organizations
- Protect the rights given songs under U.S. and international copyright laws

Music publishing is a highly specialized profession, and publishing Christian music is an even more specialized field within that profession. The owners, managers, and employees of music publishing companies are very skilled people, both creatively and in a business sense. Just as songwriters write for different reasons, publishers publish for different reasons, though commonly both songwriter and publisher are driven by the same passions. In order to equip themselves to promote and use songs to their greatest potential, publishers, like songwriters, must also know their reason for publishing and the potential life that a published song may have.

The songwriter-publisher relationship is truly a partnership, one that is based in mutual need. Publishers are in need of talented songwriters and great songs. Songwriters are in need of creative and business collaborators who will use their resources to guide them and their songs to their full potential. The songwriter-publisher relationship can flourish when both parties see the mutual benefit of their association. That must be the basis for everything that is to follow.

> The commercial outlets for songs and the legal matters related to the protection and licensing of songs are common to all genres of music.

Is General Music Publishing Different?

The publishing activities listed earlier are common to most publishers, whether publishers of Christian music or music for the general market. The commercial outlets for songs and the legal matters related to the protection and licensing of songs are common to all genres of music. For instance, there are four general ways that songs are commercially used, and they each require a certain kind of license from the publisher:

"Mechanical" licenses are issued when a song is recorded on a cassette tape, compact disc, or other mechanical device.

"Performance" licenses are issued when a song is publicly performed in concerts, on radio, or on television.

"Synchronization" licenses and/or "fixation" licenses are used when songs are combined with some visual image such as in movies, television, and multi-media presentations.

"Print" licenses are issued when a song, or the lyric or music alone, are printed in books, sheets, or hymnals.

Much can be said regarding these four license agreements that would be excessive in an overview chapter such as this. However, there are many books that delve into this topic and related matters in great detail. If you are interested in better understanding these matters, I encourage you to read some of the materials suggested at the close of this chapter.

328 Getting Started in Christian Music

The kinds of licenses that are used when songs are commercialized, the ways royalties are generated and collected for the use of those licensed songs, and the rights in songs that publishers seek to protect are common for all types of songs. Because the copyright laws throughout the world are conceived in order to govern the business parameters of intellectual property and because license agreements are constructed to operate within those laws, it is only practical that all Christian music publishers operate under many of the same business and financial guidelines as publishers of pop, rock, urban, country, and other general market music.

How Christian Songs Are Being Used Today

Using the four kinds of licenses commonly applied when a song is commercially exploited, let's observe the ways that Christian music is being promoted and developed today.

Mechanical Uses

Probably the most common use of songs in the Christian marketplace is on cassettes and CDs. Today, songs are being "mechanically reproduced" or recorded on artist recordings, praise and worship recordings, choral recordings, accompaniment track recordings, and on many other types of recordings. The songs appearing on an artist recording are selected by a combination of people: the artist, the producer, the A&R representative of the record company, and the artist's manager. Music publishers make it a practice to regularly call A&R representatives, producers, and artists to stay abreast of the kinds of songs for which they are looking. Then, that information is provided to songwriters who may attempt to target a particular musical style or a certain message which meets the needs of the artist, or the publisher may pull from their catalog a previously composed song they believe will appeal to the artist along these same lines. Next, the publisher will prepare a demonstration recording and a lyric sheet for each of the songs that they've compiled. Finally, those materials are presented to the recording's decision makers in the hope that one or more of them will like a song enough to include it on the recording.

Today, many artists write or co-write their own songs, and the opportunity to have a song recorded by an artist may be somewhat limited. However, for those artists who are more dependent on material from songwriters and publishers, it is not uncommon for a producer or A&R representative to listen to several hundred songs before they find 10 or so "right ones" for the recording.

Because Christian music is such a "message-conscious" music, artists are quite particular in what they want to say and in what musical style they feel is the best conveyance for that message. Getting songs recorded by artists is often a difficult thing to accomplish because so many things have to be right: the message, the music, the style, and the pacing of the recording (a mixture of different types and tempos of songs is usually preferred). If you, the songwriter, are also the artist, then things may be a little easier. You, maybe better than anyone else, know what you feel led to communicate and what kind of music best carries that message.

In Christian music, recording artists are often also songwriters. I would encourage you to take a look at some of the radio airplay charts and note the percentage of songs on those charts written and performed by the same person. Since, again, Christian music is such a "message-conscious" music, it requires more than just a talented person singing a good song—it requires an intelligent artist who is able to communicate deep thoughts, concepts, and ideas.

Praise and worship recordings are often constructed by the same process as an artist recording; however, the song is subject to a different scrutiny. Worship recordings require a conceptual flow throughout. This is not to say that artist recordings don't have a flow to them (because they do), but worship recordings are more focused on the emotional and lyrical passage from song to song rather than the fabric created by the mixture of musical styles, tempos, and lyrical content generally found in an artist recording.

Choral recordings require still another song selection process. When you consider the great diversity of worship styles expressed in different denominations and churches, it is easy to understand that the music embraced in those places is often unique and exclusive to this use. In today's church, the choir and congregation sing songs that generally share little or no affiliation with what is currently "popular" on contemporary Christian music charts. Songs commonly used in the church tend to be less personal and introspective and are generally written in the third person, thereby creating a more "corporate" expression. They tend to be less rhythmic and musically difficult so that there is a greater opportunity for harmonious singing by many people. As a result, songs used on choral recordings have a style all their own.

Consider again the idea that each song has its own life. If you write a song that you think is perfect for an artist recording, then that particular song will have a journey of its own as it is processed by all of the decision makers, and the journey will be quite different from that of a song written for a worship recording or a choral recording. Assuming your song is selected for the artist recording, then its life continues—on to the actual album and then to public performances by the artist. Alternatively, assuming your song is selected for a worship or choral recording, then its life also continues—on to the actual album, maybe into a printed edition, and then to public performances by congregations and choirs.

Performance Uses

Let's continue to follow the illustration about the song that is recorded by an artist. Again, your song has made it to the record, and public performances are just around the corner. If your song is selected by the record company to be a single, they will promote it to radio stations and other broadcasters, soliciting them to play it. Additionally, the artist may begin performing the song in arena concerts or at other licensed public performances venues. When a song is being publicly performed as in these two examples, that is when the performance license comes into play. In the United States, there are three Performing Rights Organizations (PROs) who, by arrangement with songwriters and publishers, license and monitor the public performances of songs: ASCAP (American Society of Composers, Authors and Publishers), BMI (Broadcast Music Inc.), and SESAC (originally chartered as the Society of European State Authors and Composers, though the acronym is no longer appropriate). Commonly, when a songwriter begins to be commercially published, he or she will affiliate with one of these three organizations, and most established publishers will already have a relationship with all three.

When a song is commercially released, the music publisher will register or "index" the song with the Performing Rights Organization with whom the songwriter is affiliated. The indexing form will require, among other details, the name of the song, the name of the songwriter(s) with their respective percentages of authorship, and the name of the publisher(s) with their respective percentages of ownership. The PRO, then, is responsible to license radio stations, television stations, concert halls, arenas, and other venues where songs are publicly performed. The PRO will monitor the use of licensed songs by these organizations, and, out of the license fees collected from the public performance facilities, the PRO will pay the songwriter and the publisher according to its individual method for calculating and disbursing royalties. Each of the three PROs also has relationships with similar organizations in other countries around the world. Through those connections, the performances of your song will be monitored around the world and paid back to you and your publisher through your respective PRO.

> A basic knowledge of the [song licensing] organizations can be gained by asking for information from them or by visiting their respective sites on the Internet.

Each of the three Performing Rights Organizations also has a staff attentive to the needs of Christian music songwriters and publishers. If you have written songs that are being publicly performed, you should begin to talk directly with a representative from each of the PROs in order to determine with which you will align. A basic knowledge of the organizations can be gained by asking for information from them or by visiting their respective sites on the Internet.

Synchronization Uses

The two most common synchronization uses of songs in Christian music today are in music videos and on television. Simply stated, synchronization involves the process of "synchronizing" some audio form of a song with a visual image. It includes, among other things, the use of a song on a video, in a movie, on television, in a multi-media presentation, or on the Internet. Given the wide range of audio-visual formats and the myriad commercial and business opportunities for them, synchronization licensing is a very complex matter. The range of license fees may extend from a few cents per unit for manufacturing and selling a videotape recording to a flat fee of thousands of dollars for the use of a song in a feature film.

Synchronization licensing is an area that is often confused with performance licensing. If an audio-visual recording is broadcast or otherwise publicly performed, you might conclude that the PRO's license to the performance facility covers the use. In the instance of live television, it generally does. However, other public broadcasts of audio-visual performances are typically prerecorded or "fixed" prior to airing. For instance, a made-for-TV movie is certainly filmed and edited before it is broadcast, and the music is fixed in synchronization with the image in that process. Therefore, the creator of the fixed version is obligated to secure from the publisher a fixation and/or synchronization license for their use, and that license will generally require the payment of a royalty. In addition, a performance fee also may be collected for the actual public performance of that film when it is subsequently aired or broadcast. For a broader understanding of this topic, I would encourage you to read some of the other suggested material mentioned later.

Print Uses

Printing Christian music is a niche within the field of Christian music publishing though there are a wide variety of opportunities for songs in printed music products. For example, one may see songs used in all of these types of publications:

- Songbooks that match artist recordings
- Collections of arrangements for adult choir, senior adult choir, youth choir or children's choir
- Praise and worship music collections
- Hymnals
- Piano, organ, and other solo instrumental arrangements
- Arrangements for band or orchestra
- Lead line and lyric inserts to accompaniment trax
- Curriculum products
- Lyrics reprinted in books
- Sheet music

Looking over this list of publication types, it is easy to see the need for a wide assortment of songs. Further, the process for song selection varies greatly among print music companies, especially for those creating print music products for customers according to the worship and musical styles embraced by different denominations. Keep in mind that songwriters and publishers may find more life in a song if they are able to identify the reason for its creation. On the one hand, a song that is fitting for performance by a contemporary Christian music artist at a festival may have a limited print music life. On the other hand, the life of a song written for choral or congregational singing may be sustained longer in print than by an artist recording.

> For many songwriters, it is not just a matter of learning to bloom where you are planted, but realizing that there is the opportunity within Christian music for a wide variety of colorful blooms.

Though there are songwriters who are driven only to write songs for contemporary Christian music recording artists, there are many more who have found success, even commercial success, in writing songs only for children, youth groups, church choirs, and congregations. For many songwriters, it is not just a matter of learning to bloom where you are planted, but realizing that there is the opportunity within Christian music for a wide variety of colorful blooms. Not only knowing how to write good songs but knowing the fields where a song is most likely to bloom is very important for a songwriter to learn if he or she ever expects to find commercial success.

Types of Publishers

I stated earlier that music publishing is a highly creative field. It is not uncommon to find experienced musicians and songwriters working as professionals in a publishing company. It is quite natural for creative people to be drawn to work with other creative people.

As you begin to look for the kind of publisher who will be the best match for your abilities and your songs, it is important to remember that the "character" or "personality" of a publisher is greatly determined by the talents and gifts of the people who work there. Though some publishers do different things, most publishers do the same things, differently. Given the unique set of talents that can be found at each company, the approach of one publisher for promoting a song or using it may be greatly different from that of another publisher. Though there may be as many different types of publishing companies as there are ways to promote and use songs, the following represent the most common:

There are many publishers who are free-standing, independent companies who develop and exploit songs for use anywhere and everywhere. Generally these publishers are pursuing every opportunity they can uncover, but they are rarely using songs themselves in products that they are creating or selling. If you are a songwriter who is unlikely to record your own songs, this type of publisher may be an option you want to consider.

Some publishers are associated with a recording company. In addition to pitching songs to outside companies, these publishers are plugging songs internally to the record company's artists or are in some other way seeking to enhance the efforts of the A&R department. Commonly, these publishers are at work assisting in the development of a songwriter who may be a future recording artist. If you are a songwriter who is an artist hoping to land a deal with a record company, this may be an option you want to consider.

Sometimes publishers are formed to be holding companies. This is commonly done when the songwriter is also the artist as their songs are unlikely to be promoted or used in any other way than on their own recordings. In this case, the songwriter generally accepts the fact that their recording may be the only use that a song ever gets; therefore, they do not need anything more than an administrator who will handle copyright registration, licensing, and royalty collection for their holding company.

There are some publishers who need songs only for their own projects. Therefore, they publish individual songs rather than develop a formal relationship with a songwriter who may deliver lots of songs, many of which the publisher cannot use. Often, these particular publishers work in specialized fields or genres of music.

There are some publishers whose primary objective is to create printed editions of original compositions. These publishers tend to focus their attention on individual choral music songs, children's music songs, and praise and worship songs, and on songwriters who primarily deliver material that lends itself to printed editions.

Occasionally, you will find publishers who specialize only in licensing and royalty collection for songwriters. They are more correctly referenced as "copyright administration companies." Generally, these companies do not have a "creative" staff to develop writers and exploit songs. Instead, they tend to primarily handle matters that arise after a song is used.

> Doing your homework as a songwriter to understand the areas of focus held by the publisher you might be considering is critical as you begin your career as a songwriter.

There are some publishers who do a combination of some or all of the things above. These generally large organizations can provide a wide range of opportunities for using songs and for promoting them to others. Though these companies can be the best solution for a songwriter who writes a wide range of songs, they can seem unwieldy to a writer who has a singular focus.

All of these types of publishers approach the task of using and promoting songs from different perspectives. What can be difficult for songwriters to determine is which type of publisher really best fits their needs. Doing your homework as a songwriter to understand the areas of focus held by the publisher you might be considering is critical as you begin your career as a songwriter. My personal experience causes me to believe that when the songwriter and publisher connect on what it is that they can bring to each other, then you have the makings for a successful creative and business relationship.

The Structure of a Music Publishing Company

Most publishing companies are divided into a number of separate but interrelated departments. Depending on the size of the publishing company, these "departments" range in size from one individual wearing many hats to several large corporate divisions comprised of many people. Each of these departments is important to the success of the company as they are all vital to maximizing the opportunities for a songwriter and his songs.

Creative Department

The creative department is probably the most critical interface between a songwriter and a publisher. The personnel in this department listen to new songs, they help songwriters fine-tune what they've written, they record demos of the songs, they nurture collaborative opportunities for songwriters, and they plug songs for potential users.

Copyright Department

This department is responsible for filing copyright registrations, distributing correct copyright notices, indexing songs with the Performing Rights Organizations, and handling all other procedures that ensure the worldwide protection of a song.

In many cases this department is also responsible for the licensing of the songs. This may entail the negotiation of royalty rates or fees for a particular use of a song and the issuance of any license agreements to the user of the song.

Royalty Department

This department is responsible for reviewing the royalty statements provided by licensed song users, making sure that the proper royalties are paid pursuant to the license agreement, and following up with companies who have either not paid or paid incorrectly. Commonly, this department is also responsible for compiling and calculating the royalty statements due to songwriters from funds that have been collected and/or from the publisher's own uses of the songs.

Executive Department

This department is generally responsible for the overall direction of a music publishing company, anything from the negotiation of songwriter contracts to the motivation and oversight of the entire staff. Depending on the character and sometimes the size of the organization, this department can set a very creative direction yet oversee a sound business operation.

Other Departments

Some publishing companies have a business and legal affairs department that may assist in the negotiation of agreements or handle the drafting or approval of all contracts entered into by the company. Sometimes a publicity department is included in a publishing company to promote newsworthy items about the company's songs or songwriters to the press and the industry.

Publishing Contracts

Once you have determined which type of publisher best fits your needs and have begun a dialog about a creative and business relationship with the publisher, your next step is to negotiate a contract.

During the course of a songwriter's career, he is likely to encounter many different types of publishing agreements. The four most common are an individual song contract or single song agreement, an exclusive songwriter's agreement, a co-publishing agreement; and an administration agreement. Most music business books delve into all of these agreements in great detail. I suggest you look into some of the additional reading material recommended at the end of this chapter or contact any professional songwriter group if you want further information.

Single Song Agreement

A single song agreement is just that—a contract whose subject matter is an individual song. A single song agreement creates a basic publishing relationship, and it is often adopted when a songwriter and a publisher are trying to determine whether to form a long-term, more formal association. By working on an individual, song-to-song basis, a writer and publisher can begin to get a sense of the other, as if they were "dating before getting married."

In addition to basic contract provisions, a standard single song agreement will generally address these items: name of the song, authors and percentages of authorship, assignment of copyright, representations/warranties, and royalty and accounting provisions. The nature of a few of these is evident by their name, but allow me to expound upon a few.

ASSIGNMENT OF COPYRIGHT

The U.S. Copyright Law grants a copyright for a song at the time a lyric and/or a melody is "fixed" in a tangible form. (Commonly, a song is "fixed" when it is written down in some basic form or recorded on even the simplest of recording devices.) Additionally, unless there is a written agreement signed by the songwriter stating otherwise, the author of a song owns the copyright for that song from the moment

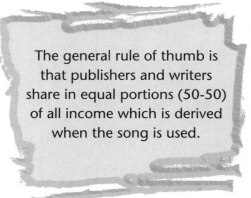

The general rule of thumb is that publishers and writers share in equal portions (50-50) of all income which is derived when the song is used.

that it is created. However, a publisher may require the songwriter to transfer the ownership of that copyright as a condition of their relationship, and that transfer is required by law to be in writing. Therefore, an assignment of copyright is either included in the single song agreement or is occasionally attached as a separate document.

REPRESENTATIONS AND WARRANTIES

A publisher will require a songwriter to give certain assurances, representations, and warranties regarding both the song they have written and their ability to enter into the contract. At minimum, the songwriter must pledge that the song is their original work and that it does not infringe upon the copyright that another songwriter or publisher may have in some other song. Additionally, the publisher may want the songwriter to confirm that they have not entered into an agreement with anyone else regarding that particular song.

ROYALTY AND ACCOUNTING PROVISIONS

Given the overview nature of this chapter, I have chosen to not address the range of royalty rates, earnings splits, and income potentials. Again look into the suggested reading material at the end of the chapter for more information.

The general rule of thumb is that publishers and writers share in equal portions (50-50) of all income which is derived when the song is used. Perhaps you have heard of the so-called "writer's share" and the "publisher's share." These are simply references to the fact that money generated by the use of the song will be distributed between the songwriter and the publisher. Additionally, the royalty provisions will ordinarily set out what rate of royalty the publisher will pay to the songwriter when it makes use of the song.

Rather than pay the songwriter their share of royalties as monies are received, a publisher is apt to make an accounting and payment of royalties due on some regularly scheduled basis. This schedule of payment ranges from monthly, to quarterly, to semi-annually, to annually, depending on each publisher's business practice.

> Though a songwriter may not be required to return the advance if royalties are never generated, the advance is commonly paid back or recouped out of the songwriter's share of royalties as they are earned.

OTHER PROVISIONS

At times, other provisions are negotiated between the songwriter and the publisher. A reversion clause and an advance are two of the most common. Given that single song agreements are sometimes used during a "courtship" period, a songwriter may request a reversion clause in his contract. This proviso allows for the ownership of the copyright to be returned to the songwriter upon the occurrence of certain events or if certain events have failed to unfold as of some date—the most common being the lack of any commercial uses of the song within a specific time period. Such time period might be anywhere from three to 10 years. Some established publishers are reticent to include such a stipulation as their track record is evident. Newer, aggressive companies may be more apt to allow this condition. Remember, though, if you are getting started as a songwriter and a publisher has shown a genuine interest in your work, it is best to allow them a reasonable period of time to generate some activity.

An advance provision might also be negotiated as a feature of a single song agreement. An advance is like a loan that a publisher makes to a songwriter in anticipation of royalties that will be earned in the future. Though a songwriter may not be required to return the advance if royalties are never generated, the advance is commonly paid back or recouped out of the songwriter's share of royalties as they are earned.

Exclusive Songwriter's Agreement

When a songwriter and publisher have determined that their match is right and that they want to move to a deeper level of commitment to each other, they will usually choose to formalize their relationship by executing an exclusive songwriter's agreement. Where a single song agreement contemplates only one song, an exclusive songwriter's agreement contemplates all of the songs a songwriter will compose during a period of time.

Most of the provisions contained in a single song agreement can also be found in an exclusive songwriter's agreement; but again, the biggest difference is that the exclusive agreement sets out the fact that everything a songwriter creates during a period of time, not just one specific title, is subject to the agreement. That period of time will vary with publishers, but a writer should expect no less than two years and more often between three and five. Given that the exclusive songwriter's agreement creates a commitment between the songwriter and the publisher, there are often business and relational issues that might be discussed or negotiated.

For instance: 1. How will demos of songs be created and who will pay for them? 2. Should there be any guarantees to exploit the songwriter personally, much less their songs? 3. Should the songwriter guarantee to write a certain number of songs during the term of the agreement? Remember, all of these things are negotiable and should be addressed in ways that encourage both parties to perform to the best of their abilities.

Co-Publishing Agreement

Co-publishing is a term that has at least two popular uses. In some instances, when a song is written by more than one writer and each writer is signed to a different publisher, the term denotes the understanding and agreement between those multiple publishers who each represent their respective writer. In this chapter, though, we will allow the word another common use—that is to identify the relationship between two publishers who share an interest in one songwriter's contribution to a song. Frequently, this type of co-publishing takes place between a publishing company and a songwriter who may retain a portion of ownership in their copyrights to place in their own publishing company.

This co-publishing agreement is very much like an exclusive songwriter's agreement in that all of the songs created by a writer during a fixed period of time are subject to the agreement. The key difference is that rather than assigning to the publisher a 100 percent ownership interest in the copyright to each song, the songwriter will retain some percentage for themselves. There is no set practice for what that percentage is, though it is generally a function of how much of the "publisher's job" is being done or can be done by the songwriter. Typically, the publishing company (as opposed to the songwriter) will want to control all matters affecting the copyright, including licensing and royalty collections, on behalf of itself and the share retained by the songwriter. In this case, all royalties are collected by the publisher, but 50 percent of those receipts are paid to the songwriter in recognition of the so-called "writer's share," and the other 50 percent is divided between the publisher and the songwriter's publishing company in accordance with their co-publishing percentages.

Administration Agreement

An administration agreement is fundamentally different from any of the three previous agreements in that no transfer of the ownership of

344 Getting Started in Christian Music

the copyright is included. Instead, the songwriter retains his copyright and only vests in the publisher certain rights and responsibilities as pertains to the paperwork, licensing, and royalty aspects of publishing. Given that there is generally no ownership or long-term benefit to the administrator, it is uncommon for them to bear any responsibilities to assist in the development of the songwriter or to use or promote their songs. Rather, they accept the fact that the songwriter may generate the sale or primary uses of the songs, and their responsibility is to oversee the administrative functions of managing the song.

An administration agreement will generally have a term of three to five years, and it will pertain to all of the songs owned by a songwriter. During that period, the publisher will register copyrights, index songs, license uses, and collect license fees. Then, after deducting either its fixed retainer or a percentage of all license fees collected, the publisher will pay the songwriter the remaining balance.

The Most Important Thing About Publishing Contracts

All music publishing contracts are negotiable and should be entered into with a mutual respect for what each party brings to the other. A good contract is intended to: 1. Define the parameters of the relationship; 2. Set forth the responsibilities of each party to the other; 3. Determine how the ownership of copyrights and the financial rewards and expenses are split; and 4. Create a partnership that encourages both parties to perform to their best ability. When you achieve these intentions, you have the foundation for a relationship that can truly flourish.

Some Frequently Asked Questions

Q: "Do I need a publisher if I perform my own songs?"

A: Perhaps not, especially if you don't perceive there are additional uses for your songs besides your own recordings and performances. Let me suggest, though, that you consider the following.

First, pursue a relationship with a PRO. Chances are that if you have a recording, especially one that you are distributing to the public, there may be some public performances of your songs of which you are not aware. More importantly, though, I recommend that you set up a publishing company to "hold" your copyrights and account to you for royalties generated by your own use of your songs. For instance, if you're selling copies of your recordings, pay yourself mechanical royalties and reinvest that income in your songwriting. Setting up your own publishing company may involve nothing more than clearing your company name with your PRO and consulting with an attorney or an accountant regarding possible legal and tax implications to your business.

Q: "How do I pursue a publisher if I don't live near one?"

A: Let me first tell you what not to do. Don't mail publishers copies of your songs without their permission. This is called sending "unsolicited material," and publishers (as well as record companies) are generally either unwilling to accept it or lack the time to listen through all they receive. Instead, let me suggest that you assemble a list of 20 to 30 publishers whose names you find associated with songs that bear some lyrical or stylistic resemblance to yours. Write a brief letter to the creative director at these companies notifying them of your writing experience and success and requesting their permission to forward three of your best songs to their attention. I've heard some publishers recommend that you include in such a letter a self-addressed, stamped postcard with boxes to check such as "Yes, send three songs," or "No, not right now, but check back in six months," or "How did you get my address? I told you never to write me here." (Okay, that last one's optional!) Sometimes you can acquire the same approval by placing a phone call to their office and requesting permission to send your material.

Though long term, a more proven method is to build a network that begins where you already are. Start by networking with all of the people in your vicinity who are in some way involved in Christian music. Perhaps it's the music buyer at the store where you buy recordings or the programmer at your favorite radio station. Consider all of the people these individuals know and who they know—in time, you can create quite a network. In the interim, keep perfecting your craft. Find every opportunity you can to write songs and to share the good ones with your network. Experience says that the good songs and the good songwriters find their way through that kind of network to the attention of a publisher. What radio station personnel wouldn't want to boast of having been the guy who passed along a tape of the writer whose song is currently in the Top 10? Consider how much more effective your query letter to publishers will be if it includes or comes upon the recommendation of "so and so" from the sales and distribution side of the company who knows the music buyer at the store where you shop. Networking is most important! Attending songwriter and music conferences is another way to build your network. Not only do you learn more about the craft of songwriting and performing, but most likely you will meet others who are networking as well. Who knows what new contact might open that last door you're looking to enter?

Q: "In what form should I submit material to publishers?"

A: Again, first have their permission. Songs they aren't expecting don't generally find their way to a tape or CD player. But, assuming a publisher has said "send it on," do all you can to present a professional image. This pitch may be your only opportunity to make an impression on the publisher, so don't waste it. Consider these things: Send a typed lyric sheet for each song. Handwritten sheets won't do. Pay attention to spelling, and be sure to include the names of all the authors.

Invest in quality audio equipment. I'm not saying to build a studio, but on the other hand, don't make third and fourth generation cassette copies on a boom box. Develop a letterhead and J-card or CD jewel case cards with your name and contact information profession-ally printed on them. Be creative in your mailing. Why does everyone use plain manila envelopes? Find some way to be unique.

Q: "Should I create a demo of each of my songs?"

A: Yes, but let me explain. A demo can mean anything from a micro-cassette tape recording of someone singing a melody to a fully produced master, complete with strings, brass, and background vocals. Should you make a recording of your song? Absolutely. Does it need to be an expensive recording? Absolutely not. Song demos (as opposed to artist demos), should be simple, inexpensive recordings. They are intended to showcase the song, not a producer or a percus-sionist or a vocalist. If you need to just archive your songs, a cassette tape is sufficient. If you're planning to pitch your songs, a clean, pro-fessional-sounding guitar-vocal recording or a piano-vocal recording is very effective.

Q: "Should I pay someone to 'publish' my songs?"

A: In my experience, I have not seen any commercial success come from paying someone to publish your songs. Notwithstanding the dis-cussion about single song agreements, publishing is not generally about an individual song but rather a relationship where both parties share in risk and reward. In these scenarios, you end up, at best, with a demo recording or a lead sheet prepared by that "publisher." At worst, you transfer ownership of your song and pay hundreds or thousands of dollars without any serious return. A "publisher" who requires a payment to "publish" is bearing no risk in your song and is not likely investing in your relationship.

Learn More About It

In an overview of music publishing, it is impossible to fully explore all of the information that pertains to the topic. Go to any bookstore or library and you are likely to find hundreds of books on the topic of songwriting and music publishing. The organizations and suggested reading material listed here all provide excellent resources for your continuing education.

Organizations

NACAS—*The National Association of Christian Artists and Songwriters*

200 Countryside Drive
Franklin, TN 37069
Telephone: (800) 79-NACAS or (615) 731-3169
Fax: (615) 361-3582
E-mail: NACAS3@aol.com   Web site: place2b.org/nacas

NSAI—*Nashville Songwriters Association International*

1701 West End Ave., Third Floor
Nashville, TN 37203
Telephone: (800) 321-6008 or (615) 256-3354
Fax: (615) 256-0034
E-mail: nsai@songs.org   Web site: www.songs.org/nsai

ASCAP—*American Society of Composers, Authors, and Publishers*

Los Angeles office:
7920 Sunset Blvd., Ste. 300
Los Angeles, CA 90046
Telephone: (213) 883-1000

New York office:
1 Lincoln Plaza
New York, NY 10023
Telephone: (212) 621-6000
web site: www.ascap.com

Nashville office:
Two Music Square West
Nashville, TN 37203
Telephone: (615) 742-5000

BMI—*Broadcast Music Inc.*

Los Angeles office:
8730 Sunset Blvd., Third Floor
Los Angeles, CA 90069
Telephone: (310) 659-9109

New York office:
320 West 57th St.
New York, NY 10019
Telephone: (212) 586-2000
web site: www.bmi.com

Nashville office:
10 Music Square East
Nashville, TN 37203-4399
Telephone: (615) 291-6700

SESAC—SESAC, Inc.

Nashville office:
55 Music Square East
Nashville, TN 37203
Telephone: (615) 320-0055

New York office:
421 West 54th St.
New York, NY 10019
Telephone: (212) 586-3450
web site: www.sesac.com

AGMA—The Academy of Gospel Music Arts

The Gospel Music Association
1205 Division St.
Nashville, TN 37203
Telephone: (615) 242-0303
Fax: (615) 254-9755   Web site: www.agma.net

CMPA—Church Music Publisher's Association

P.O. Box 158992
Nashville, TN 37215
Telephone: (615) 791-0273
Fax: (615) 790-8847
Note: This organization can provide a listing of addresses for many music publishers.

U.S. Library of Congress

Washington, DC 20559
Telephone: (202) 707-3000
Forms Line: (202) 707-9100
Web site:www. loc.gov

Don Cason is vice president and general manager of Word Music. He was president of the Church Music Publishers Association from 1992 to 1994 and has been directly involved in the songwriting careers of Carman, Cindy Morgan, Greg Nelson, Keith Thomas, and Wayne Watson.

Suggested Reading

The Art of Music Licensing—Al Kohn, Bob Kohn

This Business of Music—M. William Krasilovsky, Sidney Shemel (Contributor)

More About This Business of Music—M. William Krasilovsky

The Music Business (Explained in Plain English)—David Naggar, Jeffrey D. Brandstetter

Music, Money, and Success—Jeffrey Brabec, Todd Brabec

Music Publishing—a Songwriter's Guide—Randy Poe

All You Need to Know About the Music Business—Donald S. Passman

If you are interested in obtaining more information about the Gospel Music Association, you can contact us at:

1205 Division Street, Nashville, TN 37203
Fax: 615-254-9755

INFORMATION